D1206319

"Every page in this very entertaining book leaves the reader thirsty for more. I highly recommend that you first turn straight to page 82 and fix yourself one of the two Daiquiri recipes you'll find there. And be prepared to fix more drinks as you read on. There's nothing quite like literary drinking."
—Gary Regan, author of *The Joy of Mixology*

"His recipes are proven and the histories are true. Papa would have been on the stool next to Phil Greene in any bar, from Paris to Key West to Havana."
—Benjamin "Dink" Bruce, Hemingway expert and son of close Hemingway friends Betty and Toby Bruce

"If wine is bottled poetry, Greene's book is a mixologist's moveable feast."
—Dave Gonzales, Events Director, Hemingway Home and Museum, Key West

TO HAVE AND HAVE ANOTHER

A Hemingway Cocktail Companion

REVISED AND EXPANDED

Philip J. Greene

A PERIGEE BOOK

PERIGEE
An imprint of Penguin Random House LLC
375 Hudson Street, New York, New York 10014

Revised Perigee hardcover ISBN: 978-0-399-17490-2

The Library of Congress has cataloged the first Perigee hardcover edition as follows:

Greene, Philip, 1961–
To have and have another : a Hemingway cocktail companion / Philip Greene.—First edition.
pages   cm
Includes bibliographical references and index.
ISBN 978-0-399-53764-6 (hardback)
1. Cocktails.   2. Hemingway, Ernest, 1899–1961.
3. Drinking of alcoholic beverages in literature.   I. Title.
TX951.G784   2012   2012027662
641.87'4—dc23

PUBLISHING HISTORY
First Perigee hardcover edition / November 2012
Revised Perigee hardcover edition / November 2015

PRINTED IN THE UNITED STATES OF AMERICA

10   9   8   7   6   5   4   3   2   1

Text design by Tiffany Estreicher

To my beautiful bride, Elise.
Thanks for your love, courage, guidance, and patience,
and for indulging my occasional bursts of foolhardy ambition.
And to our girls, Hannah, Madeleine, and Olivia, who inspire
and amaze me every day. Finally, to Mom and Dad,
for the love, support, example, and inspiration
they'll always provide.

CONTENTS

FOREWORD

There are two types of writers. One will write, for example, "She walked up to the bar and ordered a drink. It came and she took a cautious sip. The morning was looking up." The other kind will say something more along these lines: "She walked up to the bar and ordered a Martini, very dry, whereupon the bartender filled a large glass with ice, poured a long stream of Gordon's gin over it, cast a regretful glance at the vermouth bottle, and set the ice rotating with a long silver spoon. Finally, he strained the silver liquid into a chilled, *V*-shaped glass, and she took a sip. She preferred Burrough's gin in her Martinis, but the drink was still crisp and cold and strong, and it made what she had to do next seem entirely possible." In the first category, you'll find a good many great writers, from St. Augustine to Dashiell Hammett, Samuel Beckett to Virginia Woolf. In the second, there are the likes of Rabelais and Dickens, P. G. Wodehouse, Raymond Chandler, and Ian Fleming. And, of course, Ernest Hemingway.

I suppose, when looked at from a certain perspective, the minute details of what people—be they fictional or historical or even sitting down the bar from you—eat and drink are rather trivial; a North African campaign, as it were, compared to the Russian front that is our perpetual struggle to make our way through an indifferent world. What does it matter what kind of goddamn whiskey a man likes in his Manhattans when he has just come to the realization that his entire life is a sham? And yet, more than twenty-four hundred years ago, Aristotle stated one of the fundamental principles of fiction when he said in Section XV of his *Poetics* that decisions define character. Every drink we order represents a small decision, and often more than one. Individually, they might be minor, but they add up, as do all the little decisions we make. The campaign in North Africa might have been a sideshow in World War II, but the decisions made there meant that the troops and tanks Hitler lost at El Alamein weren't there to save his Sixth Army at Stalingrad a few weeks later, and after Stalingrad, the Götterdämmerung of 1945 was inevitable. And, if I may compare small things to great, to decide to order a Mimosa in the morning is a very, very different thing from ordering a no-vermouth dry Martini.

If you're willing to accept that argument, fortunately there is a third type of writer: the one who writes about what the second one writes about drinks. I am one of those, and, more importantly, Philip Greene is one, too—and, as this book demonstrates, a very good one indeed. Ernest Hemingway is an icon in many fields of human endeavor. Writing, of course (he won a Nobel Prize for that). Hunting, fishing, war (although he was more of a witness than an actual combatant). Beard growing. Womanizing. Drinking. Indeed, as Mr. Greene so ably demonstrates in the book you hold, Hemingway was a drinker without peer in his age. That's not to say he was a degenerate alcoholic; he drank a lot, but not when he was writing, and he did that all the time. What's more, as this book teaches us, he was a discriminating and curious drinker, always seeking the precise drink to complement his particular circumstances. Likewise, Mr. Greene, who appears to have read every single word Hemingway ever wrote, taking bibulous notes all along, demonstrates how Hemingway used this affinity to illuminate the characters in his fiction.

Not that this is a dry study (indeed, how could it be). Mr. Greene is an admirably thorough and clear-eyed guide to his topic, but fortunately an amiable and witty one as well. He illuminates obscurities and dispels myths (and creates a few new ones), but most of all, he inspires thirst. A mixographer can receive no higher praise.

—David Wondrich

HEMINGWAY CHRONOLOGY

JULY 21, 1899: Ernest Miller Hemingway born in Oak Park, Illinois

1917: Graduates high school; cub reporter for *Kansas City Star*

1918: Joins Red Cross Ambulance Corps; is severely wounded in Italy; romance with nurse Agnes von Kurowsky ends in heartbreak

1921: Reporter for *Toronto Star*; marries Hadley Richardson and they move to Paris in December

1923: *Three Stories and Ten Poems*

1926: *The Sun Also Rises*

1927: Divorces Hadley and marries Pauline Pfeiffer; *Men Without Women*

1928: Begins extended visits to Key West; eventually moves there in 1931

1929: *A Farewell to Arms*

1932: *Death in the Afternoon*

1934: Buys thirty-eight-foot boat, *Pilar*

1935: *Green Hills of Africa*, based on 1933 safari

1937: *To Have and Have Not*; covers Spanish Civil War

1939-40: Moves to Cuba; divorces Pauline and marries Martha Gellhorn

1942-43: Runs "Crook Factory" in Cuba; intelligence and subhunting operation using *Pilar*

1944: Covers war in France; "liberates" the Ritz; is said to lead troops in battle

1945-46: Divorces Gellhorn and marries fourth wife, Mary Welsh

1950: *Across the River and Into the Trees*

1952: *The Old Man and the Sea*

1953: Wins Pulitzer Prize for *The Old Man and the Sea*

1954: Wins Nobel Prize in Literature; survives two plane crashes in Africa

JULY 2, 1961: After enduring electroshock therapy, and suffering from depression, diabetes, and hypertension, Hemingway takes his own life, not three weeks shy of his sixty-second birthday

INTRODUCTION

This is a book about Ernest Hemingway and what he liked to drink, what he wrote about those drinks, and how to make the drinks that he and his characters enjoyed. Like many writers, Hemingway was no teetotaler, but perhaps more than any other writer, he engaged his characters in the act of eating and drinking—be it at a café or a campfire, fishing the Gulf Stream or on safari in Africa—and he described it in such rich detail, readers can almost smell and taste the scene.

Like many, I was introduced to Hemingway in high school. Along with other required reading, I read *A Farewell to Arms*. I enjoyed it, as I recall, but it didn't grab me like the short story "Big Two-Hearted River."

It's the story of a young man, Nick Adams, on a backpacking trip on Michigan's Upper Peninsula. Coincidentally, I'd taken a similar trip the summer before, and the story appealed to me immediately. Hemingway described it all so thoroughly—how Nick fished for trout, his trek across the rugged landscape, the aroma of the campfire, the sound of the river, the way his canned spaghetti bubbled in the pan, how the hot food burned his tongue—that I was compelled to seek out his other works.

Ironically, Nick doesn't have a drop to drink, just coffee. Yet it was that story that launched me on a lifelong appreciation of

Hemingway and the rich detail he devoted to describing the simple act of eating and drinking.

Hemingway's formal education ended with high school; he'd often say he attended the university of the world. In all his life's travels—summers spent in the Michigan woods, service with the Red Cross in Italy during World War I, working as a reporter for the *Kansas City Star* and *Toronto Star*, living as an expatriate American writer in 1920s Paris, traveling throughout Europe and Africa, serving as a war correspondent during the Spanish Civil War and World War II, his life in Key West and Cuba, and his final years in the mountains of Idaho—Hemingway sought to learn from the locals, the customs and folkways, but more important, to get the flavor of the place. He is quoted as saying, "Don't bother with churches, government buildings or city squares; if you want to know about a culture, spend a night in its bars."

A wine enthusiast calls it *terroir*, the flavor of the region. Hemingway's descriptive style offers that additional perspective, allowing the reader another way to become immersed in the scene. As a history buff, I found myself wanting to know more, the backdrop, the geographical, cultural, and historical context. As a lover of good food and drink, I also wanted to know more about what the characters were enjoying in those cafés and bars.

In *The Sun Also Rises*, Jake Barnes drinks a Jack Rose while waiting in vain for Brett Ashley to meet him. In *A Farewell to Arms*, Frederic Henry enjoys a couple of Martinis, noting how "cool and clean" they taste, how they make him "feel civilized." In *Across the River and Into the Trees*, two lovers have a Martini, and they feel it "glow happily all through their upper bodies." In "The Strange Country," Roger relaxes with a drink in his New Orleans hotel room, reading the papers while listening to the noises from the street below. It reminds him of when he lived in Paris, the evenings he'd spend at the café, alone, perusing the evening papers with his aperitif. In *The Garden of Eden*, David and Catherine Bourne enjoy a decadent lunch, including a cold bottle of "good light, dry, cheerful unknown white wine" that the restaurant was proud of.

And in *For Whom the Bell Tolls*, it is the ritual of dripped absinthe that gives Robert Jordan temporary solace from the rigors of war: "one cup of it took the place of the evening papers, of all the old evenings in cafés, of all chestnut trees that would be in bloom now in this month, . . . of all the things he had enjoyed and forgotten and that came back to him when he tasted that opaque, bitter, tongue-numbing, brain-warming, stomach-warming, idea-changing liquid alchemy."

Upon reading Hemingway, I wanted to know more about that Jack Rose, to drink a Martini and feel those same feelings, to read the evening papers with my aperitif, experience the ritual of absinthe, and taste that "cheerful unknown white wine," putting myself in those scenes, if only for a moment.

I somewhat soberly note that Hemingway drank too much, and his drinking took years off his life. His was a life full of pain, both emotional and physical, and alcohol was often his anesthetic. According to biographer Carlos Baker, Hemingway "explained the nights of drinking as a necessary counterforce to the daily bouts of writing which left him as whipped, wrung out, and empty as a used dishrag." It was a "release," "the irresponsibility that comes after the terrible responsibility of writing." I don't wish to celebrate Hemingway's excesses, or apologize for his flaws. Rather, not wanting to throw the baby out with the branch water, so to speak, this is meant as a celebration of both his life and his writing, and the sensory aspect of his writings with respect to drink. It's not about how much he drank, but *what* he was drinking, and how he wrote about it.

This book will teach you how to make those drinks, tell you

about their history and folklore, and offer some interesting and colorful anecdotes about drink and drinker, be they Hemingway or someone else. It will also offer excerpts from Hemingway's works that will allow you to embrace the *terroir* and taste the scene. Cheers!

WHAT YOU'LL NEED

In order to fully appreciate this book, I recommend that you have a decent set of bar tools, the ingredients and glassware identified herein, plus of course some Hemingway. Above all, find yourself a clean, well-lighted place to enjoy it.

Bar Tools

A jigger or measuring glass. A typical double-ended jigger measures 1½ ounces on the larger end and ¾ ounce on the smaller.

Cocktail shaker. You can use a three-piece cobbler shaker (all in one, with built-in strainer under the cap) or a two-piece Boston shaker (combination pint glass and metal bottom half). For drinks to be stirred, use a pint glass.

Long-handled cocktail stirring spoon

Hawthorn or julep strainer

Muddler

Citrus squeezer/juicer

Knife

Works of Hemingway

In a perfect world, I'd present for you here page after page of vintage Hemingway. However, because of copyright restrictions, I am not able to reproduce as much as I'd like, so what I offer to you instead is a road map directing you to all the choicest scenes, and notable excerpts found within.

You'll want his major books: *The Sun Also Rises*, *A Farewell to Arms*, *Green Hills of Africa*, *To Have and Have Not*, *For Whom the Bell Tolls*, *Across the River and Into the Trees*, *The Old Man and the Sea*, *The Dangerous Summer*, *Islands in the Stream*, *A Moveable Feast*, *The Garden of Eden*, *True at First Light*, and *Under Kilimanjaro*, and his short stories, found in *The Complete Short Stories of Ernest Hemingway: The Finca Vigía Edition*. You might also want to have a look at his play *The Fifth Column*, as well as his journalistic efforts, found in his *Esquire* articles and in *Dateline: Toronto* and *By-Line: Ernest Hemingway*. And don't forget *Ernest Hemingway: Selected Letters, 1917–1961*, as there are some gems in there as well, including his inimitable Bloody Mary recipe, and how to make ice for your Martini that's fifteen degrees below zero!

December 1937. Hemingway in his Valencia hotel room, filling his flask prior to covering the battle of Teruel, one of the decisive actions of the Spanish Civil War. The photo was taken by renowned photojournalist Robert Capa, also covering the war. Although they were friends, years later Hemingway and Capa would have a falling-out over Hemingway's perception that Capa was always shooting him while engaged in the act of drinking. Courtesy Magnum Photos.

Absinthe

DRIPPED ABSINTHE

1½ oz. absinthe

1 cube sugar (optional; Hemingway did not use it)

Small pitcher ice water or absinthe dripper

Slotted absinthe spoon

Place a sugar cube on a slotted absinthe spoon atop a small glass of absinthe. Slowly drip ice water onto the sugar to dissolve it. When it has reached the desired strength or sweetness—both matters of taste—sip it slowly.

SUGGESTED READING: *The Sun Also Rises* (Chapter 18), *For Whom the Bell Tolls* (Chapters 4 and 16), *The Garden of Eden* (Chapter 13), "The Strange Country," "Wine of Wyoming"

Absinthe is a high-proof distilled spirit, flavored with a variety of herbs, notably wormwood (*Artemisia absinthium*). It is said to have been invented in the 1790s by Pierre Ordinaire, a French physician who lived in the Swiss commune of Couvet, having recently fled the French Revolution.

It was demonized (and banned) around the turn of the last century, for a variety of reasons. Without any quality control or labeling laws, there were a lot of (sometimes toxic) spirits being labeled as absinthe. Further, the Temperance movement was looking for an easy victim, and in absinthe it found it. The final nail in the coffin was a horrific incident in 1905, when a French peasant killed his family in a drunken rage. Temperance leaders blamed it on absinthe, though the man had been drinking wine and brandy all day. The decade that followed saw absinthe's near-global ban. It was outlawed in the United States in 1912; the other shoe, known as Prohibition, dropped in 1919.

When properly made, absinthe is no more addictive or dangerous than any other distilled spirit, and understanding this has aided its revival. The key ingredient is thujone, found in wormwood, previously thought to be hallucinogenic and toxic. Today's absinthe still contains thujone, but at safe "parts per million" levels. During the ban, wormwood-free absinthe substitutes filled the void, such as Pernod and Herbsaint.

Absinthe was immensely popular during the nineteenth century, especially among the world's poets, writers, artists, and bohemians. Poets waxed, well, *poetic* under its influence, and its color inspired the name "La Fée Verte." Paintings by Manet and Degas depicted the Green Fairy, or its dissipating effects on consumers.

Hemingway likely discovered absinthe during his first year in Paris. In a tongue-in-cheek article in the *Toronto Star* in 1922 titled "The Great 'Apéritif' Scandal," he told of the brouhaha that erupted in Paris when police discovered absinthe being sold under the name Anis Delloso. Unlike the "beautiful green color that minor poets have celebrated to the driest corners of the world," Anis Delloso was a pale yellow. Nevertheless, it tasted like absinthe, and it had that same milky cast when diluted with water. Alas, once the police caught on, it was reduced to a common anisette (sans wormwood).

Because of the ban, you'll find Hemingway's characters engaging in evasive tactics when drinking it in public, including the use of a dummy bottle of Pernod. In *The Garden of Eden*, Catherine has to "engulp" her absinthe to avoid detection by the police. David explains that to drink absinthe properly, one should have the correct setup, with iced water and a means by which to drip it into the absinthe, but "everybody would know what it was then."

Hemingway vividly depicts the ritual of absinthe. One does not just pour and sip. There is a process, a method, a *ceremony* almost, with the patient dripping of the water, at just the proper rate and amount. "It breaks up and goes to pieces if the water pours in too fast," which makes it worthless, he explains in *The Garden of Eden*. But if you conduct the ritual correctly, the drink is transformed with that magical opalescent hue; the Green Fairy will have arrived.

Hemingway also viscerally describes its effects on the drinker. In Chapter 4 of *For Whom the Bell Tolls*, Robert Jordan drinks it during the Spanish Civil War, describing it as a medicine that

Vintage Pernod ad. Courtesy Pernod Ricard USA.

"cures everything." Not only that, it will transport you away from your troubles and bring back things you enjoyed in the past.

One of Jordan's compatriots asks for a taste of his absinthe and is repulsed, declaring it to be "bitter as gall," adding, "It is better to be sick than have that medicine." Jordan explains that the bitterness comes from the wormwood and tells him, "It's supposed to rot your brain out but I don't believe it. It only changes the ideas."

By Chapter 16, Jordan's Whiskey & Water just isn't the same; as he puts it, "it does not curl around inside of you the way absinthe does."

Note also in "The Strange Country," where Roger describes "feeling the warmth of the alchemist's furnace starting at the pit of his stomach." As Helena tastes it, she notes, "It is strange and wonderful. But all it does so far is just bring us to the edge of misunderstanding," and "it makes you feel as though you could do anything."

In a 1931 letter to Guy Hickok, Hemingway tells of an evening with absinthe in Key West:

> Got tight last night on absinthe and did knife tricks. Great success shooting the knife underhand into the piano. The woodworms are so bad and eat hell out of all furniture that you can always claim the woodworms did it.[1]

It's not just a play on words; his home was plagued by woodworms, so much so that it's the only former Hemingway residence not to have any original furniture in it (though tour guides might tell you otherwise).[2]

Absinthe is an ingredient in many classic cocktails, including Death in the Afternoon, Absinthe Suissesse, Absinthe Frappé, the Sazerac, and the Corpse Reviver (No. 2). If you do indulge in absinthe in any form, I can't guarantee that it will serve as a "wormwood-tasting truth serum," warm your brain, change your ideas, cure anything that is wrong with you, or even make the Green Fairy appear, but I'd like to think you'll have a nice drink all the same.[3]

Aguardiente

Raw, unaged spirits

SUGGESTED READING: *The Sun Also Rises* (Chapters 11 and 12)

he Sun Also Rises (1926) concerns a circle of friends in post–World War I Paris and features the fiesta of San Fermín in Pamplona. While in Spain, Jake Barnes and Bill Gorton do a little trout fishing on the Irati River near the village of Burguete. In Chapter 11 they board a double-decker bus full of jovial Basque peasants and head up into the Navarre hill country. On this boozy bus trip, Jake and Bill learn the art of drinking from a leather wineskin, called a bota. They're taught how to direct a long stream from the wineskin into their awaiting mouths, to the cries of *"Arriba! Arriba!"* During a brief stopover in a small village, Jake and Bill then enjoy a local drink called aguardiente. Their new Basque friends buy them a round, so they feel obliged to buy a round, and amid much backslapping, more rounds are bought and tossed back.

Aguardiente literally means "firewater," a term universally used to describe raw, unaged spirits. When made from sugar, it's *aguardiente de cana*, a crude rum, said to have been the basis for El Draque, the predecessor of the Mojito. I suspect that it was the grape-based *aguardiente uva* that Jake and Bill enjoyed.

In his epic 1948 book, *The Fine Art of Mixing Drinks*, David Embury describes aguardiente as "seldom seen in the United States, which is perhaps just as well, but is quite popular in Spain and the various Latin American countries with those who want a cheap, high-powered liquor, regardless of taste."[4]

Hemingway and his first wife, Hadley, twice visited Burguete to fish the Irati River. The 1924 trip followed their first visit to Pamplona, where they enjoyed the fiesta with Donald Ogden Stewart, Robert McAlmon, Chink Smith, John Dos Passos, and Bill and Sally Bird. They traveled in a double-decker bus "jammed with Basque farmers drinking wine from leather wineskins."[5] Hemingway fell in love with the countryside, the cold mountain streams, the rugged terrain, the virgin pine and beech forests, and the hearty people. Spain "was the real old stuff."[6]

You can still stay at the Hostal Burguete, where Hemingway stayed (room 23, for those planning a pilgrimage). If any Basque peasants buy you a round of aguardiente, please do return the favor. *Topa!*

Americano

1 oz. Campari
1 oz. Italian (sweet) vermouth
1–2 oz. seltzer (to taste)

Add all ingredients to a rocks or highball glass filled with ice. Stir. Garnish with an orange wedge or a lemon twist. Enjoy.

SUGGESTED READING: "The Good Lion"

Hemingway was likely introduced to both Campari and vermouth in Italy during World War I, while serving as a Red Cross ambulance driver. In fact, during a conversation with Gertrude Stein in *A Moveable Feast*, he mentions an old man who used to visit him in the hospital in Milan when he was recuperating from nearly being killed by an Austrian trench mortar. The man would bring him bottles of Marsala or Campari, which was all well and good until one day he went a bit too far with his alleged friendship, forcing Hemingway to bar the man from the room. Stein dismissed the man's behavior, saying, "Those people are sick and cannot help themselves and you should pity them." Hmmm. Despite whatever happened in that hospital room, Hemingway's love for Campari endured.[7]

Campari is an aperitif bitters invented in the 1860s by Gaspare Campari in Turin, Italy. It is a secret blend of herbs, spices, bark,

1926 Campari ad. Courtesy Davide Campari-Milano.

fruits, and fruit peels. Its distinctive carmine hue derives (at least originally) from dye extracted from the cochineal, a beetle-like insect. It's one of two types of bitters. *Aperitif* bitters (Campari, Amer Picon, Fernet-Branca, and Averna, to name a few) are typically enjoyed as a beverage, while *cocktail* bitters (including Angostura, Peychaud's, and Fee Brothers) are used only a dash at a time. It's easy to remember: aperitif bitters = big bottle, cocktail bitters = small bottle.

Hemingway offered a further primer on aperitifs in a 1922 article in the *Toronto Star Weekly*, in which he described them as "those tall, bright red or yellow drinks that are poured . . . by hurried waiters during the hour before lunch and the hour before dinner, when all Paris gathers at the cafés to poison themselves to a cheerful pre-eating glow."[8]

The Americano is a simple drink, equal parts Campari and Italian (sweet) vermouth, with a splash of seltzer for effervescence. It was originally called the Milano-Torino (Campari from Milano, Cinzano vermouth from Torino). It became the Americano in the early twentieth century, as many American tourists favored the drink, especially during Prohibition. Perhaps that was because Americans had acquired a taste for Campari stateside, as the U.S. government had classified it as a medicinal product, available to savvy Americans by prescription (!). Substituting gin for the seltzer yields another delightful drink, the Negroni.

In *Across the River and Into the Trees*, in a rare mixological mix-up, Hemingway appears to confuse the Negroni with something more resembling the Americano: "They were drinking negronis, a combination of two sweet vermouths and seltzer water." The thing is, as I say, the Negroni contains gin in place of the seltzer. Of all ironies, how could Hemingway leave out the gin?

He also mentions the Negroni and the Americano in his short story "The Good Lion." Intended as a children's story, it tells of a lion who exists on a higher moral plane; whereas "the bad lions would roar with laughter and eat another Hindu trader," the good lion would "ask politely if he might have a Negroni or an Americano and he always drank that instead of the blood of the Hindu traders."

The Americano has also found its way into other works of prose, notably in the Ian Fleming novel *Casino Royale*. In this first of the James Bond series of thrillers, the Americano carries the distinction of being the first cocktail ever to grace the lips of 007.

Both the Americano and the Negroni are an excellent introduction to aperitif bitters, an acquired taste, indeed, but well worth the

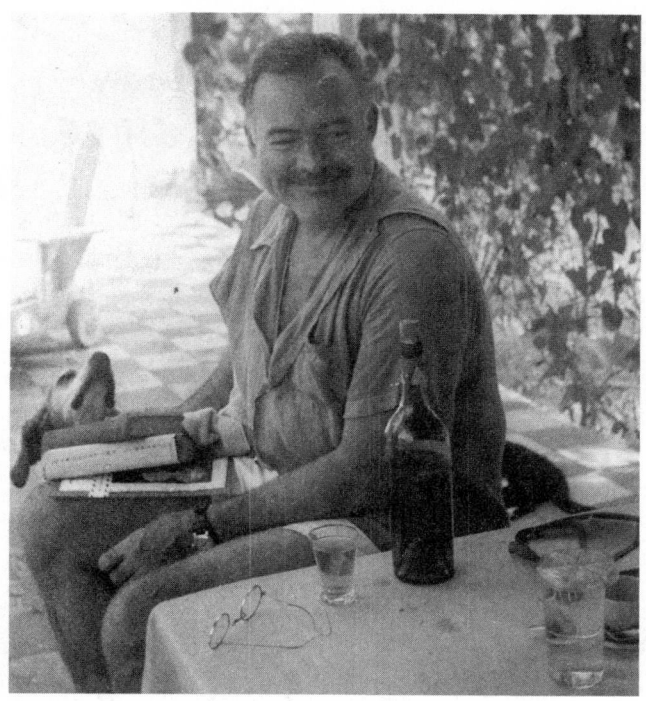

Hemingway relaxing with his dog Negrita at the Finca Vigía, Cuba, circa 1942. Ernest Hemingway Photograph Collection, John F. Kennedy Presidential Library and Museum, Boston.

acquisition. Indeed, it took even Hemingway some time to embrace them; in the 1922 dispatch he wrote for the *Toronto Star Weekly*, he described them as tasting "like a brass doorknob."[9] I'll drink to that.

Anis del Mono

2 oz. Anis del Mono

2 oz. chilled water

Serve over crushed ice.

SUGGESTED READING: *The Sun Also Rises* (Chapter 15), "Hills Like White Elephants"

Anis del Mono is yet another anise-flavored spirit found in the Hemingway bar, along with absinthe, Pernod, and Ojen. It has been produced since 1870 by Vincente Bosch in Badalona, Spain.

Anis del Mono appears in *The Sun Also Rises*, where the characters of this 1926 novel throw themselves into the nonstop pace of Pamplona's fiesta of San Fermín. During the calm before the storm, the characters are having a quiet glass of Sherry at a café. Then all hell breaks loose. At noon sharp, a skyrocket is launched into the air to announce the start of the fiesta, and all at once the square is full of people. Music and dancers are everywhere, and the café tables are filling up. More friends join the group, and everyone becomes caught up in the frenzy of the fiesta. Robert Cohn passes out after drinking Anis del Moro, and Jake tries the drink himself: "It tasted of licorice and warmed all the way. I could feel it warming in my stomach."

In the short story "Hills Like White Elephants," Hemingway

Anis del Mono ad, circa 1938; Floridita menu. Vicki Gold Levi collection.

tells the story of a young couple at a railway café, seemingly at a crossroads of their own. As they wait for a train, they decide to have a drink, since, after all, "That's all we do, isn't it—look at things and try new drinks?" They order an Anis del Toro, diluted with ice water.

The girl has a sip, noting that it tastes like licorice; she says, "Everything tastes of licorice. Especially all the things you've waited so long for, like absinthe."

Beneath the conversation, it seems that the man is trying to convince the woman to terminate her pregnancy. He comes off as a bit of a cad, dismissing it as no big deal, just a simple medical procedure, with the pregnancy being the root cause of any problems they might have. The girl appears to give in, but does she?

Near the end of the story, perhaps it is the man who is relenting.

He's taking the bags across to the other side of the station. She smiles at him. He then ducks into the café for another quick Anis del Toro, perhaps to brace himself for what the future holds.

One wonders why Hemingway has renamed Anis del Mono as Anis del *Toro*. Was he just being funny, or was there some symbolism at play? Maybe he changed the name to evoke the übermasculine imagery of the bullfight. Or maybe it was intended to represent the virile bull, rather than the emasculated steer. Or maybe . . . maybe I should just focus on the drinks and leave the critical analysis to the English majors (I only minored). Perhaps Hemingway would want it that way, anyway. Indeed, when asked by George Plimpton if there were symbols in his works, Hemingway replied:

> I suppose there are symbols since critics keep finding them. If you do not mind I dislike talking about them and being questioned about them. It is hard enough to write books and stories without being asked to explain them as well. Also it deprives the explainers of work. If five or six or more good explainers can keep going why should I interfere with them? Read anything I write for the pleasure of reading it. Whatever else you find will be the measure of what you brought to the reading.[10]

Works for me.

Armagnac & Soda

2 oz. Armagnac

4 oz. sparkling water (Hemingway called for Perrier)

Add all ingredients to a collins glass filled with ice, stir, and serve.

SUGGESTED READING: *The Garden of Eden* (Chapters 2 and 10)

This drink is essentially a Brandy & Soda, but with Armagnac, produced in southwestern France. Along with Cognac, it is thought by connoisseurs to be among the finest grape brandies in the world. It's a bit ironic that both are distilled from the otherwise pedestrian grapes Ugni Blanc, Folle Blanche, and Colombard. That such a common wine could be distilled and aged to yield such uncommon brandies is a testament to the resourcefulness of their makers.

Armagnac is steeped in tradition. Many Armagnacs are aged for decades in barrels crafted from the dark oak trees of the nearby Monlezun forest, which imparts a rich color to the finished product. Some producers never get to taste their finest wares, but are able to enjoy what their ancestors laid down, just as their own children and grandchildren will savor their labors. Some evaporation takes place during aging; this lost portion is romantically called "the angel's share."

Hemingway drank his share of Armagnac during World War

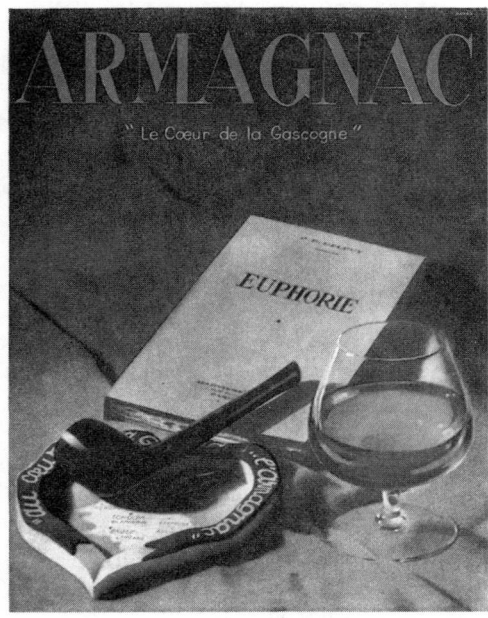

1948 Armagnac ad. From the author's collection.

II, once noting that he "fought best and clearest headed on Armagnac (couldn't even taste champagne no matter how brut after first 50 days)."[11] Of course, he was known to eat and drink as the locals did, as happens in *The Garden of Eden.*

In Chapter 2 David and Catherine Bourne enjoy this classic highball in the coastal commune of Le Grau du Roi. David is a writer, and he and his new bride, Catherine, are on an extended honeymoon on the Mediterranean. David is having a vermouth at a café and is soon joined by Catherine. They both agree that the vermouth is "dull" and want something "real." David asks, "Did you ever drink Armagnac and soda? That's real enough." So they ask the waiter to bring them a bottle of Armagnac and a chilled bottle of Perrier, instead of the seltzer bottle of ordinary charged water. "This will fix us," David says. "It's a hell of a thing to drink before lunch though." Catherine tastes it, describing it as having "a fresh clean healthy ugly taste." Hemingway notes that "The cold Perrier had made the heavy brandy alive."

It's also featured in Chapter 10, in what is perhaps the turning point of the story. We're introduced to Marita, the beautiful girl who forms the third part of the novel's love triangle. We find David and Catherine at a café; David is having a Haig Scotch & Perrier, while Catherine has another Armagnac & Perrier. Sitting nearby, Marita has a *fine à l'eau*; her friend, a Chambéry Cassis. In addition to their drinks, they're having a fight, arguing over the propriety of whether they should ask David and Catherine where they got their hair cut. After her friend storms off, Marita joins David and Catherine, first at their table, then a bit more than that.

In the chapter that follows, Catherine befriends Marita, while David works on his novel. Marita soon falls in love with both David and Catherine, and the three begin a rather odd and passionate ménage à trois. Marita takes a room at the hotel, they eat and drink together, and they swim together (sometimes au naturel). Before you know it, David has two girls, and then Catherine finds herself the odd girl out.

Once again Hemingway has based his fiction on real-life events. In the summer of 1926, when his second wife, Pauline, was beginning to pry him away from his first wife, Hadley, it began as a friendship between the two women, and the three did a lot together. Following the Hemingways' visit to Gerald and Sara Murphy's Villa America in Cap d'Antibes (see the Bailey and the Villa America Special), the trio rented two rooms at the Hôtel de la Pinède in nearby Juan-les-Pins, not far from Cannes, the general locale for this portion of *The Garden of Eden*. According to biographer Carlos Baker:

It was near the beach and had a small garden where the *ménage à trois* took most of their meals. Each morning they spent on the beach, swimming and taking the sun. . . . [A]t the hotel there were three of everything: breakfast trays, bicycles, bathing suits drying on the line—and worst of all two women in love with the same man. Hadley was at some pains to pretend that nothing was amiss.[12]

Pamplona, the "dangerous summer" of 1926. Seated from left to right, Gerald Murphy, Sara Murphy, Pauline Pfeiffer, Ernest, and Hadley. Hemingway was married to Hadley but having an affair with her eventual replacement, Pauline. Here he learned the wisdom he'd later share in his bullfighting treatise *The Dangerous Summer*, that "Pamplona is no place to bring your wife." Ernest Hemingway Photograph Collection, John F. Kennedy Presidential Library and Museum, Boston.

Pauline, of course, prevailed. Ernest and Hadley divorced in 1927, and Pauline and Ernest wed shortly thereafter. In many respects, Hemingway's memoir *A Moveable Feast* was a tribute not only to Paris, but also to Hadley, a bit of an idealized homage to both.

Bailey

1½ oz. gin
½ oz. grapefruit juice
½ oz. fresh lime juice
1 tsp. simple syrup (optional)
1 sprig mint

Gerald Murphy instructs (from a letter to Alexander Woollcott):[13]

The mint should be put in the shaker first. It should be torn up by hand as it steeps better. The gin should be added then and allowed to stand a minute or two. Then add the grapefruit juice and then the lime juice. Stir vigorously with ice and do not allow to dilute too much, but serve very cold, with a sprig of mint in each glass.

Serve in a chilled cocktail glass or wineglass.

The Bailey is one of two Gerald Murphy cocktails featured herein. He and his wife, Sara, were wealthy expatriates who, feeling stifled by American culture, abandoned New York for Paris in 1921. Soon the couple began to make the acquaintance of the great writers, artists, and bohemians of 1920s Paris. They bought a home on the French Riviera, Villa America, where they were all but credited with inventing the summer season on the Côte d'Azur. Here, during the 1920s, they were the focal point of a large circle that included Zelda and F. Scott Fitzgerald, the Hemingways, Pablo Picasso, Robert Benchley, Dorothy Parker, and many others.

The Murphys would throw legendary dinner parties, which Sara called a "Dinner-Flowers-Gala," a term borrowed from ocean liners of the day. They began with Gerald's cocktails on the terrace (never more than two). It was said that "even the most mundane act—the way Gerald prepared a cocktail, or a walk from the Murphys' house to the beach—was somehow transformed into a memorable event."[14] While watching him make drinks, playwright Philip Barry noted: "Gerald, you look as though you're saying mass."[15] In *A Moveable Feast*, Hemingway (somewhat derisively, I might add) described the Murphy approach to life: "that every day should be a fiesta."[16]

And Gerald was known for his one-liners, as well; he might toss back a well-made cocktail and comment, "This drink has gone straight to my head, which is just what I intended it to do." One of his quips even made it into an Oscar-winning film. When asked what went into one of his classic cocktails, he might coyly reply, "Just the juice of a few flowers." Philip Barry ended up using that line in *The Philadelphia Story*. It's in the scene where Cary Grant offers Katharine Hepburn a stinger as a hangover remedy.

It occurs to me that the Bailey resembles another classic, called the Southside, said to have been the favorite drink of Chicago's Southside mob during Prohibition. Somehow that drink made its way to the Hamptons, Long Island, where it remains popular to this day. Both Sara and Gerald were from the Hamptons and lived their last days there. Is there a connection? It has stumped cocktail geeks for decades, how a drink popular with Chicagoland gangsters became embraced by genteel country club types back east. Did Gerald have anything to do with it? It's one of life's delicious mysteries.

As for the Bailey, *Wall Street Journal* columnist Eric Felten speculates that perhaps it was this drink that first introduced Hemingway to the idea of marrying grapefruit and lime juice in a tart, sugarless cocktail (see the Papa Doble), and he notes that adding "just a teaspoon of sugar or simple syrup makes the drink sing."[17] I happen to agree on both counts. I further submit to you that the Bailey might just be about as close to a Mojito as Hemingway would ever come, the possibly forged scribbling on the wall at La Bodeguita del Medio notwithstanding. But that is a discussion for another chapter.

In May 1926, Hemingway was off writing in Madrid, and the Murphys persuaded Hadley and toddler son Bumby to come to Villa America. Hemingway was to join them when his work was done. A party was planned for the evening of his arrival, and Hadley and the Murphys dutifully met him at the train station. Also tagging along, I should mention, was a young Paris editor of *Vogue* magazine named Pauline Pfeiffer, who'd joined their circle of friends. The Murphys loved her keen wit and sense of style. Hemingway did, too, and more. See, he'd been having an affair with her for several months.

The Murphys' party that evening was particularly memorable, though not for all the right reasons. Pauline, Hadley, and Sara were all doting on the newly arrived and suntanned Hemingway, much to the chagrin of Fitzgerald, who was jealous not only of Hemingway's success, but of Sara's attentiveness to him. Fueled by envy and alcohol, Fitzgerald started tossing ashtrays off the terrace, then harassing other women guests. He then wrapped himself in a rug and crawled around the party, whining, "Sara's being mean to me."[18] He tied it up in a bow by insulting Gerald on how silly and affected the party was.

For Hemingway, the evening was only the beginning of the

long, painful process of replacing Hadley with Pauline. The three of them would extend their holiday to nearby Juan-les-Pins. But just as happened with the ménage à trois in *The Garden of Eden*, it couldn't last forever; one of the women would have to leave. It was the summer of their discontent, indeed.

The Bellini

4 oz. chilled prosecco (an Italian sparkling wine)
2 oz. white peach puree

In a mixing glass, add the peach puree and ice, then slowly add the prosecco. With a teaspoon, carefully dredge up the puree from the bottom, until the components are well mixed. Strain into a chilled champagne flute.

Originally, I wasn't sure I was going to include this chapter. I had the idea that I wouldn't offer any drink that I couldn't actually place in Hemingway's hand, wanting to avoid mere speculation. Integrity and all that. But that would have barred, for example, the two offerings from Gerald Murphy, the Bailey and the Villa America Special. Call me unreliable . . .

What we do know is that the Bellini was invented at Harry's Bar in Venice in 1948, when owner Giuseppe Cipriani was inspired by the delicate pink glow of a garment as depicted in a painting by Italian Renaissance painter Giovanni Bellini. He wanted to replicate that lovely hue in a cocktail and to capture the magic of the local produce. As the story is told by his son, Arrigo Cipriani, "Peaches are in abundance throughout Italy from June to September, and my father had a predilection for the white ones. So much so, in fact, that he kept wondering whether there was a way to transform this magic fragrance into a drink he could offer at

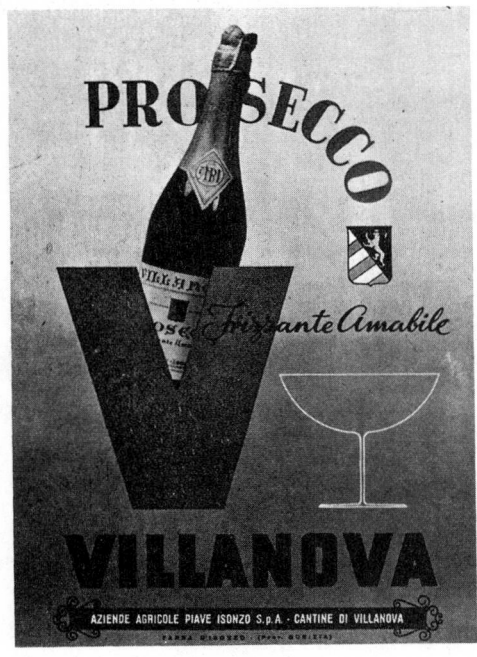

Vintage prosecco ad from 1948. From the author's collection.

Harry's Bar. He experimented by pureeing small white peaches and adding some *prosecco* (Italian champagne). Those who tested this new concoction gave it rave reviews. . . ."[19]

We also know that Hemingway became more or less a regular at Harry's the following year, while writing *Across the River and Into the Trees*. "One of our most faithful regulars in 1949 and 1950 was Ernest Hemingway. . . . He burst into Harry's Bar for the first time in the fall of 1949."[20]

And we also know that, well, Hemingway liked to drink. Your honor, the state rests.

Seriously, beyond the circumstantial evidence, you'll also find a few newspaper accounts that claim that Cipriani actually invented the drink as a way of offering his friend Hemingway a lower-alcohol alternative to all those powerful 15:1 Montgomery Martinis he was throwing back. In a syndicated column in October of 1986, United Press International's John DeMers stated that "[a]ccording to legend, Giuseppe Cipriani invented the Bellini cocktail at Harry's Bar in Venice to help his pal Ernest Hemingway cut back on his martinis. . . . Whenever Hemingway was drinking in more than atmosphere in Venice, he knocked back both Bellinis and martinis."[21]

Additionally, in an interview with Hemingway's granddaughter Mariel Hemingway, she was asked, "Is there a popular Hemingway family dish that is still occasionally prepared when you get together with relatives?" Mariel replied, "My grandfather truly loved foods of all kinds. He left a legacy of drinks behind more than anything else. I am not a drinker, but I suppose if I were I would have to say it would be a Bellini. That would be a pure Hemingway drink."[22]

I'm offering these more for anecdotal purposes—heck, call it wallpaper. You likely know by now that I have a healthy disdain for newspapers, especially when it comes to "cocktail history." I could line a thousand canary cages with the "news stories" that depict Hemingway drinking Mojitos at La Bodeguita del Medio. So, I offer the decision to you, dear reader. The Bellini is a very nice drink, a classic, and if you want to join the lovely Mariel Hemingway in considering it "a pure Hemingway drink," I'll not argue with you!

Bloody Mary

MAKES 1 PITCHER

16 oz. vodka
16 oz. tomato juice
1 Tbsp. Worcestershire sauce (or A.1.)
1½ oz. fresh lime juice
Celery salt (to taste)
Cayenne pepper (to taste)
Black pepper (to taste)
Large lump of ice

SUGGESTED READING: *A Moveable Feast* ("A False Spring" and "The End of an Avocation"), *Ernest Hemingway: Selected Letters*

There seem to be as many stories relating to the origin (and naming) of the Bloody Mary as there are variations on the recipe. Perhaps the most popular one attributes it to Fernand "Pete" Petiot, who tended bar at Harry's New York Bar in Paris, circa 1921. The name was allegedly coined by Roy Barton, an American entertainer, after a Chicago club called the Bucket of Blood. As the story goes, Petiot brought the drink to the St. Regis Hotel in New York, where he renamed it the Red Snapper.

Legendary bartender Dale DeGroff tells of a conversation with Harry MacElhone's grandson Duncan, who said that Petiot named the drink "Bloody Mary" after a woman "who sat at the bar for long hours pining for a boyfriend who seldom kept appointments with her."[23]

The Hemingways at the Stork Club with Nancy Hawks, Spencer Tracy, Leland Heyward, and George Jessel, self-proclaimed father of the Bloody Mary. Courtesy Getty Images.

Another story tells us that entertainer George Jessel invented the Bloody Mary in Palm Beach in 1927, to fight a wicked hangover. In a 1939 item in the *New York Herald Tribune*, gossip columnist Lucius Beebe noted that "George Jessel's newest pick-me-up . . . is called a Bloody Mary: half tomato juice, half vodka." The name came from Jessel's friend Mary Warburton, of the Wanamaker department store family. After spilling it on her white evening dress, she blurted out, "Now, you can call me Bloody Mary, George!"[24]

But like any drink worth its celery salt, there are multiple claims of inventorship. Yet another story surrounds, you guessed it, a fellow named Hemingway. According to Colin Peter Field, head bartender of the Ritz Paris's Hemingway Bar:

Bernard "Bertin" Azimont, the bartender of the Ritz Paris's Petit Bar . . . told me one day over lunch how he invented the Bloody Mary in the 1950s: he had, he said, concocted it for Ernest Hemingway. The doctors had forbidden the writer to drink. Mary, Hemingway's wife, had taken the interdiction very seriously and had placed him under close watch. Stealth and cunning were needed, and so it was that Bertin devised the ingenious mixture, a drink packed full of alcohol that could not be detected on the writer's breath. Hemingway, he said, was so pleased that he had got the better of his "bloody wife" that he named the drink after her. . . . If only it were that easy: there exists a letter written by Hemingway himself in 1947 giving the precise recipe for the Bloody Mary, offering information that he had enjoyed it in China as early as 1941.[25]

Now that you mention it, here's a bit of that letter, written to his friend Bernard Peyton, in which he shares the recipe for a pitcher of Bloody Marys (noting that any lesser quantity was "worthless"):

[T]ake a good sized pitcher and put in it as big a lump of ice as it will hold. (This is to prevent too rapid melting and watering of our product.) Mix a pint of good russian vodka and an equal amount of chilled tomato juice. Add a table spoon full of Worcester Sauce. . . . Stirr [*sic*]. Then add a jigger of fresh squeezed lime juice. Stir. Then add small amounts of celery salt, cayenne pepper, black pepper. . . . If you get it too powerful weaken with more tomato juice. If it lacks authority add more vodka. Some people like more lime than others. For combatting a really terrific hangover increase the amount of Worcester sauce—but don't lose the lovely color.[26]

Speaking of the Paris Ritz, in 1950 Hemingway "adopted the bar as his Head Quarters and spent many hours there planning his strategies for the horse races at Auteuil." All of this was done "under the profound inspiration of Bertin's Bloody Marys."[27]

As a final note, Hemingway's recipe says nothing about garnish. Celery, of course, is a standard adornment, and other options abound. My own favorites include pickled string beans (as is served at the Columns Hotel in New Orleans) or pickled okra.

All the Tea in China

In the letter referenced above, Hemingway also claimed to have introduced the Bloody Mary to Hong Kong in 1941, noting that only the Japanese army had more to do with its downfall. While that might have been a boast, he did in fact visit the Far East with his third wife, Martha Gellhorn; they were covering the war between Japan and China. While on that arduous assignment, Hemingway faced innumerable challenges when looking for a decent drink. He had to endure such bizarre local "delicacies" as rice wine having either a dead snake or bird in the bottle (much like the worm in tequila).[28]

In Chungking (Chongqing), Hemingway met a young navy lieutenant named Lederer, who'd purchased two cases of whiskey at an auction. Hemingway wanted to buy some, but Lederer was saving them for a farewell party. Hemingway adopted the role of Epicurus and advised him to "never delay kissing a pretty girl . . . or opening a bottle of whiskey." He made a deal with Lederer, swapping six writing lessons for six bottles of whiskey. At the end of the course, Hemingway told Lederer that a writer above all should never laugh at another's mistakes, and he should roll with the punches. He then suggested that the young man go home and sample his whiskey.

When Lederer did so, he discovered that he'd been swindled: the bottles contained tea, not whiskey. Carlos Baker writes, "Hemingway had known the truth for nearly a week. Yet he had neither laughed at the victim nor evaded his part of the bargain. Lederer salted his story away for twenty years. From that day in Chunking he always remembered Hemingway as a civilized man."[29]

Brandy & Soda
(*Fine à l'Eau*)

2 oz. brandy (Cognac if *fine à l'eau*)
4 oz. club soda or sparkling mineral water

Combine ingredients in a collins glass filled with ice. Stir and serve.

SUGGESTED READING: *The Sun Also Rises* (Chapters 1 and 10), *A Moveable Feast* ("Ford Madox Ford and the Devil's Disciple"; "With Pascin at the Dôme"), *The Garden of Eden* (Chapters 3 and 4)

ll Cognacs are brandies, but not all brandies are Cognacs. So a Brandy & Soda uses any grape brandy, whereas a *fine à l'eau* has Cognac. The word *fine* is short for *Grande Fine Champagne*, a blend of Grande Champagne and Petite Champagne Cognac. This drink was immensely popular in the 1920s and '30s. But by the 1950s, the *fine à l'eau* had fallen out of fashion somewhat; even Ian Fleming was throwing dirt on the casket, observing in *For Your Eyes Only* that a "*Fine à l'Eau* is fairly serious, but it intoxicates without tasting very good." But in 1920s Paris, Brandy & Soda and *fine à l'eau* were all the rage, and you'll find Hemingway's characters tipping 'em back quite a bit.

In *The Sun Also Rises*, he writes about a group of rather dissipated young people in 1920s Paris. Jake Barnes is in love with Lady Brett Ashley, an unrequited love at that. One evening, Jake is out for the

evening with a woman he's just picked up, and he runs into a group of friends. By this point, he's lost all interest in the girl and the evening and is pretty much just going through the motions. The girl, by the way, is a *poule*, a polite term for a prostitute. Jake has a *fine à l'eau* and is "a little drunk. Not drunk in any positive sense but just enough to be careless." Brett shows up, only adding to Jake's gloomy mood. Brett's in fine spirits, however, saying, "I say, give a chap a brandy and soda."

Hemingway in front of his apartment, 113 Rue Notre-Dame-des-Champs, circa 1924. Ernest Hemingway Photograph Collection, John F. Kennedy Presidential Library and Museum, Boston.

The Brandy & Soda makes more appearances throughout *The Sun Also Rises*, with Jake or Brett "getting brandy and soda and glasses" or reaching for the siphon (seltzer bottle) to make a short one at home. It's as much a part of the background as the drapes and the furniture, one of the go-to cocktails of the Lost Generation, it seems.

The *fine à l'eau* is also found in *The Garden of Eden*. David Bourne and his newlywed wife, Catherine, are on holiday. They've had a decadent lunch, featuring a bottle of cold white wine, celery ré-moulade, and grilled sea bass. They retire to their room, and afterward, David goes for a walk and ends up at a café, ordering a *fine à l'eau* "because he felt empty and hollow from making love." He notes that it is the "first time since they had come on the wedding trip that he had taken a drink of brandy or whiskey when they were not together."

Brandy and Cognac are something of an acquired taste. The Brandy & Soda is an excellent "gateway" drink to help to begin to appreciate these complex flavors. The Sidecar is another one, a classic cocktail that showcases the brilliance that is the distilled fruit of the vine (see also the Villa America Special).

The Sense of Place

Hemingway understood the societal and communal role of the café, the watering hole, and the accompanying sense of place that is part of the human condition. Indeed, he spends the first six paragraphs of the short story "The Denunciation" extolling the virtues of Chicote's in Madrid, and its role as a place of refuge for a wartime city under siege. It was "the place where you dropped in to find out who was in town, or where they had gone to if they were out of town. And if it was summer, and there was no one in town, you could always sit and enjoy a drink because the waiters were all pleasant." Hemingway notes, "All we old clients of Chicote's had a sort of feeling about the place." This was no more true than in the case of the doomed Luis Delgado, who risked his life to spend an afternoon at Chicote's in "The Denunciation." "He just wanted to have a drink in the old place. Knowing him, and knowing the place in the old days, it would be perfectly understandable."

In *Across the River and Into the Trees*, that place is Harry's Bar in Venice. In one scene, Colonel Cantwell is making his way across Venice, an arduous walk made all the more difficult by his chest pains. But then, "he was pulling open the door of Harry's bar and was inside and he had made it again, and was at home."

In *A Moveable Feast*, Hemingway writes of such a spot in Paris, the Closerie des Lilas: "It was warm inside in the winter and in the spring and fall it was very fine outside with the tables under the shade of the trees."

Years later, with a few more francs to rub together, his "home" in Paris would be a bit more upscale: "When I dream of afterlife in heaven, the action always takes place in the Paris Ritz."[30]

Perhaps my favorite example of the societal role of the café is in the short story "A Clean, Well-Lighted Place." This is the poignant tale of a lonely old man. He spends his evenings at a café. "In the day time the street was dusty, but at night the dew settled the dust and the old man liked to sit late because he was deaf and now at night it was quiet and he felt the difference."

One of the waiters at the café is young and too selfish and callous to understand the old man's loneliness. The other waiter does understand and is compassionate. He further knows the role of the café in the wee small hours; he knows the old man is like himself, one of "those who like to stay late at the café. . . . With all those who need a light for the night." He "disliked bars and *bodegas*. A clean, well-lighted café was a very different thing."

A final comment on this story concerns the title, a matter of dispute between Hemingway and *Esquire* publisher Arnold Gingrich. "Contrary to your estimable opinion 'A Clean Well Lighted Place' is a damned fine title and 'Give Us a Night Light' is lousy," wrote Hemingway.[31] We can only be thankful that the story was published in *Scribner's* magazine, not *Esquire*.

The Bronx Cocktail

¾ oz. London dry gin

¾ oz. dry vermouth

¾ oz. sweet vermouth

⅔ oz. fresh orange juice

Shake well with ice, strain into a chilled cocktail glass. Garnish with orange peel.

NOTE: This recipe is from *Dining in Chicago: An Intimate Guide*, by John Drury (1931), which instructs us to "shake well, and then note the results upon imbibing."[32]

Since this chapter deals with the Bronx, I'll obviously spend most of my time talking about one of the greatest of American cities . . . Chicago. The Bronx cocktail is an all-time classic, going back over a century; the recipe likely debuted in the 1908 edition of William "Cocktail" Boothby's *The World's Drinks and How to Mix Them*. As is often the case with the classics, you'll find wide variations in the recipe and proportions of each ingredient. Sometimes the vermouth is on equal footing with the gin, sometimes far less. David Embury noted that in the somewhat similar Orange Blossom (gin and orange juice), which he considered "one of the horrors of Prohibition," the juice is the modifier, whereas

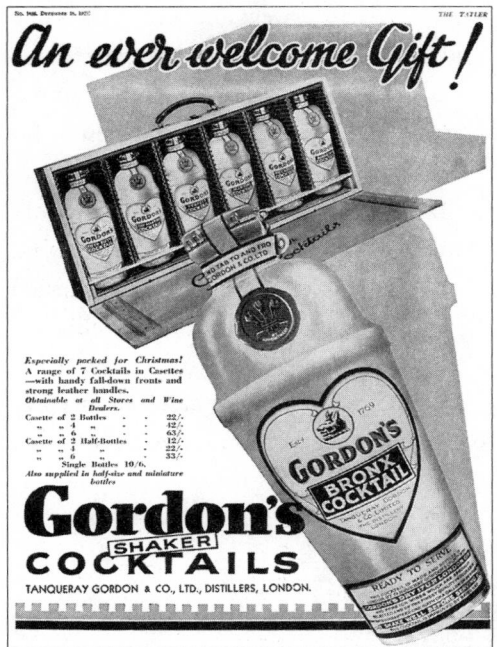

1929 Gordon's Gin magazine ad (UK). From the author's collection.

vermouth played that role in the Bronx, with the orange merely adding flavor and color.[33] Note that by adding Angostura bitters to the Bronx, it becomes an Income Tax cocktail. Now you know.

F. Scott Fitzgerald included the Bronx in his 1920 classic novel *This Side of Paradise*, where it factors in a rather drunken evening for protagonist Amory Blaine. He's at the old Knickerbocker Bar in New York, drowning his sorrows after a romantic breakup, and having more than a few belts with some fellow Princetonians. He's drinking Bronxes, "his head spinning gorgeously, layer upon layer of soft satisfaction setting over the bruised spots of his spirit."

The Bronx cocktail claims a degree of infamy, as well. After all, it was the first drink ever enjoyed by a nervous young World War I lieutenant named Bill Wilson who, during a party in Newport, found that the Bronx "tasted wonderful, sweet and airy at the same time. . . . My gaucheries and ineptitudes magically disappeared. . . . I had found the elixir of life." Well, perhaps that's a bit of a mischaracterization; booze became something other than an elixir for Bill Wilson. See, he went on to found Alcoholics Anonymous.[34]

For Hemingway, it was likely that his first taste of the almighty Bronx came around the same time as both Fitzgerald's novel and Bill Wilson's Newport soiree. In October of 1920, having returned from World War I and after spending some time "up in Michigan," Hemingway moved to Chicago. He shared an apartment with his friend Bill Horne, at 1230 North State Street. Nineteen twenty was a big year for him; he also began writing stories for the *Toronto Star*.

The College Inn, Chicago, where young Ernest and Hadley, fortified with "two Rounds of Bronix's [sic]," danced the night away in October, 1920, and fell in love. Postcard, 1919. From the author's collection.

And it was in Chicago that Hemingway would meet his first wife, Hadley Richardson, that very same October.

According to a letter Hemingway sent to his pal Bill Smith on October 25, Horne "throwed a party the other nocturnal at which a group of young people" were present, notably Katy Smith, Hadley, Horne, and Hemingway. After dinner at the Victor House, which included "two Rounds of Bronix's [sic]," they then "went to the College Inn and danced. We were in the finest of shape. It was a jovial affair."[35]

Note that it was October of 1920, and Prohibition was supposed to have been in force. Not so in Chicago. Indeed, in a November 16 letter to his friend Grace Quinlan, Hemingway observed, "The town is in no sense dry. In fact it's a long ways wetter than this time last year."[36] A month later, writing in the *Toronto Star Weekly*, Hemingway noted that "the Wild West hasn't disappeared. It has only moved. Just at present it is located at the southwestern end of Lake Michigan, and the range that the bad men ride is that enormous smoke jungle of buildings they call Chicago." At the core of this evil, of course, was the rapid rise in organized crime in the wake of Prohibition. "Chicago is supposed to be a dry town," he observed. "But anyone willing to pay twenty dollars a quart for whiskey can get all they want. . . . Now most of the whiskey you buy has a Kentucky label. Canadian whiskey costs too much and there is too much American liquor on hand."[37] Everybody, sing with me . . . *"Myyyy kind of town, Chi-ca-go is . . ."*

Anyway, Ernest and Hadley's love blossomed. They married the following November and moved to Paris thereafter. Perhaps it was the "Bronix's" that helped warm Ernest to Hadley, and finally expunge the pain from his World War I romance with Agnes von Kurowsky, his nurse in Milan while he recuperated from that Austrian mortar attack.

Hemingway and Hadley became quite the drinking buddies;

you see that throughout *A Moveable Feast* and his letters, and he often boasted about her prowess. In a letter to John Dos Passos sent from Paris in 1925, he wrote, "Wish you were here to drink. There's a girl named Hadley that's showing a lot of promise as a drinker and she wants to meet you."[38] And to think, "the Paris Wife" got her start in Chicago with the Bronx. You can't make this stuff up.

Campari & Gin

1–2 oz. London dry gin
1 oz. Campari

Pour over ice in a highball glass, stir. Garnish with orange peel.

CAMPARI, GIN & SODA
1–2 oz. London dry gin
1 oz. Campari
2–4 oz. soda water (to taste)

Pour over ice in a highball glass, stir. Garnish with orange peel.

SUGGESTED READING: *Across the River and Into the Trees* (Chapter 8), *True at First Light* (Chapters 1, 4, 5, 10, and 18), *Under Kilimanjaro* (Chapters 2, 9, 10, 11, 13, 19, 38, and 40), "Get a Seeing-Eyed Dog"

For more background on Campari, please see the Americano and the Negroni.

These two drinks complete the circle, so to speak; the Americano has Campari, vermouth, and seltzer, and the Negroni swaps out gin for the seltzer. Here we see the vermouth dropping out. They're all lovely drinks, and they highlight the versatility of Campari in cocktails.

The short story "Get a Seeing-Eyed Dog" is the poignant tale of a man facing the rest of his life having lost his sight, while apparently experiencing an enhancement of his other senses. As his companion walks up the stairs to his room, he can tell she's carrying drinks as opposed to walking empty-handed. When she enters, he reaches out his hand for the drink, and of course he finds it there. As his hand closes around it, he feels the gentle tap of her glass against his, as if to toast.

"It's our old drink for out here," she said. "Campari and Gordon's with ice."

"I'm certainly glad you're not a girl who would say 'on the rocks.'"

1909 Campari ad. Courtesy Davide Campari-Milano.

"No," she said. "I wouldn't ever say that. We've *been* on the rocks."

Campari is also featured in the 1950 novel *Across the River and Into the Trees*, Hemingway's story of an aging army colonel, Richard Cantwell, and his final days in Venice with his lover, Renata. In Chapter 8, we find him checking into his room at the Gritti Palace Hotel. He asks the bellman to ring Renata, but she is not there. When told that she might be at nearby Harry's Bar, the Colonel remarks that you can find anything at Harry's, including happiness, because happiness "is a movable feast."

The bellman then offers Colonel Cantwell a drink: "I have brought Campari bitters and a bottle of Gordon Gin. May I make you a Campari with gin and soda?"

Vintage 1937 Gordon's gin ad. From the author's collection.

"You're a good boy," the Colonel said.

He really shouldn't be drinking, but he takes the drink "with his old wild-boar truculence, as he had taken everything all of his life." Hemingway appears to be making an inside joke, perhaps referring to the wild boar on the Gordon's label.

"You find everything on earth at Harry's."

Colonel Cantwell spends a good bit of time in Harry's Bar. Hemingway became quite fond of Harry's and its owner, Giuseppe Cipriani, while writing the novel in 1949–50.

Harry's has an interesting story. Back in 1927, Cipriani was a bartender in the Italian resort town of San Remo. He foolishly lent a large sum of money to a customer, who promptly skipped town. He didn't exactly learn his lesson, and soon he loaned ten thousand lire to another customer, an American named Harry Pickering. Harry was visiting Italy with his aunt, her boyfriend/gigolo, and the aunt's dog. The four of them spent a lot of time and money in Cipriani's bar; even the little

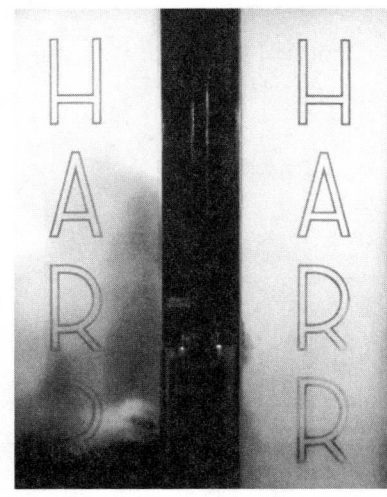

The iconic front doors of Harry's Bar in Venice. Courtesy Arrigo Cipriani.

dog came to the bar! When Harry's money ran dry, he borrowed from Cipriani.

Harry returned to the United States, leaving Cipriani to wait.

Months dragged by, and Cipriani concluded that he'd been fleeced again. But one day, behold! Harry returned, flush with good tidings, not to mention cash. "Cipriani, thank you so much. Here is your money. And to show you how grateful I am, take this as well. We can use it to open a bar together," Harry gushed. He not only repaid the ten thousand lire, but added an additional thirty thousand lire as interest.[39] Harry's Bar officially opened May 13, 1931.

Over the years, customers would remark about the good publicity Hemingway brought to Harry's. Cipriani's son Arrigo sees it differently: "You've got it the wrong way around; we gave *him* good publicity. It is no accident that he got the Nobel Prize after he wrote about Harry's Bar, not before."[40] Harry's is still there, along with Captain Tony's and Sloppy Joe's (Key West), the Floridita (Havana), and the Ritz Paris, a must-see stop on any Hemingway cocktail pilgrimage.

Capri with Fresh Peaches & Strawberries

1 bottle of Capri white wine
2-4 ripe peaches, sliced
6-10 strawberries, sliced

Add all ingredients to a tall glass pitcher, add ice and stir. Serve on the rocks.

SUGGESTED READING: *A Moveable Feast* ("A False Spring"), *A Farewell to Arms* (Chapters 7 and 18)

This is a lovely, light, and refreshing drink, perfect for a Sunday brunch or warm afternoon. The classic Italian wine, Capri bianca, is the basis for this charmer.

It seems to me that for Hemingway, in both his life and his prose, certain wines play a certain role. In *The Garden of Eden*, Tavel "is a great wine for people that are in love." In *The Sun Also Rises*, a bottle of Château Margaux was an apt companion while dining alone. "It was pleasant to be drinking slowly and to be tasting the wine and to be drinking alone," Jake Barnes noted. "A bottle of wine was good company." For Hemingway, Capri was a wine for

Vintage souvenir postcard from the Galleria Vittorio Emanuele II, showing Biffi Caffè, circa 1957. From the author's collection.

love, for reminiscing, and for closing your eyes and being somewhere else.

In *A Moveable Feast*, Ernest and Hadley reflect on their happy times together, when they "ate well and cheaply and drank well and cheaply and slept well and warm together and loved each other." They reminisce about "having fruit cup at Biffi's in the Galleria with Capri and fresh peaches and wild strawberries in a tall glass pitcher with ice." They're recalling one of their visits to Milan, Italy, in either 1922 or 1923, when they dined at the Biffi Caffè.

But this is not the only time we see Capri bianca in Hemingway's prose. The wine plays a starring role in *A Farewell to Arms*, where ambulance driver Frederic Henry has fallen in love with an American nurse, Catherine Barkley. He wishes not to be at the front in war-torn Italy, but with Catherine, in Milan. He longs to take her to dinner at the Cova, and then enjoy a nice, evening stroll with her down the Via Manzoni, along the canal, to their hotel. Once there, the porter would take them up the elevator to their room, the anticipation building as the elevator ascends, "very slowly clicking at all the floors and then our floor," and then Frederic would "take down the telephone and ask them to send a bottle of Capri bianca in a silver bucket full of ice and you would hear the ice against the pail coming down the corridor." When the boy arrived with the Capri, he'd knock on the door, but Frederic would ask that he leave it outside the door, because Frederic and Catherine would be making love, which they would do all night long, and they "would drink the Capri and the door locked and it hot and only a sheet and the whole night and we would both love each other all night in the hot night in Milan. That was how it ought to be."[41]

Phew . . .

Both Capri and Biffi's pop up again later on in *A Farewell to Arms*. In Chapter 18, Frederic is recuperating in the military hospital after nearly being killed by an Austrian trench mortar. He's allowed brief outings away from the hospital with Catherine. "We had a lovely time that summer. When I could go out we rode in a carriage in the park." He would take her to dinner "at Biffi's or the Gran Italia," where George the headwaiter would wait on them, and they "drank dry white capri iced in a bucket." Clearly, the marriage of the ice bucket and the cold bottle of Capri had a romantic connotation in Hemingway's mind; one can almost hear the metallic sound when the bottle rattles against the icy water. It's a sound of luxury, of living well, of the good life.

Once again, we see Hemingway's real life being carried out in the pages of fiction. Catherine Barkley is based on the real-life nurse Agnes von Kurowsky, Hemingway's first true love. She cared for him as he recovered from the near-fatal wounding. Of course, life isn't so bad; he's safe now, away from the war, having a little

"Swank[ing] about a bit." Hemingway in Milan, Italy, 1918. That's Agnes to his right, along with two other American Red Cross nurses at the San Siro horseracing track. Ernest Hemingway Photograph Collection, John F. Kennedy Presidential Library and Museum, Boston.

R&R while falling for a beautiful woman. In a 1923 *Toronto Star* column, he noted that "I do not mind being blown up in the trenches so much; it has its good side, you leave the trench and go to a hospital, you convalesce, you even swank about a bit."[42] Hey, when in Rome . . . er, I mean Milan . . .

Carburetion

3 oz. Cognac

Instructions from Hemingway's friend Grant Mason:

Take a large mouthful, but don't swallow it now. Swish it around in your mouth half a minute or so. Hold it. Now exhale through your nose—completely deflate your lungs. That's right. Then swallow the cognac to get it out of the way. Open your mouth. Quickly! Inhale as deeply as you can.[43]

Carburetion is not a drink, but rather a method of drinking good Cognac. It goes back to a sultry night near Havana in the early 1930s. Hemingway had been fishing for several weeks with his Key West buddies Charles Thompson and Joe Russell (owner of Sloppy Joe's) aboard Russell's boat *Anita*. They'd caught nearly a thousand pounds of marlin when bad weather forced them into the port town of Jaimanitas. So, looking for a good time, they went in search of Hemingway's friend Grant Mason.

Mason was a wealthy executive with Pan American Airlines, which had capitalized upon Prohibition by opening air routes to Havana. He was married to the gorgeous twenty-two-year-old Jane Mason. Jane was away, so the four set about cooking up some fun, and "got an entire suburb of Havana cockeyed—on the finest vintage brandy in the world. That party lasted two solid days and into a third."[44]

Hemingway having a drink with Charles Thompson, near Dry Tortugas, circa 1928. Courtesy Waldo Peirce Collection—Colby College, and Karin Peirce.

It started innocently enough. Grant announced that he had "a new way to drink called carburetion, . . . based on the principle of carburetion in good engines. What you need most is a good mixture, . . . such as a fine Cognac." It so happened that Grant had recently purchased five dozen cases of vintage Cognac, salvaged from a sunken French schooner.

Grant instructed Hemingway as described above, to hold the Cognac in his mouth, then exhale, swallow, and inhale sharply. As Hemingway did so, and the pleasing results registered on his face, Grant noted that "it enters your lungs in a fine mist that way. Goes into your blood stream faster, like a carburetor that gives the best mixture for burning in an engine."

They embraced carburetion with gusto, and "soon the room was filled with exhaling sounds like those of dying porpoises." Russell and Thompson soon retired, but Hemingway and Mason were determined not only to keep on drinking, but to preach the gospel to the locals. Hemingway reasoned, "Why should the honest fishermen of this barrio sit playing dominoes over who slugs the next stranger when they could be enjoying this boon to humanity?" So, "like a pair of jolly Santas, weighted down with cases of fine cognac, Ernest and Grant headed down the streets of Jaimanitas, knocking on rickety wooden doors." Before they were done, they'd distributed some three dozen cases, no doubt knocking back some of that themselves. Mason became infamous among the locals that night as "the gringo who invented *carbinacion*."[45]

Pan Am Clipper leaving Miami. From the author's collection.

Vintage Cognac label. Courtesy Alexandre Gabriel/Cognac Ferrand.

Jane Mason

Jane Mason was not your typical American housewife. According to a friend, she was "one of the wildest, hairiest, most drinking, wenching, sexy superwomen in the world. . . . She was proud of being the model for the Macomber woman in 'The Short Happy Life of Francis Macomber.'"[46]

Beginning in 1932, Hemingway began going over to Havana from Key West to fish and write. He and Pauline soon befriended the Masons, and Jane gave Pauline two pink flamingos to dress up the yard on Whitehead Street. Not the ornamental ones, mind you, *live* flamingos! Jane and Hemingway soon became fishing buddies, drinking buddies, and, many believe, lovers. Ernest liked to brag that Jane would sneak through the transom of his hotel room at the Ambos Mundos Hotel in Havana. Pauline, getting a bit worried about all the time Ernest was spending with her, jokingly wrote to him from Key West, "Am having large nose, imperfect lips, protruding ears and warts and moles all taken off before coming to Cuba. Thought I'd better, Mrs. Mason and those Cuban women are so lovely."[47] Pauline even dyed her hair blond to try to compete with Jane.

As a final note, in *To Have and Have Not*, Hemingway likely based the characters of Tommy and Helene Bradley on Grant and Jane. In the original draft, Grant as Tommy is "an impotent playboy," and Jane is "his nymphomaniac wife, Helene, who collects writers."[48] Yet another instance of where if you're a friend of Hemingway's, you might end up in one of his stories, for better or for worse.

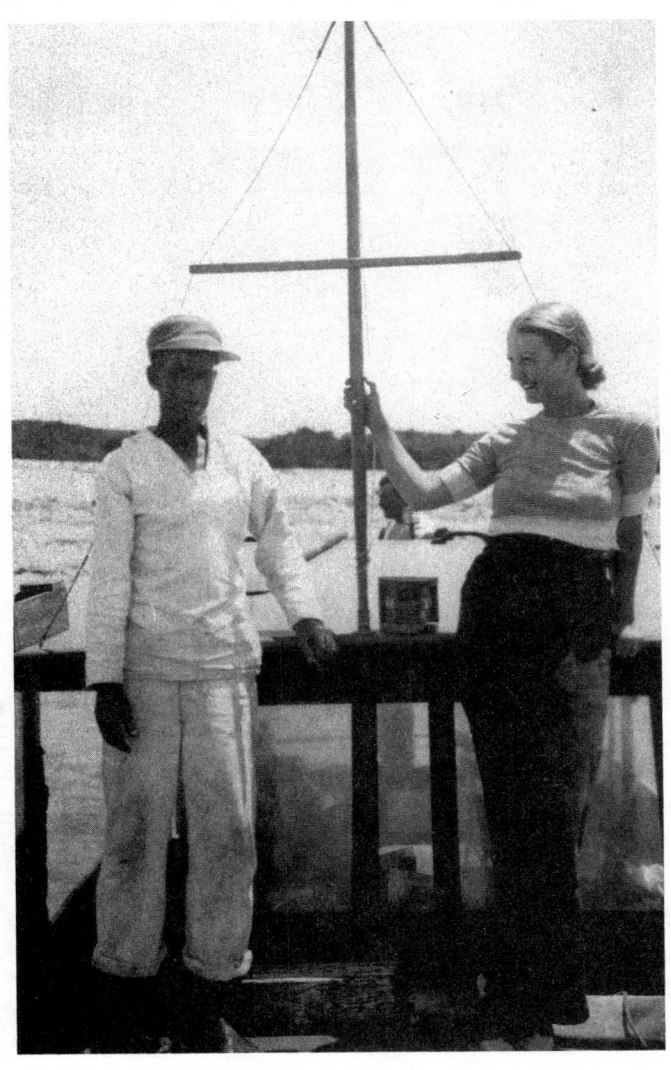

Carlos Gutierrez and Jane Mason aboard Joe Russell's boat *Anita*, 1933 (Hemingway is in background). Ernest Hemingway Photograph Collection, John F. Kennedy Presidential Library and Museum, Boston.

Cayo Hueso La Floridita

2 oz. white rum
½ oz. lime juice
3–4 oz. grapefruit soda

Add all ingredients to a highball glass filled with ice. Stir, garnish with a lime wedge, serve.

Adapted from Betty Bruce's recipe.

SUGGESTED READING: "A Key West Girl"

Canada Dry matchbook cover. From the author's collection.

Cayo Hueso is the original name for Key West, literally meaning "island of bones," named for the many bones said to have been encountered by Spanish explorers.

Betty and T. Otto "Toby" Bruce were Key West friends of the Hemingways. This recipe was given to me by their son, Benjamin "Dink" Bruce. Per Betty's recipe, "the drink is similar in flavor to a daquarie [sic], especially in the punch form." She refers to it as a "variation highball," in other words, a highball version of the Hemingway Daiquiri. It's a lovely little drink, perfect for the warm Key West climate.

Meet the Bruces

Pauline's family home was in Piggott, Arkansas. During a visit there, Hemingway came to know Toby Bruce, who lived nearby. Hemingway brought Toby to Key West to help renovate the house at 907 Whitehead Street in the early 1930s. Toby fell in love with Betty Moreno, married her, and became a fixture in the Hemingways' lives.

Toby and Betty lived for a while near San Francisco during the war, but Key West beckoned them back. The lure of the island on a young man such as Toby was captured in a Hemingway short story fragment titled "A Key West Girl," said to have been based on Betty. It tells of the strong pull that the island exerts on its natives. A man from up north who marries a Key West girl might be able to take her away from the island, but

Toby Bruce at the Hemingway home bar in Sun Valley, with the ubiquitous bottles of Gordon's gin, Noilly Prat vermouth, and White Horse Scotch, not to mention Papa's battered "Ginny Flask." Bruce Family Archive.

only for a while; Key West will inevitably draw them back. Hemingway wryly notes that it's the likely reason why a Key Wester never conquered the world.[49]

According to Ernest's son Gregory, "it was with Toby Bruce . . . that Hemingway had his most enduring Key West friendship."[50] Hemingway described Toby in a 1948 letter to Malcolm Cowley: "Otto is a very good guy. . . . He has been a completely loyal friend and he has wonderful talents for very varied things. He is also very fine company and we have wonderful times driveing [*sic*] across the country."[51]

Toby had many talents: he built the wall around the Hemingway house in Key West, designed the dust jacket of *For Whom the Bell Tolls*, and negotiated the purchase of the Finca Vigía in Cuba. After Ernest's death, Toby was of invaluable assistance to his widow, Mary, leading her to a Sloppy Joe's storeroom where Ernest had stashed a treasure trove of letters, photos, manuscripts, and other materials.

Chambéry Cassis (Vermouth Cassis)

3 oz. dry Chambéry vermouth
½ oz. crème de cassis liqueur
1–2 oz. club soda (to taste)

Fill a highball or collins glass with ice, add ingredients, stir well.

SUGGESTED READING: *A Moveable Feast*, restored edition ("Ford Madox Ford and the Devil's Disciple" and "Secret Pleasures"), *The Garden of Eden* (Chapter 10), *A Farewell to Arms* (Chapter 13)

Although relegated to a supporting role in many cocktails, vermouth gets top billing in this classic, which often goes simply by the name Vermouth Cassis. Chambéry is a city in the foothills of the French Alps, where this lighter, drier style of vermouth is made.

Vermouth is a fortified wine (alcohol is added to it), infused with a variety of herbs, spices, and botanicals, even traces of wormwood (after all, *vermouth* comes from the German *wermut*, for wormwood). Most vermouth recipes are trade secrets.

In the Chambéry Cassis, vermouth is paired with crème de cassis, a liqueur made from black currants. The Vermouth Cassis was a popular drink in the 1920s and '30s, and it is found in such classics as Harry Craddock's 1930 *Savoy Cocktail Book.*

The Chambéry Cassis is featured twice in *A Moveable Feast*, Hemingway's memoir of his days as a young writer in 1920s Paris. The first instance takes place in a comical essay titled "Ford Madox Ford and the Devil's Disciple." Hemingway was at the Closerie des Lilas. He often went there to write, to warm up, and to escape from his noisy flat. Hemingway was sitting at a table, just enjoying the evening, watching the light change, taking in the sights of the world passing by on the broad Parisian boulevard. And then Ford Madox Ford showed up and ruined the evening.

Ford was a well-known English writer. He was somewhat instrumental in launching Hemingway's career, hiring him in 1924 to help run the *Transatlantic Review.* Nevertheless, Hemingway saw fit to ravage him in *A Moveable Feast*, describing him as "breathing heavily through a heavy, stained mustache," noting that his breath was "fouler than the spout of any whale," and adding that "I had always avoided looking at Ford when I could and I always held my breath when I was near him in a closed room." Hemingway even worried that Ford's presence might ruin the taste of his drink; to his immense relief, he sampled it and it was still good.

Yet Hemingway felt obliged to invite him to join him for a drink. Initially Ford ordered a Chambéry Cassis, but then he changed his mind to a *fine à l'eau.* When the waiter returned with his drink, Ford corrected him, saying he'd ordered a Chambéry Vermouth and Cassis. Not wanting to see the drink go to waste, Hemingway told the waiter he'd take it. "Bring Monsieur what he orders now," he said to the waiter. "What I ordered," insisted the stubborn Ford. Later, as Hemingway was drinking what Ford refused to admit he'd ordered, Ford admonished him. "Don't you know it's fatal for a young writer to start drinking brandy?" And so it went, with Ford pontificating on what separates a gentleman from a bounder from a cad, and Hemingway joking that he very well could end up a cad, since after all he was intent on drinking brandy.

Chambéry Cassis is featured again in the restored edition of *A Moveable Feast*. In the chapter "Secret Pleasures," Hemingway tells of how he and Hadley finally decided to embrace the bohemian lifestyle and dress. As a reporter for the *Toronto Star*, Hemingway had to look the part, dress well, have decent clothing, and be well groomed. But he came to see how journalism might retard his creative writing. He decided to make a break; he'd quit the newspaper racket, even if they had to go without the income. Even if, he wrote, "we lived as savages and kept our own tribal rules and had our own customs and our own standards, secrets, taboos and delights." He and Hadley decided to wear their hair the same length, *long*. After this momentous decision, they celebrated with a Chambéry Cassis, with Hadley noting, "It's part of being free from all that awfulness."[52]

It seems innocent enough, but it somewhat presages the storyline of *The Garden of Eden*. Writer David Bourne and his newlywed wife, Catherine, both have their hair cut and colored the same length, and that's just the beginning of their sexual role reversal and their eventual entry into a ménage à trois with a beautiful girl named Marita. In fact, it was their shared hairstyle that caught Marita's eye. So it's somewhat fitting that the Chambéry Cassis should also appear when they first meet Marita.

The Chambéry Cassis also played a role in Hemingway's personal life, in the wake of his breakup with Hadley during the winter of 1926–27. He would do his brooding in an unknown café. "Ernest would walk into the café slowly, self-consciously, and select a table close to the windows. He felt calmed by the knowledge that he would meet no one he knew in this café. Ernest would usually

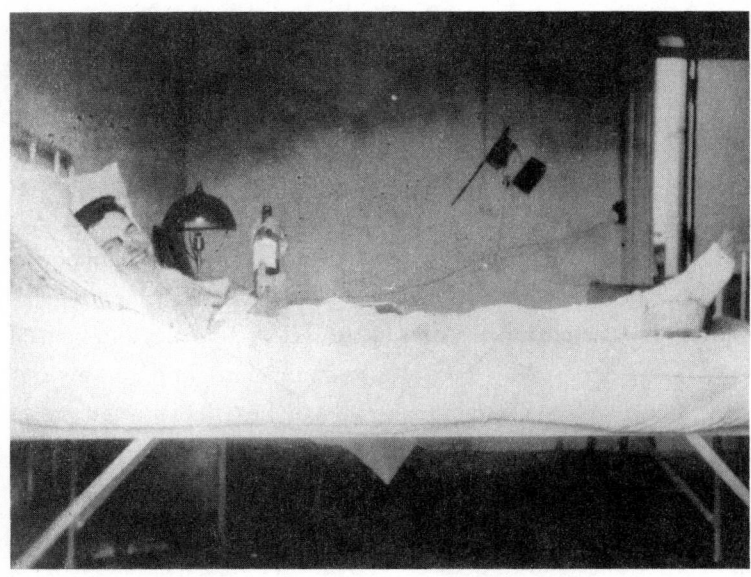

Hemingway in hospital bed in Milan, 1918, recovering from injuries during World War I. Copyright Henri Villard. Courtesy Dimitri Villard.

order a Vermouth Cassis, and when the waiter would bring it, Ernest would squirt 'charged water into the glass so that the vivid color paled and the glass filled.' Ernest would taste his drink, and, before he ordered his food, look out the window for awhile. . . . Each cassis cost Ernest two francs—little enough for a 'ticket that entitled him to stay as long as he wished in the warmth of the café.'"[53]

Hemingway developed a taste for vermouth while recuperating from his wounds in Milan in World War I. Friends would smuggle bottles of booze into his hospital room, much to the consternation of some of his nurses. He fictionalized it in Chapter 13 of *A Farewell to Arms*, where the protagonist Frederic Henry is recuperating from wounds of his own. Frederic enlists the porter to bring him a bottle each of Cinzano vermouth and Chianti, along with the eve-

ning papers. So he lay there in bed, taking sips from the vermouth while reading the war news: "I . . . reached down and brought up the bottle of Cinzano and held it straight up on my stomach, the cool glass against my stomach, and took little drinks making rings on my stomach from holding the bottle there between drinks, and watched it get dark outside over the roofs of the town."

Be it dry or sweet, make sure you either refrigerate your vermouth or decant it into smaller bottles, just as you would with any open bottle of wine. Once exposed to air, vermouth will go stale, and you don't want to ruin a good drink with bad vermouth.

Champagne Cocktail

4–5 oz. chilled Champagne
1 sugar cube
Angostura bitters

Place a sugar cube at the bottom of a champagne flute. Saturate the cube with Angostura bitters. Slowly fill flute with Champagne.

Or pour the Champagne first, then add the already saturated sugar cube.

SUGGESTED READING: *A Farewell to Arms* (Chapter 35), *The Fifth Column* (Act 3, scenes 1 and 4)

I t's somehow fitting that one of the oldest drinks in this book should have been consumed by one of the oldest of Hemingway's characters. Indeed, the Champagne cocktail is about 140 years old, and in *A Farewell to Arms*, an old gentleman by the name of Count Greffi fancies them.[54] His character was based on the real-life Count Greppi, who, like his favorite drink, was still going strong well after the century mark. Even in 1934, at the ripe young age of seventy, the Champagne cocktail made *Esquire*'s top ten list.[55]

In *A Farewell to Arms*, we find the ageless Count drinking this equally ageless cocktail. Frederic Henry and Catherine Barkley

Hemingway in his Red Cross uniform, 1918. Ernest Hemingway Photograph Collection, John F. Kennedy Presidential Library and Museum, Boston.

have escaped from the war and made their way to the northern Italian town of Stresa, en route to neutral Switzerland. Henry is still adjusting to civilian life. He's been to Stresa once before, where he played billiards and drank Champagne with the Count. In spite of his age, Count Greffi is still a master at pool.

In this scene, Frederic sits in the hotel bar and reads the papers. The bartender tells him that Count Greffi was looking for him earlier. Not only that, the Count is "younger than ever. He drank three champagne cocktails last night before dinner." The Count arrives, and they decide to play a game of pool. Count Greffi rings for the bartender. "Open one bottle please," he says. "We will take a little stimulant."

Hemingway met the real count, Greppi, in 1918 in Stresa while recovering from his war wounds; they played pool and Hemingway learned a great deal about international politics. In a letter to his parents, he wrote:

> The second night I was here the Old Count Greeo [*sic*] who will be 100 years old in March took charge of me and introduced me to about 150 people. He is perfectly preserved, has never married, goes to bed at midnight and smokes and drinks champagne.[56]

Count Greppi died at the age of 102, while attending the horse races at the San Siro track in Milan. The obituary does not say whether or not his horse won, but I rather suspect it did. Here's to you, Count.

Cognac & Bénédictine

1 oz. Cognac (Martell is called for)

1 oz. Bénédictine

Serve in an Old Fashioned glass with ice, garnished with lemon peel.

Recipe adapted from the story.

SUGGESTED READING: Hemingway unpublished manuscript, "The Mercenaries: A Story"

Perhaps it's an understatement to say that Hemingway often had his characters eating or drinking. That would be, after all, the premise on which this book is based, no? Here we have what is possibly the first such instance, from 1919. Hemingway, age twenty, returned home from his World War I ambulance corps service in Italy and set out to become a writer. He wrote a batch of stories, one of them titled "The Mercenaries: A Story." Both *Redbook* and the *Saturday Evening Post* rejected it, and he never tried to publish it again.[57]

It tells of a night spent at a dive bar in Chicago, a smoky joint filled with mercenaries, "neo-bohemians," and other shady characters. Here he has an encounter with a couple of men who invite him to join them at their table. The men, Graves and Ricaud, tell

Martell ad, circa 1938. From the author's collection.

of opportunities for professional soldiers and reveal that they are officers in the Royal Republican Peruvian Army, paid two hundred dollars a month, and they propose a toast to the war against Chile.

Graves invites him to have a drink and suggests a mixture of Cognac & Bénédictine. The protagonist is puzzled at the drink choice, since there is only one place on earth where people drink such a mixture, and it isn't Chicago. He is puzzled further when the waiter returns with the drinks; they're not served in tiny liqueur glasses, as one might expect. No, these gents ordered them in full-sized cocktail glasses. They drink again to the downfall of the hated Chile.

We come to learn that Graves discovered the drink during World War I, down in Sicily. He orders another round, careful to note that too much of it could be dangerous.

I find it a bit odd that Hemingway would not only place this

Vintage ad. Courtesy Bénédictine.

mixture of *French* Cognac and *French* liqueur in Sicily, but further that he'd comment that he knew of only one other place on earth where they drank such a drink. Sicily? Why not France? Indeed, this drink, more or less, is known today as B&B (short for "brandy and Bénédictine"), a sixty-forty blend of Cognac and Bénédictine, a French liqueur that goes back to 1510. To celebrate B&B's seventieth anniversary in 2008, the company staged an anniversary party at the '21' Club in New York City. A feature of the event was a cocktail competition. Yours truly tied for second place, with an entry titled the Claiborne Cocktail. But this is a book about Hemingway's cocktails, not Greene's cocktails. . . .

Coincidentally, the '21' Club was one of Hemingway's favorite New York watering holes. He claims to have gone to a party there one night during Prohibition, invited by co-owner Jack Kriendler. There he met an Italian girl, "the most beautiful girl—face and body," that he'd ever seen. She and Hemingway stayed beyond the end of the party, and "suddenly we were making love there in the kitchen and never has a promise been better fulfilled."

Next day, Hemingway was quite smitten; he rushed over to '21' to talk to Kriendler and find out who she was. Jack pulled him aside. "Listen, Ernie, you better lay low for awhile. I should have warned you—that was Legs Diamond's girl, and he's due back in town at five o'clock."[58] Diamond was a notorious gangster, and that was the end of that, if the story is even true. After all, Hemingway did have a knack for mixing truth with fiction. But it is a good story.

Cuba Libre

2 oz. rum (light, dark, up to you)*
4 oz. cola*
Juice of ½ lime
Lime wedge

Add rum, cola, and lime juice to a tall glass filled with ice. Garnish with lime wedge, stir, and serve. When toasting, drink to a free Cuba: *"Por Cuba libre!"*

* Use Coca-Cola and Bacardi if you want to be authentic. Use Coke sweetened with sugar rather than fructose (often available at ethnic grocery stores) and pre-Castro Bacardi if you want to be even *more* authentic. Use the circa 1900 *original*-formula Coke (with cocaine) if you want it to be *really* authentic (though you might land in jail).

SUGGESTED READING: *To Have and Have Not* (Chapter 15)

Cuba was a Spanish colony pretty much from the time that Columbus sailed the ocean blue until 1898. Like any European colony yearning to be free, revolution was inevitable, and throughout the latter portion of the nineteenth century there were many attempts to overthrow mother Spain. Several American newspapers, notably the *New York Herald* and the *New York Tribune*, in what came to be known as "yellow journalism," actively called for U.S. intervention.

In February 1895, Cuban rebels launched an all-out revolt, with the rallying cry *"Vive Cuba libre!"* As the rebels gained territory, the situation became dangerous in Havana. The United States sent the battleship *Maine*, in part to evacuate any American citizens. On February 14, 1898, the *Maine* exploded in Havana's harbor, the

The Cuba Libre, the pause that refreshes for more than a few good men, or women. Copyright © 1953 by Coca-Cola Co. From the author's collection.

cause of which remains uncertain. The U.S. government blamed Spain, and war was soon declared.

The American invasion force landed in June at Daiquiri Beach (see the Daiquiri). After Spain's defeat, the United States took control of Cuba, which gained its independence in 1902.

America's influence on turn-of-the-century Cuba was significant, as thousands of military, political, and business types flocked to the island. With them came thousands of cases of Coca-Cola, which was all the rage back Stateside. While stories vary over when rum-meets-Coke first took place, and by whom, it was a foregone conclusion that this classic highball should be invented, and so it was.

As the story goes, Coca-Cola arrived around 1900, and when folks took to mixing rum and Coca-Cola together, with a healthy wedge of lime, they'd raise their glass and toast to a free Cuba—*por Cuba libre!* And thus the drink was named.

One version of the tale concerns a U.S. Army Signal Corps messenger named Fausto Rodriguez. In 1900, he visited a local bar with an officer, who ordered a Bacardi and Coke. Nearby soldiers took notice, and before you knew it, they were all toasting this great new drink.

This story was published in a full-page ad in *Life* magazine in 1966. The ad, not to mention Fausto's salary, was covered by a little ol' rum company called Bacardi. See, our friend Fausto was Bacardi's New York director of publicity.[59] Compare this to the Daiquiri story in the 1937 *Miami Herald*, which had no fewer than *ten* references to Bacardi sprinkled throughout, and you begin to see a rather brilliant marketing theme. But I digress. . . .

The Cuba Libre makes an all-too-brief appearance in Hemingway's 1937 novel *To Have and Have Not*. The book was Hemingway's homage to Key West and its Depression-era working-class natives (called Conchs, pronounced "konks," after the mollusks common to the area), and it concerns a Conch by the name of Harry Morgan, a charter boat skipper, rumrunner, smuggler—anything that could earn a buck.

Harry Morgan was loosely based on Hemingway's friend Joe Russell, owner of Sloppy Joe's, with his boat modeled after Russell's *Anita*. Russell and Sloppy Joe's itself were also the basis for Freddy Wallace and Freddy's Bar. Richard Gordon, somewhat viciously, was modeled after John Dos Passos. Tommy and Helene Bradley were based on Grant and Jane Mason. Least flattering of all, perhaps, is the character Mrs. James Laughton. She orders a Cuba Libre. She could use one. Believe me.

In Chapter 15, the Laughtons are a couple of tourists at Freddy's Bar. Mrs. Laughton is described as having "blonde curly hair cut short like a man's, a bad complexion, and the face and build of a lady wrestler." She is fond of saying things like "double nerts to you," and "gee, you can talk as educated as the professor." A real charmer. She's based on the wife of Hemingway's friend Jack Coles. In a 1936 letter to Dos Passos, Hemingway noted that Coles's "new squaw" looks "something like one of these new style wrestlers. The hero. Not the villain. You can tell the hero always because he is pimpled. The villain is bearded."[60]

Mrs. Laughton is offering up her charming expressions when Harry Morgan comes in to see Freddy. He's a bit preoccupied and isn't in the mood for her *nertses*. After a verbal altercation with her, he orders a drink:

> "What will you have?" asked Freddy.
> "What's the lady drinking," Harry asked.
> "A Cuba Libre."
> "Then give me a straight whiskey."

One wonders if Hemingway's disdain for the woman translates into a commentary on her choice of drink. In any event, the Cuba Libre was very popular in the 1930s and '40s. In his 1946 classic, *The Stork Club Bar Book*, Lucius Beebe lists it among the top three rum drinks served at the Stork, along with the frozen Daiquiri and the MacArthur cocktail. While the MacArthur has sadly fallen into obscurity (a charming drink made with dark and light rum, Cointreau, and egg white), the Daiquiri and the Cuba Libre (and rum and Coke) remain bestsellers to this day.

"Rum and Coca-Cola"

The Cuba Libre sans lime is simply a Rum & Coca-Cola, a name made famous by a World War II–era song performed by the Andrews Sisters. It spent ten weeks as *Billboard*'s No. 1, and twenty weeks in the Top 30. Simple story, right? Wrong.

You see, we have to go back to the early stages of the war, to September 1940. Britain was the lone remaining nation fighting Hitler and the Axis powers. Churchill pleaded for U.S.

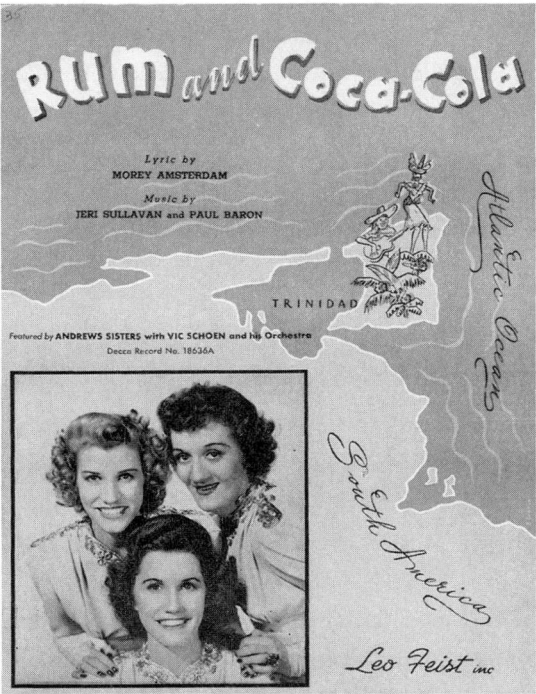

Sheet music. From the author's collection.

support, but the best Roosevelt could offer was fifty old destroyers. In exchange, Britain granted a ninety-nine-year, rent-free lease to selected parcels of land in the British realm for use as U.S. military bases. One such outpost was the tiny Caribbean island of Trinidad. What that meant to the local economy and culture was, to paraphrase the English lament in 1944, that they had too many American servicemen overpaid, oversexed, and *down here*.

In 1943, Morey Amsterdam (Buddy Sorrell on *The Dick Van Dyke Show*) went to Trinidad on a USO tour. He happened to hear a local folk song called "L'Année Passée." Amsterdam had previously seen a number of Yanks fraternizing with the local girls, drinking shots of rum chased with Coca-Cola. So he wrote a calypso song, borrowing the melody from "L'Année Passée."

The Andrews Sisters recorded it, it was a boffo smash, and Amsterdam began to rake in the dough. The song sold seven million copies, surpassed only by Bing Crosby's "White Christmas" and Patti Page's "Tennessee Waltz." Great story, right? Well . . .

When the author of "L'Année Passée," Lionel Belasco, and his record company found out, they sued for copyright infringement. Amsterdam claimed it was a public domain folk song. Belasco testified that copyright should extend to folk songs. Long story short, in 1947 a U.S. federal court judge ruled against Amsterdam, who was ordered to surrender future royalties from sales of the song to Belasco.[61]

In closing, I like to think that if Amsterdam wandered into a bar after hearing the verdict, he likely declined a Cuba Libre, opting for a *straight whiskey* instead.

Photo showing Hemingway, Carlos Gutierrez, Joe Russell, and Joe Lowe, circa 1933. Sadly, Lowe, on whom the Rummy Eddy (*To Have and Have Not*) was based, died in the Labor Day 1935 hurricane on Matecumbe Key.[62] Ernest Hemingway Photograph Collection, John F. Kennedy Presidential Library and Museum, Boston.

Daiquiri

Two versions from which to choose:

E. HENMÍWAY SPECIAL (CIRCA 1937)
2 oz. white rum
1 tsp. grapefruit juice
1 tsp. maraschino liqueur
½ oz. fresh lime juice

"Frappé" (chip or crush) some ice, add to shaker, then add remaining ingredients. Shake well, then pour contents of shaker into a chilled cocktail glass.

PAPA DOBLE (THE WILD DAIQUIRI) (CIRCA 1947)
3¾ oz. white rum
2 oz. fresh lime juice
2 oz. fresh grapefruit juice
6 drops maraschino liqueur

Blend well with ice. Serve in a large chilled goblet.

SUGGESTED READING: *Islands in the Stream* ("Cuba")

As I reached the drinking age in the early 1980s, I thought there were two types of Daiquiri—banana and strawberry—and both required a blender. Not only that, Daiquiris required

Drink coaster from the Floridita, Havana. From the author's collection.

bottled, canned, or worse, *powdered* mixes; at least, that's what I saw around my parents' suburban home. After making a lot of store-bought atrocities, or merely drinkable alcoholic Slurpees, I've learned that the Daiquiri is a very simple but elegant cocktail made with rum, fresh lime juice, and sugar. That's it.

Hemingway was a bit luckier; he moved to the Gulf Stream just as the King of the Daiquiri was getting his start, behind the bar of the Floridita in Havana. We'll come back to him in a moment.

Cocktail historians tell us that the Daiquiri was invented around 1900. It seems an American engineer by the name of Jennings Cox, in the southeastern Cuban town of Daiquiri, was preparing to host some visiting American friends. To his horror, he was out of gin. As in so many such stories based on the theme "What do I do with these seemingly surplus and incongruous ingredients?" Cox did have a good amount of rum, sugar, and limes. This was, after all, *Cuba*. Cox rolled up his sleeves, and the Daiquiri was born. Or so the story goes. . . .

Another story finds our Horatio Alger–esque hero Cox in a

Santiago saloon, the Venus Bar, tossin' 'em back with some co-workers. The following is an excerpt from the *Miami Herald* of March 14, 1937:

> One day a group of American engineers who had come into town from the Daiquiri mines were imbibing their favorite drink in this restful spot. It was one of those wonderful rum concoctions made from Ron Bacardi. A jovial fellow by the name of Cox spoke up. "Caballeros y amigos, we have been enjoying this delicious mixture for some time, but strange to admit the drink has no name. Don't you think it is about time something was done to extricate us from this sad predicament?" It was unanimously agreed that the drink should be named, without further procras-

Shown above, Jennings Cox, the man and his recipe. Courtesy Cuban Heritage Collection, University of Miami Libraries, Coral Gables, Florida.

tination. There was silence for several minutes as each man became immersed in deep thought. Suddenly, Cox's voice was heard again. "I have it, men! Let's call it the 'Daiquiri!'" And so it was christened.

Yet another Daiquiri story is also tied to this same Cuban coastal town, set during the American invasion in 1898. In his excellent book *And a Bottle of Rum*, Wayne Curtis tells of U.S. Army general William Shafter, who:

> came ashore during the Spanish-American War in 1898 near Santiago. He was not shy of girth and in poor health, and he liked food and drink more than the tedious chore of battle. When he sampled the drink of the Cuban patriot—rum, lime juice, and sugar muddled together—he found it to his liking and declared, "Only one ingredient is missing—ice." He set about remedying that omission, and, lo, the daiquiri was born.[63]

In whichever story, we're left with something of an imperialistic tale, a wise American in a foreign land, assessing the local ingredients and figuring out what the noble savages were too ignorant to see for themselves—that this holy trinity of rum, sugar, and lime juice tasted pretty damned good together! Didn't Rudyard Kipling mention the Daiquiri in his politically incorrect poem "The White Man's Burden"? Please. Rum, sugar, and lime juice had been around in the Caribbean since the seventeenth century. I rather doubt that some *Yanqui* was the one to get it sorted. Perhaps the *name* was coined in this manner, but I suspect the drink had been around for quite a while.

Witness the classic Ti' Punch in Martinique (rhum agricole, cane syrup, and lime wedge), Brazil's Caipirinha (cachaça, sugar or cane syrup, and lime wedges), or even the alleged prototype of

1930s La Florida Bar cocktail menu. Courtesy Vicki Gold Levi Collection.

the Mojito, El Draque; all have rum, sugar, and lime. Look also to the British Royal Navy, serving the trinity to its sailors going back over 250 years! Indeed, as early as 1740, Admiral Edward Vernon ordered that lemon or lime juice be added to his sailors' daily ration of rum, to dilute the strength of the spirit and improve the taste (the vitamin C prevented scurvy, too). In Vernon's honor, the men came to call this daily cocktail "grog," and the name stuck ("Old Grog" was Vernon's nickname, as he wore a coat made of grogram cloth).

Well, let's leave aside how the Daiquiri was invented and focus on the man who *perfected* it, none other than Constantino Ribalaigua, bartender and owner of Havana's La Florida Bar, affection-

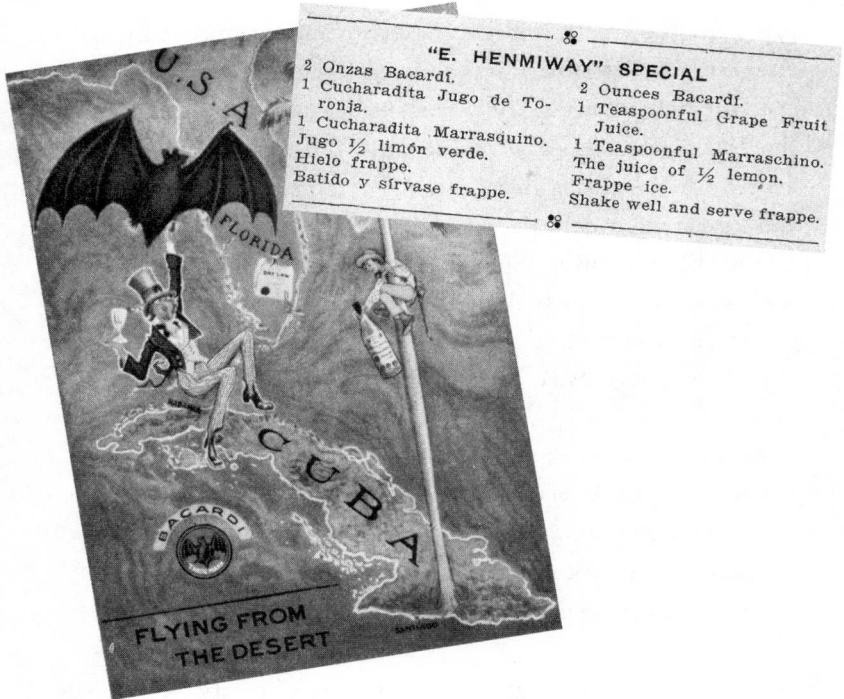

"E. HENMIWAY" SPECIAL

2 Onzas Bacardí.
1 Cucharadita Jugo de Toronja.
1 Cucharadita Marrasquino.
Jugo ½ limón verde.
Hielo frappe.
Batido y sírvase frappe.

2 Ounces Bacardí.
1 Teaspoonful Grape Fruit Juice.
1 Teaspoonful Marraschino.
The juice of ½ lemon.
Frappe ice.
Shake well and serve frappe.

FLYING FROM THE DESERT

From the 1937 Floridita cocktail menu. From the author's collection.
Prohibition-era Bacardi ad, circa 1925. Courtesy Bacardi.

ately known to locals as the Floridita. That's where Hemingway comes in. Often.

Hemingway began frequenting the Floridita in 1932, during visits to Havana from his home in Key West. He would stay at the nearby Ambos Mundos Hotel (where he is said to have written parts of *Green Hills of Africa*, "The Short Happy Life of Francis Macomber," and *For Whom the Bell Tolls*). He would visit the Floridita in the late afternoon, after mornings spent writing and afternoons fishing the Gulf Stream. He became such a regular that the

1937 edition of the Floridita's cocktail manual named a Daiquiri after him. Well, sort of. It was christened the "E. Henmiway" Special. The typo wasn't the only mistake; note the loss in translation that occurs when limes become lemons. You see, in Cuba, a lime is a *limon verde*, that is, a green lemon. The translator forgot the *verde*, and a great many defective Daiquiri recipes were launched.

The "E. Henmiway" Special evolved over the next decade, and not just to correct the spelling. By 1947 it doubled in size, got more grapefruit juice, and became the Papa Doble (as in *double*). From *Papa Hemingway*, by A. E. Hotchner:

> Requested by most tourists, a Papa Doble was compounded of two and a half jiggers of Bacardi White Label Rum, the juice of two limes and half a grapefruit, and six drops of maraschino, all placed in an electric mixer over shaved ice, whirled vigorously and served foaming in large goblets.[64]

The "double frozen daiquiri with no sugar" pretty much steals the show in the "Cuba" book of *Islands in the Stream*, which re-

EL REY DE LOS COTELEROS

Constantino Ribalaigua, the "King of the Daiquiri." From the author's collection.

Hemingway at the Floridita with his wife Mary and Spencer Tracy, during the filming of *The Old Man and the Sea*. At Tracy's right is Jack "Bumby" Hemingway, Ernest's eldest son. This is the end of the bar where Papa's statue now sits. Ernest Hemingway Photograph Collection, John F. Kennedy Presidential Library and Museum, Boston.

counts a marathon drinking session at the Floridita during which Thomas Hudson was drinking the famous frozen Daiquiris of the Floridita, "the great ones that Constante made, that had no taste of alcohol and felt, as you drank them, the way downhill glacier skiing feels running through powder snow and, after the sixth and eighth, felt like downhill glacier skiing feels when you are running unroped."

In a later scene, Hudson is in mourning. After a couple of whiskey highballs at home, followed by a Tom Collins for the road, Hudson heads for the Floridita, where he spends the afternoon with some colorful locals. The frozen, sugarless Daiquiris he drinks remind him of the sea. The frappéd part of the drink resembles "the wake of a ship and the clear part was the way the water looked when the bow cut it when you were in shallow water over marl bottom. That was almost the exact color."

The basis for that epic Daiquiri binge from *Islands* may have come from a day in 1942, as Hemingway recounted to his friend Harvey Breit years later. He claims that he spent a day at the Floridita when the weather was too bad to be out on the *Pilar*. He ran into his friend Guillermo and, beginning at 10:30 a.m., they set about doing a little drinking. "We drank seventeen double frozen Daiquiris apiece in the course of the day without leaveing [*sic*] the bar except for an occasional trip to the can. Each double had four ounces of rum in it. That makes 68 ounces of rum. But there was no sugar in the drinks and we each ate two steak sandwiches."

He went on to say that he had one more double and then went home and spent the evening reading. The next day, he met Guillermo again at the Floridita "at noon and had a couple of frozen Daiquiris. We both felt good and neither one of us had been drunk and there was no compulsion to go on drinking and neither one of us had a hangover."[65]

His boast is "corroborated" by a 1945 letter he wrote to his soon-to-be wife Mary, where he made great efforts to tell her how well behaved he'd been in her absence: "Haven't bought anything for myself except books, magazines, pop-corn and peanuts, and phonograph records for house. Never been to Floridita more than three times a week and not had more than four daiquiris (once had 34 some years ago. Still record . . .)."[66] If these were singles, not *dobles*, the seventeen number holds fast.

Whichever, that's a hell of a lot of Daiquiris, folks.

Death in the Afternoon

1½ oz. absinthe
4 oz. Champagne

Pour one jigger of absinthe into a champagne glass. Add iced Champagne until it attains the proper opalescent milkiness.

emingway loved his Champagne. Throughout his prose and letters you'll see references to esteemed houses such as Bollinger and Perrier-Jouët, and on his fiftieth birthday he bragged of having consumed an entire case of Piper-Heidsieck with some friends on board *Pilar*. In a 1950 interview with Lillian Ross, he wrily observed the "half bottle of champagne is the enemy of man. If I have any money, I can't think of any better way of spending money than on champagne."[67] So it's fitting that Hemingway would combine two of his favorite tipples, Champagne and absinthe, to form this classic.

This drink is found in a 1935 celebrity cocktail book called *So Red the Nose, or, Breath in the Afternoon*, featuring thirty cocktails from noted writers of the day. According to the text, the drink "was arrived at by the author and three officers of HMS *Danae* after having spent seven hours overboard trying to get Capt. Bra Saunders' fishing boat off a bank where she had gone with us in a N.W.

gale."[68] The *Danae*, by the way, was a British cruiser that later served as part of the Allied fleet off Normandy on D-day.

Hemingway relied on men like Bra Saunders and Joe Russell to provide a fishing boat and local knowledge in his first few years in Key West, until he purchased the *Pilar* in 1934. On one trip in 1930, Hemingway was joined by his editor, Maxwell Perkins, Mike Strater, and two others on a trip to the Marquesas and Dry Tortugas, west of Key West. They camped for a few days at Fort Jefferson and ended up getting marooned there by a huge storm.

The waves were mountainous, and they knew they weren't going anywhere anytime soon. So the men made the most of it, grew beards, and ate all kinds of fish. But it got a bit old. "First they ran out of ice, then beer, then canned goods, then coffee, then liquor, then Bermuda onions, and at last everything but fish. Ernest did not care. He said that he never ate or drank better in his life." The weather finally cleared, and they made their way back to Key West, after seventeen days. All the wives were worried sick, but for Pauline. Hemingway proudly said that it "was a damned good trait in a woman to love you and not worry about you."[69]

From *So Red the Nose*, the write-up continues:

> It takes a man with hair on his chest to drink five Absinthe and Champagne Cocktails and still handle the English language in the Hemingway fashion. But Ernest has proved his valor, not alone in his cups. Captain of the swimming team at Oak Park high school—first American to be wounded on the Italian front during the World War (with 227 individual wounds to his credit)—tossed by a bull in the streets of Pamplona while rescuing his friend Donald Ogden Stewart—deep-sea fisherman—big game hunter—and resident of Key West—Hemingway is the man who can hold his Absinthe like a postwar novelist.[70]

Drink five absinthe and Champagne cocktails? I'm reminded of Harry Craddock's classic warning in his 1930 *Savoy Cocktail Book* about the Corpse Reviver (No. 2): "Four of these taken in swift succession will unrevive the corpse again." Indeed, the editors of *So Red the Nose* saw fit to offer a similar caution: "After six of these cocktails, *The Sun Also Rises*." Be careful with this one, with or without hair on your chest.

Death in the Gulf Stream (Ernest Hemingway's Reviver)

2–3 oz. Holland gin (such as Bols genever)
Juice of 1 lime (with peel)
1 tsp. sugar (optional)
4 healthy dashes Angostura bitters

Take a tall, thin water tumbler and fill it with finely cracked ice. Lace this broken debris with 4 good purple splashes of Angostura, add the juice and crushed peel of 1 green lime, and fill glass almost full with Holland gin.

From *The Gentleman's Companion*[71]

SUGGESTED READING: *The Gentleman's Companion*, Vol. 2, by Charles H. Baker Jr.

In 1939, globe-trotting bon vivant Charles H. Baker Jr. published his two-part masterpiece, *The Gentleman's Companion*. Volume 1, *Being an Exotic Cookery Book, or Around the World with Knife, Fork and Spoon*, deals with food, while Volume 2, *Being an Exotic Drinking Book, or Around the World with Jigger, Beaker and*

Gezondheid!

ELKEN DAG EEN GLAASJE

BOLS

Vintage Bols genever ad. Courtesy Lucas Bols.

Flask, handles the drinks. Hemingway had one contribution in Volume 1, that being "Smothered Conch—Ernest Hemingway." He had two drinks in Volume 2; this is one of them.

The latter book reflected "fourteen years' liquid field work" by Baker and his intrepid wife, Pauline, from their travels around the globe, much of it done on their fifty-six-foot yacht, *Marmion*. When not abroad, they lived in Coconut Grove, Florida, where they built an art deco villa, Java Head. Baker and Hemingway were both members of the Key Biscayne Yacht Club and contributing writers for *Esquire* magazine, and so became friends during Hemingway's Key West years.

In January 1937, the Bakers sailed to Key West "to get some receipts from Hemingway for the cookery book." Along the way, they endured not only "a howling no'theaster" but also "an insane stew-

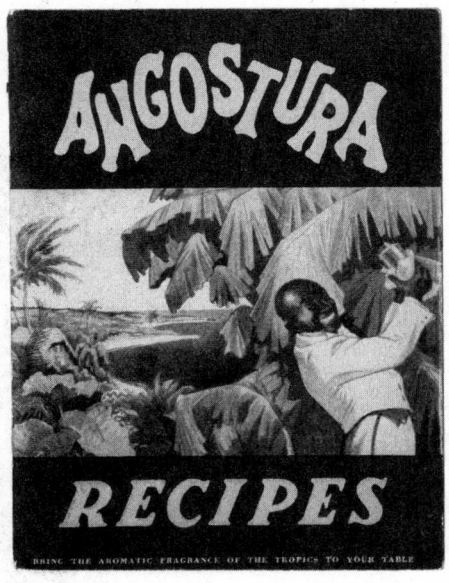

1934 Angostura cocktail recipe book. From the author's collection.

ard." They arrived intact, and with Hemingway they "fished the Gulf Stream by day, and ate and drank and talked half the night." After the rigors of their trip and a couple of days of Hemingway's hospitality, they were admittedly "withering slightly on vine." So they were offered and accepted "Hemingway's other picker-upper," and they "liked it."[72]

Notwithstanding its "picker-upper" qualities, the drink was dubbed Death in the Gulf Stream, a play on Hemingway's 1932 treatise on bullfighting, *Death in the Afternoon*, as well as his contribution to the cheeky cocktail book *So Red the Nose, or, Breath in the Afternoon*. Hemingway's friend Waldo Peirce also did a comical painting titled *Death in the Gulfstream*, which depicted Hemingway, Peirce, and another man (perhaps Bra Saunders) in a tiny rowboat, battling a fierce shark (which Hemingway dispatches with a shot from a blunderbuss).

Baker and Hemingway in Bimini with one of those legendary tuna. Ernest Hemingway Photograph Collection, John F. Kennedy Presidential Library and Museum, Boston.

Baker admits to being prejudiced against the drink at first, noting that "[d]rinking Holland gin drinks is like the fanciful *cliché* about eating olives—when you like one you always like one. For many years we had hated the stuff with a passion, holding its taste to be like fermented radishes mixed with spirits of turpentine." But Hemingway's drink made the Bakers change their tune: "No sugar, no fancying. It's strong, it's bitter—but so is good English ale strong and bitter, in many cases. We don't add sugar to ale, and we don't need sugar in a Death in the Gulf Stream—at least not more than 1 tsp. Its tartness and its bitterness are its chief charm. It is reviving and refreshing; cools the blood and inspires renewed interest in food, companions and life."[73]

I find myself agreeing with the inimitable Charles Baker; I was not much of a fan of Holland gin, not until I made this drink. I used Bols genever, plenty of Angostura, and ice crushed in a Lewis bag. It takes a couple of sips to get past the bitterness, but once you do, it's really a delightful drink.

El Definitivo

¾ oz. vodka
¾ oz. gin
¾ oz. tequila
¾ oz. rum
¾ oz. Scotch
2 oz. tomato juice
1 oz. fresh lime juice

Add all ingredients to a tall glass filled with ice. Stir well and serve.

Adapted from a recipe in *Hemingway's Cuban Son,* by René Villarreal and Raúl Villarreal.

Hemingway created this drink with his pal Winston Guest in Havana, circa 1942. Hemingway used to participate in the local boys' baseball games, even going so far as to organize a team. Often he and his friends would take part, with the kids running the bases when the adults were batting. Winston, aka Wolfie, was a regular participant (not to mention Winston Churchill's cousin and godson). Their chief rivals on the field were Don Andres and the Herrera brothers.

According to Hemingway's "majordomo" René Villarreal, Wolfie "was one of Hemingway's closest friends in Cuba and also one of his favorite drinking partners. Together they created *el definitivo,* a blend of vodka, gin, tequila, rum, whiskey, tomato juice, and a lot of lime juice. The trick drink was intended to obliterate the Herrera brothers, the jai alai players, and Don Andres, but most of the time Hemingway and Guest succumbed to their own concoction as well."[74]

Somehow Winston Guest has a connection to drinks of this sort. Hemingway wrote in a letter to his editor, Maxwell Perkins, in 1943, that one of Winston's father's favorite cocktails was a mixture of "gin with Worcestershire sauce and red pepper and that nothing ever made him feel better or more healthy." When Hemingway asked Winston how his father had died, "he said hurriedly 'Cancer of the stomach.'"[75]

Ouch.

But looking at El Definitivo's ingredients, I know what you're thinking: Papa invented the Long Island iced tea! Close, but not quite. Both drinks have vodka, gin, rum, and tequila, but whereas El Definitivo also has lime, tomato juice, and whiskey, the Long Island iced tea goes with triple sec, simple syrup, lemon juice, and cola. Either way, you're talking about a potent combination, not recommended while playing baseball, no.

The "Crook Factory," or "Our Man in Havana"

Winston Guest was one of Hemingway's cronies in Havana during World War II. While Hemingway's wife Martha was off covering the war for *Collier's*, Ernest was back in Cuba, increasingly restless about missing out on the action. Meanwhile, German U-boats were inflicting great damage on Allied shipping in the region, and there was concern that Nazi influence was on the increase in Havana. So he convinced the U.S. ambassador to Cuba, Spruille Braden, to allow him to create and lead a counterespionage ring. Hemingway initially called this group the "Crime Shop," and later the name changed to the "Crook Factory." "As might have been expected, the organization was somewhat loose. It was held together by the force of Ernest's personality and liberal infusions of wine, spirits and pesos."[76]

Hemingway's role had two elements. Initially Braden authorized him to establish "a makeshift intelligence service," to monitor the approximately three hundred thousand Spanish citizens of Cuba, some 10 percent of whom Braden believed to be Nazi sympathizers. Braden later recalled that Hemingway "enlisted a bizarre combination of Spaniards: some bar tenders; a few wharf rats; some down-at-heel pelota players and former bullfighters; two Basque priests; assorted exiled counts and dukes; several Loyalists and Francistas. He built up an excellent organization and did an A-One job."[77]

Ultimately Hemingway convinced the U.S. embassy to allow him to outfit the *Pilar* as a so-called Q-boat, to search for German U-boats. As part of what was called Operation Friendless,

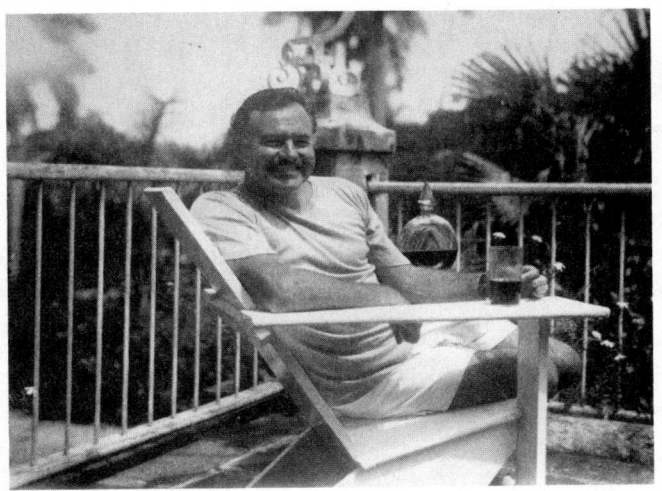

Hemingway relaxing at the Finca Vigía, circa 1942. Ernest Hemingway Photograph Collection, John F. Kennedy Presidential Library and Museum, Boston.

named for a Hemingway cat (!), *Pilar* would be equipped "with a well-trained crew and a supply of bazookas, grenades, short-fuse bombs, and two or three 50-calibre machine guns."[78] The plan called for them to pose as a fishing boat or research vessel, and when confronted by a surfacing U-boat, they'd toss a bomb down its open hatch. Sounds simple enough to me. The *Pilar*'s missions were conducted from mid-1942 until early 1944.

Thankfully, perhaps for both sides, they never engaged with a German sub. They did, however, conduct extensive patrols along the Cuban coast, searching the offshore cays for spies who might be relaying information on passing convoys to nearby U-boats. This portion of Hemingway's life is played out in fiction, in "At Sea," the final book of *Islands in the Stream*, where Thomas Hudson leads an expedition to track the crew of a German submarine among the islands off the northern coast of Cuba and, of course, have an occasional Tom Collins.

Notwithstanding the merits of Hemingway's activities, Martha saw the entire enterprise as being a way for Hemingway to "play" combat and to spend weeks at sea with his drinking buddies, using scarce government-issued gasoline. Her disgust with the whole operation was part of the reason the two split apart. Marriage with Martha would be Hemingway's shortest lived, lasting only five years.

A Farewell to Hemingway

2¼ oz. kirsch (cherry brandy)
¼ oz. cherry syrup
Juice of 1 large lime

Shake well with ice, transfer contents into a collins glass, drop in a spiral lime peel, and fill glass nearly full with chilled club soda. Enjoy.

SUGGESTED READING: *The Gentleman's Companion*, Vol. 2, by Charles H. Baker; *A Moveable Feast* ("Miss Stein Instructs")

As noted in the comments to Death in the Gulf Stream, Hemingway's friend Charles Baker published a two-part masterpiece titled *The Gentleman's Companion*, covering both food and drink. Volume 2 includes two Hemingway drink recipes; this is the second of the two. Baker also wrote *The South American Gentleman's Companion*, and I commend all his writings to you.

This drink was created one night in January 1937. Hemingway and his bullfighter friend Sidney Franklin visited the Bakers in Coconut Grove, a stopover visit from Key West on their way to Madrid. Hemingway would report on the Spanish Civil War, not to mention continue his affair with Martha Gellhorn.

According to Baker, "There is no reason to this drink. It just happened because Ernest prefers *kirschwasser*, and it was a muggy, half-breathless sort of night." He refers to it as "being a sort of Kirsch Collins."[79] Indeed, Hemingway did like his kirsch, a dry cherry brandy popular in Germany and the Alps. Hemingway likely acquired a taste for it in 1924, during a ski holiday with first wife, Hadley, in Schruns, Austria. Much to his delight, the locals referred to him as the "Black Kirsch-drinking Christ," due to his suntan, long hair and beard, and taste for the local brandy. Much as he liked kirsch, however, it still didn't take the place of Scotch. During one of his visits to Schruns, he groused a bit to his friend Howell Jenkins:

> Have had some swell ski ing [*sic*] today. Feel tired. Wish for some good old Scotch. Wish you were here and we could uncork a bottle. You'd have to bring it from Paris. No good hootch in Mittel Europa. But great beer—38 different kinds—Swell Beer from here to Budapest then it gets Bum again until you hit Constantinople.[80]

As a final comment, Baker notes that the "cherry syrup sweet, of course, can be varied to taste," and that "[w]e've later found that raspberry syrup is very decent, also."

A hale and hearty Hemingway, in a photo sent from Gstaad, Switzerland, to his publisher Scribner's in February 1927. The note on the back reads, "This is to re-assure you if you hear reports of another of your authors dying of drink." Meanwhile, on a skiing holiday in Schruns, Austria, the locals called him the "Black Kirsch-drinking Christ." Ernest Hemingway Photograph Collection, John F. Kennedy Presidential Library and Museum, Boston.

Gambler's Delight

1½ oz. sweet (Italian) vermouth
1½ oz. Cognac

Serve on rocks in an Old Fashioned glass, garnished with orange or lemon rind. Liven up with a splash of seltzer, if desired.

Recipe adapted from the description in the letter.

It's 1919, and Hemingway has just returned home from World War I ambulance corps duty in Italy. He was nearly killed by an Austrian mortar and was dumped by his first true love, nurse Agnes von Kurowsky. So he's back in Oak Park, wounded, heartbroken, and, well, thirsty. See, during his time abroad, he's acquired quite a taste for a variety of drink.

In a letter to his ambulance corps friend Jim Gamble, he notes that America "isn't such a bad place now with the exception of the coming aridity," referring to the looming Prohibition. He describes his bedroom:

> On the left is a well filled book case containing Strega, Cinzano Vermouth, kummel and martell cognac. All these were got after an exhaustive search of Chicago's resources. If it were not nine o'clock in the morning, I would suggest compounding of a Gamblers Delight. Cinquante martell and vermouth.[81]

Vintage ad. Courtesy Martini.

Hemingway was quite the drink inventor, and this is likely one of the first drinks he created. With respect to the recipe, I'm assuming that *cinquante*, French for "fifty," means a fifty-fifty mixture of vermouth and Cognac. I'm also guessing that he's naming the drink in honor of his war buddy Jim Gamble.

This is actually a nice little drink; it reminds me of the classic Vieux Carré cocktail, from the Hotel Monteleone in New Orleans. The Vieux Carré starts with the Gambler's Delight, adds another

Bénédictine, liqueur exquise, tonique, digestive.

1932 menu. Courtesy Bénédictine.

measure of rye whiskey and a couple dashes each of Angostura and Peychaud's bitters, plus a float of Bénédictine.

Warning: Be careful looking up the "Gambler's Delight" on the web; a contemporary offering is made with Red Bull and vodka. No, thanks; that's too much of a gamble for me.

The Hotel Monteleone, New Orleans

NEW HOTEL MONTELEONE, NEW ORLEANS

The Hotel Monteleone, Hemingway's favorite hotel in New Orleans. Vintage postcard, circa 1930s. From the author's collection.

Hemingway visited New Orleans on more than one occasion, usually staying at the historic Hotel Monteleone in the French

Quarter (the rooftop suite is named in his honor). The hotel boasts other literary giants as its guests, among them Truman Capote (who claims he was born there), William Faulkner, and Tennessee Williams, to name a few. Hemingway saw fit to mention the Monteleone in the short story "Night Before Battle," and it's probably also featured in "The Strange Country." He and fourth wife, Mary, stayed there in the 1950s. In her autobiography, she wrote of a time when they drove "along the old storm-battered Gulf Coast road of Louisiana to New Orleans. Staying at a hotel of frayed glories in Royal Street, we took a day's break there, wandered the French Quarter, lunched lavishly at Galatoire's, loitered in bookshops and antique shops."

Gimlet

2 oz. London dry gin

1 oz. Rose's Lime Juice Cordial (more or less to vary sweetness)

Shake well with ice; strain into chilled cocktail glass.

SUGGESTED READING: *Green Hills of Africa* (Chapters 1 and 3), *True at First Light* (Chapters 12 and 19), *Under Kilimanjaro* (Chapters 17, 19, 24, 25, 38, and 40), "The Short Happy Life of Francis Macomber"

As with so many drinks, we're not 100 percent sure who invented the Gimlet. Heck, show me a timeworn drink with an undisputed lineage and I'll buy you a round. The likeliest story concerns a Royal Navy surgeon, Sir Thomas Gimlette, who encouraged men at sea to mix lime juice with their gin rations, circa 1880 (see also the Daiquiri).

The Gimlet appears to be Hemingway's go-to cocktail while on safari, along with Campari, Gin & Soda and the Whiskey & Soda.

Essential to an authentic Gimlet is the use of Rose's Lime Juice Cordial, patented in 1867 by a Scot by the name of Lauchlin Rose. It became a staple on board ship, in part because of its long shelf life. Perhaps Hemingway chose the Gimlet for the same reason, not wanting to worry about fresh fruit perishing under the hot African sun. Hemingway mentions Rose's by name in *True at First Light*, referring to a mixture of "half and half Rose's Lime Juice and whisky that would ease the throat."

In *True at First Light*, based on Ernest and Mary's 1953–54 safari, Mary is ill and asks, "Would it be terrible to have a gimlet for my morale?" Hemingway naturally obliges, noting, "You're not supposed to drink but I always did and I'm still here."

In *Green Hills of Africa*, based on Ernest and Pauline's 1933–34 safari, the Gimlet makes a few more appearances. In one instance it helps rescue Hemingway from a conversation, about writing, that has grown tedious. When asked to recite the things that might harm a writer, Hemingway profoundly states, "Politics, women, drink, money, ambition. And the lack of politics, women, drink, money and ambition." To change the subject, he adds, "Let's all have a gimlet."

The Gimlet is central to the opening scene in "The Short Happy Life of Francis Macomber," published in *Cosmopolitan* in 1936. We find Francis and Margot Macomber on safari with their professional hunting guide, Robert Wilson. While lion hunting earlier, Macomber panicked and ran away, leaving Wilson to kill the charging lion. If that weren't enough, on top of needling him for having fled, his wife Margot has been adding to his misery by having a fling with Wilson. The story begins in the aftermath of the scene with the lion, as they're having lunch, trying to act as though nothing has happened. While Macomber offers a nonalcoholic lime juice or lemon squash, Wilson decides to have a Gimlet.

"I'll have a gimlet too. I need something," Macomber's wife said.
"I suppose it's the thing to do," Macomber agreed. "Tell him to make three gimlets."

Wilson knows that his friendly relationship with the Macombers cannot survive the day, what with the lion incident, his dalliance with Margot, and her cruel treatment of her cuckolded husband. He decides to insult Macomber, ensuring there will be a

1947 movie poster. From the author's collection.

break. "Then he could read a book with his meals and he'd still be drinking their whisky. That was the phrase for it when a safari went bad. You ran into another white hunter and you asked, 'How is everything going?' And he answered, 'Oh, I'm still drinking their whisky,' and you knew everything had gone to pot."

It should be noted that Macomber later recovers his courage, standing tall in the face of fearsome, charging buffalo. It is but a momentary redemption, though (not wanting to spoil the plot).

Hollywood saw fit to cinematize the story in 1947, renaming it

The Macomber Affair. According to the movie poster, Gregory Peck "makes that Hemingway kind of love to Joan Bennett," whatever the hell *that* means. What's ironic is that his depictions of lovemaking were often lampooned in the media. Critics howled at the notion of two people making love in a sleeping bag (*For Whom the Bell Tolls*) and on a gondola in the canals of Venice (*Across the River and Into the Trees*). But who am I to question the Hollywood PR machine?

Hemingway isn't the only author to feature the Gimlet. Perhaps the most memorable instance is in Raymond Chandler's *The Long Goodbye* (1953). The drink plays an integral role in the relationship between detective Philip Marlowe and his friend Terry Lennox:

> We sat in a corner of the bar at Victor's and drank gimlets. "They don't know how to make them here," he said. "What they call a gimlet is just some lime or lemon juice with a dash of sugar and bitters. A real gimlet is half gin and half Rose's Lime Juice and nothing else. It beats martinis hollow."

As a final note on the Gimlet, I encourage you to try both the *traditional* version (using Rose's), and the *natural* version (using freshly squeezed lime juice and simple syrup). You might find that the natural version tastes better, but if you want authenticity, you've got to use the Rose's. While I don't share Terry Lennox's view that "it beats martinis hollow," the Gimlet is still a pretty good drink.

Gin & Coconut Water

2 oz. London dry gin
4 oz. chilled coconut water

Add ingredients to a collins glass filled with ice. Stir. Garnish with a wedge of lime.

A true "when-in-Romer," Hemingway tended to drink locally. He likely discovered coconut water in Key West in 1928. Fresh coconuts were a staple on board his boat *Pilar*; he stowed as many as four dozen during a long voyage. As early as April 1930, he was drinking something you might have seen thirty-five years later on *Gilligan's Island*.

While entertaining John and Katy Dos Passos, Hemingway invented "a new drink, made by boring a hole in a fresh coconut, pouring in six or eight ounces of gin, and sipping the mixture through a straw."[82] His love for the drink continued throughout his life; it was one of the house drinks at the Finca Vigía in Cuba, where, according to Mary Hemingway, they entertained guests who "came to the Finca for extra-dry martinis made by the host or gin in iced coconut water . . . accompanied by three or four courses of the most interesting food I could dream up, and ample pouring of Spanish or Italian wines."[83]

Gin & Coconut Water is popular throughout the Caribbean.

Hemingway in Key West, circa 1932. Ernest Hemingway Photograph Collection, John F. Kennedy Presidential Library and Museum, Boston.

More recent versions, perhaps wanting to resemble the piña colada, also contain rum and sweetened condensed milk. Stick to the original, mon.

The postwar years saw a Stateside fascination with all things tropical. The tiki boom, led by Donn "the Beachcomber" Beach and "Trader Vic" Bergeron, was in full swing, as GIs returning from Pacific and Caribbean outposts were nostalgic for the flavors and ambience of the islands, including the music. Nat sang his "Calypso Blues" and Harry had his "Banana Boat Song," but before all that there was a cat named Wilmoth Houdini who, with his

Royal Calypso Orchestra, released a hit tune in 1946 by the name of "Gin and Cocoanut Water." The song was later covered by none other than Robert Mitchum, on his 1957 album *Calypso Is Like So.*

Interestingly enough, Gin & Coconut Water is said to be an aphrodisiac in the islands and, perhaps fittingly, it even made its way into a bit of marital advice Hemingway gave to his friend Harvey Breit in 1955:

> When you're married you can't afford champagne and brandy and anyway sooner or later the champagne will make your stomach sour and the brandy will make you mean. So take it from here Ecclesiasties [*sic*]. I am not against american womens [*sic*] because Miss Mary and I were just on a fine long trip and went to bed every night by ten o'clock at the latest and slept well every night and drank good gin and coco-nut water. . . . And we're happy as before we were ever married and drank champagne and brandy always . . . and that's been eleven years and it was as lovely as always![84]

While I'm not sure I'd want to take marital advice from someone who's on wife number four, the man *does* know a thing or two about drinks, I have to say.

Gin, Lemon & Wild Strawberries

2 oz. London dry gin

¾ oz. fresh lemon juice

1 tsp. powdered sugar (avoid confectioner's sugar, which can contain cornstarch)

2–4 wild strawberries

In a shaker, muddle the strawberries with the other ingredients, shake well with ice. Strain into a chilled cocktail glass, keeping the strawberry pulp in the shaker. Serve either up or on rocks. Cut with a little soda water, if you'd like (if so, use a collins glass).

rnest Hemingway once said there were only two places he loved, Africa and Wyoming."[85] Nearly every summer from 1928 to 1939, Ernest (and usually Pauline) would escape the oppressive heat and humidity of Key West for the wilds of northwest Wyoming, where he could write, hunt, and fish. It was here that he wrote portions of *A Farewell to Arms*, *Green Hills of Africa*, and *To Have and Have Not*. They'd rent a cabin at the L-Bar-T Ranch, about twelve miles south of Cooke City, Montana, up against Yellowstone Park's eastern border. Hemingway would fish for cut-

Circa 1928, a pretty good day's catch of trout in Wyoming. Ernest Hemingway Photograph Collection, John F. Kennedy Presidential Library and Museum, Boston.

throat trout on the Clark's Fork of the Yellowstone River. "This is the most beautiful country you ever saw," he told his friend Mike Strater.[86]

According to local Polly Copeland, during the Hemingways' 1938 stay in Wyoming, "Every now and then, Pauline Hemingway would pick wild strawberries in the woods on a late afternoon, which she would brew with gin, powdered sugar and lemon, making a powerful drink that we would be invited to sip, sitting on the cabin steps, looking up to the glorious sunset color radiating over Beartooth Butte while Ernest Hemingway would read to us his latest chapter of *The Fifth Column*."[87]

This drink appears to be a variation on Scotch with Lemon & Wild Strawberries, with gin in place of the Scotch. Who knows, maybe it was Pauline's invention that Hemingway modified for use in "The Strange Country," that story of a road trip from Miami to New Orleans. This is a really nice drink, and you can cut it with some soda water and make it into a tall drink, almost like a Collins. Delicious.

Getting Away from It All

Hemingway was no homebody. Looking back on his life, one sees a restless soul, always looking to escape from the mundane, far from the madding crowd. It comes as no surprise that he considered Mark Twain's classic *Huckleberry Finn* as the progenitor of "all modern American literature."[88] After all, that novel closes with the immortal line, "But I reckon I got to light out for the Territory ahead of the rest."[89]

As noted in the Mint Julep chapter, Hemingway discovered the Great American West in 1928, and would come for extended visits throughout the rest of his life. In the February 1939 issue of *Vogue* magazine, Hemingway penned an homage to this region telling of the excellent fly-fishing that could be had in early September on the Clark's Fork of the Yellowstone River. He spoke of horseback riding in the mornings, or lazy afternoons sitting in the sunshine on the front porch of the cabin, where he could look across the valley and see "the line of quaking aspens along the river, now turning yellow in the fall." When winter came, you'd try to keep yourself warm as you rode on horseback to the cabin, and you'd feel "the sharp, warming taste of whiskey when you hit the ranch and changed your clothes in front of the big open fireplace. It's a good country."[90]

This corner of the world held a certain promise of escape for Hemingway. "But these few log cabins, frame houses, filling station, and general store are west of the mail, west of publishers, west of gossip, west of mothers, siblings, in-laws, west of almost everything," said biographer Michael Reynolds.[91] Hemingway longed for a place away from everyone else, away from civilization, tourists, and distractions. In a 1928 letter to Guy Hickok, while completing *A Farewell to Arms*, he vowed to "find a place where [I] can fish and work and finish the bloody book."[92] He found it in Wyoming.

But not at first. His first stop was the Folly Ranch outside Sheridan, Wyoming. Alas, there were too many dudes, tourists, and Easterners for his tastes. "Came to a ranch of a friend where there were 15 girls! Shit," he complained to Waldo Peirce.[93] Thankfully, he found his sanctuary at the L-Bar-T. "This is a cockeyed wild country, looks like Spain, swell people," he told Peirce.[94]

He later thought he'd found that "end of nowhere" escape in Key West in the late 1920s, but by the late 1930s, tourists had ruined that oasis for him as well. After all, the Overseas Highway, connecting Key West with the Florida mainland, opened to auto traffic in early 1938. In a 1932 letter to John Dos Passos, Hemingway facetiously spoke of Key West seceding from the Union!

> *It may be well if the South Western Island Republic secedes from the Union at once. I have organized cutting the cables, blowing up Bahia Honda viaduct, burning bridges, destroying all buoys and lighthouses and the seizing of enough tramp steamers to feed the ungry [sic] populace. We will be a free port, set up gigantic liquor warehouses and be the most PROSPEROUS ISLAND IN THE WORLD. The PARIS OF THE SOUTHWEST.*[95]

The letter goes on another fifteen or so sentences, each one more politically incorrect than the last, but the point is made:

Hemingway was decades ahead of his time with respect to talk of the so-called Conch Republic and Key West secession.

It's clear that Hemingway was no stranger to the road; by age twenty-nine, he'd already traveled extensively throughout North America, Europe, and the Near East, and he's now pressing westward as far as a road will take him. This was according to plan, it seems. Indeed, at the tender age of nine, Hemingway emphatically wrote in his diary, "I intend to travel and write." He's living the example he gave to his sister Marcelline back in 1919 when, just home from the Great War, he exhorted, "[D]on't be afraid to taste all the other things in life that aren't here in Oak Park. This life is all right, but there's a whole big world out there full of people who really feel things. They live and love and die with all their feelings. Taste everything, Sis." Oak Park, after all, was a place of "broad lawns and narrow minds," a quote attributed to him. Even if he never said it, he had to have believed it.

Gin & Tonic

2 oz. London dry gin

4 oz. tonic water

2 dashes Angostura bitters

Fill a tall glass with ice, add ingredients, stir, and garnish with a lime wedge or peel.

SUGGESTED READING: *Islands in the Stream* ("Bimini," Chapter 3), "The Denunciation," "The Butterfly and the Tank"

The Gin & Tonic is a classic highball, a no-nonsense, easy-to-make combination of a distilled spirit and a nonalcoholic, carbonated beverage. Think of it as a cocktail with training wheels. But according to David Embury, a highball shouldn't contain citrus juice; if so, "it becomes a Buck or a Collins or a Rickey and is no longer a Highball."[96] You've been warned.

The Gin & Tonic is based on a centuries-old tandem. In the seventeenth century, quinine was found to have medicinal value against malaria and yellow fever. In India, British subjects would add a dose of quinine to their gin. This combination became popular in warm-weather climes, where such illnesses were common. So, as a law student in steamy New Orleans, a city historically known for outbreaks of fever, I was careful to supplement my diet with the occasional Gin & Tonic. That's my story and I'm sticking to it.

Indeed, Charles Baker notes in *The Gentleman's Companion* that the Gin & Tonic was "originated to combat fevers, real or alleged." Baker further adds that it "became accepted over here by American hosts who wanted to impress folk with having combed the Orient."

As a final note, Baker warns that "it is a medicine and not primarily a stimulant only. On more than one occasion we have temporarily showed aberration on this subject, with the result that our ears rang unmercifully and next day we felt like Rameses II, *rechauffe*. We suggest from 2 to 4 drinks of gin and tonic as being plenty for any one sitting."[97] You heard the man.

In *Islands in the Stream*, Thomas Hudson is at Mr. Bobby's bar, enjoying a "gin and tonic water with a piece of lime peel in the glass and a few drops of Angostura in the drink." Hudson is an artist living in Bimini. The loyal British subjects thereabouts are drinking to celebrate the Queen's Birthday, which is still observed in

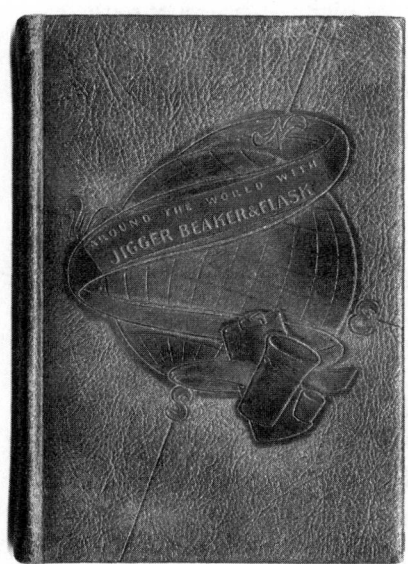

Cover of Charles Baker Jr.'s epic work, *The Gentleman's Companion*, Vol. 2. Courtesy Ted Haigh collection.

1935 Schweppes ad. From the author's collection.

Commonwealth nations, typically on a date having nothing to do with her actual birth date. Indeed, in New Zealand they celebrate it on the first Monday in June, while the Aussies do so the *second* Monday, neither caring one whit that her actual birthday is in *April*. Why quibble over details when the result is a three-day weekend, eh? A moveable feast, indeed.

At Mr. Bobby's, Hudson got his Gin & Tonic and "stood there, holding the long, pleasantly bitter drink, tasting the first swallow of it, and . . . he had a sudden nostalgia for Africa."

Bobby's not so enamored of tonic water, however: "Man can

drink anything he wants. He has money to pay for it. He's supposed to be taking his pleasure and he spoils good gin by putting it into some kind of Hindu drink with quinine in it."

The Gin & Tonic also appears in the short story "The Denunciation," set during the Spanish Civil War. In the mid-1930s, Hemingway was chafing a bit at comments from the left that success had made him forget the writer's role as a voice of the downtrodden. After all, he'd just published *Green Hills of Africa* (safari) and *Death in the Afternoon* (bullfighting), seen by some as travelogues penned by a wealthy globe-trotter, oblivious to the Depression. Perhaps this inspired him to write *To Have and Have Not*, with a bona fide working-class hero, and to also take up a cause. So when Spain erupted in civil war in 1936, he decided to join the war correspondent ranks. But he wasn't a neutral observer; rather, he supported the Loyalist fight against Franco's fascists.

Hemingway's motives weren't entirely altruistic. His marriage to Pauline was on the rocks, and he was having an affair with a young writer named Martha Gellhorn, also covering the war. The conflict gave him a convenient excuse to escape Pauline's watchful eye and to hole up with Martha in Madrid's Hotel Florida.

Yet Hemingway was praised for a 1937 speech in which he noted, "There is only one form of government that cannot produce good writers, and that system is fascism. For fascism is a lie told by bullies. A writer who will not lie cannot live or work under fascism."

You can see the echoes of his mind-set taking place in the short story "The Denunciation," which takes place in Chicote's bar in Madrid. The protagonist, Henry Emmunds, has stopped in for a Gin & Tonic after work. His waiter is very troubled by the fact that a fascist, Luis Delgado, has come to the bar in a Loyalist uniform and is sitting with some Loyalist pilots, who are unaware of his duplicity. The waiter decides that he must report, or *denounce*, Delgado. Emmunds gives him the number of the counterespionage

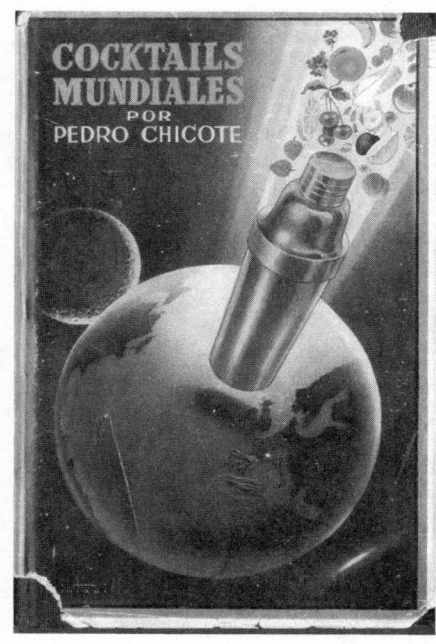

Chicote's 1946 cocktail book.
Courtesy Siegel's Books.

bureau. The waiter derives no pleasure from denouncing Delgado, an old client. But he must, as it is for "the *Causa*." During the exchange, Emmunds is drinking his Gin & Tonic. It has been the drink of the moment at Chicote's, it seems, ever since someone discovered that the bar still has plenty of Schweppes Indian tonic water and Booth's yellow gin, both of which are in short supply as a result of the war.

Emmunds then has a comical conversation with a Greek officer, still recovering from nearly being killed in an air raid. He offers him a Gin & Tonic and informs the Greek of the drama unfolding around the denounced fascist.

Later, the Greek notices that Delgado is also drinking a Gin & Tonic, and he worries, if "[w]e drink that other people think we fascists, eh?" Not too concerned, the Greek later says, "What you

1940 Gordon's gin ad. Courtesy Gordon's Gin.

say we drink some more this fascist drink?" which they naturally proceed to do.

We learn that Emmunds knew Delgado before the war; in fact, he won a hefty sum of money from him four years earlier. Then, as now, they both drank Gin & Tonics, and after winning all that cash, Emmunds says, "a gin and tonic never tasted better to me in all my life." Perhaps Delgado was as big a fan of the drink as Emmunds. Indeed, in the story's introduction, Emmunds speculates that it was the draw of Chicote's and its excellent drinks that proved too much for Delgado to resist. See, by this point in the war, all the good liquor in town was gone. But because it was Chicote's, and because in "November of 1937 they still had the yellow gin and they still had Indian quinine water," Delgado saw fit to take the chance and pay a visit to the place. It was a gamble that this time cost him his life.

At the end of the story, Emmunds fears that Delgado will be told of the waiter's betrayal. So he telephones his contact at the counterespionage bureau, asking him to tell Delgado that it was Emmunds who'd done it. His contact doesn't see the point, since, as a spy, Delgado will be summarily shot. But his contact finally relents, to Emmunds's immense relief. Fully cognizant of Delgado's fatal attraction toward Chicote's, Emmunds doesn't want Delgado, in his final moments before he faces the firing squad, to know he was betrayed by a waiter at the bar he so loved.

Say what you will about your Applebee's or T.G.I. Friday's, a place just doesn't engender that kind of loyalty every day. Here's hoping you've known a place like Chicote's in your own life.

Glühwein

1 quart dry wine
Peel of 1 lemon and 1 orange
Spices to taste
1 Tbsp. sugar

If ground spices are used, cook 1 to 2 teaspoonfuls of them with the lemon and orange peels and sugar in 1 cup water until flavor is well dissolved and then add the wine. It is even better to use 1 crushed, but not grated, nutmeg, 2 to 3 inches stick cinnamon, and a half dozen whole cloves; boil them with sugar and lemon and orange peels in the wine and strain out. Do not allow the wine to boil as this detracts from the flavor.

From David Embury, *The Fine Art of Mixing Drinks*

SUGGESTED READING: *A Farewell to Arms* (Chapter 39)

Glühwein ("glowing wine" in German) is a mulled, spiced wine popular in German-speaking countries. Like any punch or seasoned drink, the choice of spice, sweetener, and other flavorings is up to you. Options include orange zest, cloves, vanilla pods, nutmeg, cinnamon, honey, apples, currants, peppercorn, and ginger. Some folks even fortify their Glühwein with rum or a liqueur.

Glühwein is featured in *A Farewell to Arms*, Hemingway's tale of ambulance corps officer Frederic Henry and nurse Catherine

Barkley, set in Italy during World War I. Frederic and Catherine make their escape from the war and travel by rowboat into Switzerland. When the snows come, they spend much of their time indoors, planning what they'll do when their baby is born.

By mid-January, Frederic has grown a beard, and the couple go for long walks along snow-packed roads. On one of these outings they stop for a drink, sitting inside an inn and drinking "hot red wine with spices and lemon in it. They called it glühwein and it was a good thing to warm you and to celebrate with."

They have a happy winter together, waiting for the arrival of spring and the birth of their baby. When the spring finally comes, so does the rain, perhaps presaging the novel's ending.

Glühwein is a classic winter warmer, and while it is typically made with red wine, white may also be used. As with other Hemingway drinks like the Bloody Mary, sangria, and hot rum punch, there are many good recipes out there, so improvise as you see fit. *Prost!*

Green Isaac's Special (The Tomini)

2 oz. London dry gin
4 oz. green coconut water (not milk)
Juice of 1 lime (about 1 oz.)
2–4 dashes Angostura bitters, to taste

Shake all ingredients well with ice, then transfer contents of shaker into a collins glass, adding more ice as needed. Garnish with a lime wedge or peel.

SUGGESTED READING: *Islands in the Stream* ("Bimini," Chapter 7; "Cuba" and "At Sea," Chapters 7 and 19)

This is yet another Hemingway creation, basically a modified Tom Collins. Hemingway discovered the joys of mixing gin, lime, and coconut water while living in Key West (1931–39, though he began visiting the island for extended periods in 1928). In a 1931 letter to his editor, Max Perkins, concerning his new home on Whitehead Street, he noted, "This is really going to be the hell of a fine house. . . . Will plant more limes and coconuts. Wish you could plant a gin tree."[98]

The Green Isaac's Special debuts in *Islands in the Stream*, a poi-

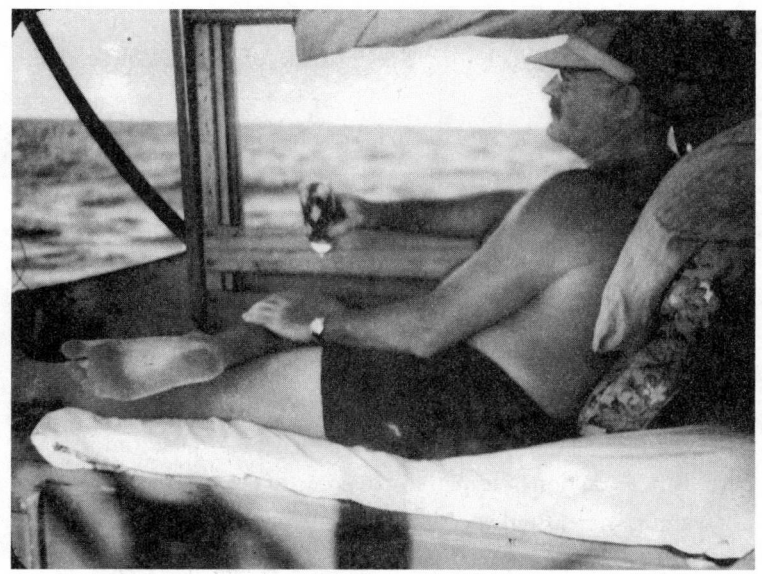

In a photo reminiscent of the scene, Hemingway enjoys a drink in the cabin of *Pilar*. Ernest Hemingway Photograph Collection, John F. Kennedy Presidential Library and Museum, Boston.

gnant story of an artist with three sons (by two mothers, like Hemingway). It is named for a pair of islands north of Bimini, Great Isaac and Little Isaac. In the opening book, "Bimini," Thomas Hudson enjoys the summer with his three sons, Tom, David, and Andy, and his friend Roger Davis.

In Chapter 7, they're all out fishing on Hudson's boat. Eddy, the first mate, offers Hudson a drink they refer to as the Green Isaac's Special. Hudson relaxes in the shade, enjoying "the tall cold drink made of gin, lime juice, green coconut water, and chipped ice with just enough Angostura bitters to give it a rusty, rose color," and gazes out over the Gulf Stream.

Later on, while David is engaged in an epic battle with a sailfish, his brother Tom makes Hudson this same drink. Hudson feels "the sharpness of the lime, the aromatic varnishy taste of the Angostura and the gin stiffening the lightness of the ice-cold coconut water."

The funny thing about this drink is that it has a different name in each of the novel's three books. In "Bimini," Eddy calls it the Green Isaac's Special. In "Cuba," Hudson asks for "a Tom Collins with coconut water and bitters." In "At Sea," he asks Antonio to make him a drink containing "[g]in and coconut water with Angostura and lime," which Antonio calls a "Tomini." What is this, *Three Faces of Eve*?

By whatever name, I've had the pleasure of making this drink with water fresh from the coconut on two occasions, and it is superb. But if you don't happen to have a coconut palm nearby, coconut water is increasingly available at the grocery store. One wonders what Hemingway would think of the recent popularity of coconut water, and the marketing claims that it's a better way to rehydrate, restoring electrolytes and sodium lost to perspiration. Perhaps he figured that out a long time ago, out on the Gulf Stream.

Gregorio's Rx

1–2 oz. rum (to taste)

2 Tbsp. honey

2 oz. lemon or lime juice

1 mint leaf

Muddle honey and mint in a collins glass. Add ice, juice, and rum, and stir well. Garnish with a wedge of whatever citrus you're using.

Gregorio's Rx was concocted by Gregorio Fuentes, a longtime crew member on Hemingway's boat *Pilar*. He was more than just a first mate, cook, and bartender; after all, Hemingway reportedly left his beloved boat to Fuentes in his will.

Fuentes was born in the Canary Islands and lived to be 104. Many believe he's one of two or three Cuban fishermen who formed a composite for the character of Santiago in *The Old Man and the Sea*, another being Carlos Gutierrez. According to Hemingway folklore, he hired Fuentes to replace Gutierrez, who'd been lured away by Hemingway's presumed lover Jane Mason to retaliate for Hemingway's affair with Martha Gellhorn. Hell hath no fury like a woman scorned, eh?

While at sea, "Hemingway gave full command of the bar to 'Gregorine,' as he called Gregorio. As they sailed past the Morro of Havana, Hemingway would invariably say: 'Captain Gregorine, please take charge of the Ethyline Department.' Gregorio had his rules in this area, claiming 'that a drink should be held in the hand no longer than half an hour. Once the sun makes it lukewarm, it should be discarded.'"[99]

It seems that "Gregorio had his own special prescription, which he considered very effective to prevent or cure a cold: 'Take a clean glass and put two tablespoons of honey in it, add the juice of two lemons, a mint leaf, two ice cubes and rum to taste. Nothing like it,' he says."[100]

I know what you're thinking, this sounds an awful lot like the Mojito, doesn't it? But it's not clear if "lemons" actually means lemons, or *limon verde* (lime), a "loss in translation" we've seen before (see the Daiquiri). It's a very nice drink either way, and along with the Bailey, it's perhaps as close as Hemingway ever came to a Mojito.

Hemingway and Prohibition

According to Gregorio Fuentes, not only did Hemingway purchase illegal booze and consort with rumrunners like Joe Russell, Hemingway himself was a bootlegger! More on this in a moment, but first a word about the Noble Experiment.

Prohibition ran from 1920 through 1933. Like many Americans, Hemingway wasn't much deterred by it. Of all things, it began the year he turned twenty-one. At nineteen he had already served in the ambulance corps in World War I in Italy, getting a taste for a variety of potent potables. During Prohibition's thirteen-year duration, Hemingway lived in a place that either didn't have it (Paris) or didn't particularly recognize it (Key West). Unlike many other American expatriates, he didn't go to Paris for the booze or the cafés; he went there to further his writing career (though it no doubt improved its "livability"). And Key West, which he began visiting in 1928 (he moved there in 1931), was nearly as free and easy as the Left Bank; this according to a 1940 newspaper account:

> *Key West has never felt the restraint of prohibition or gambling laws. It has more saloons and jooks than you can shake a well-rounded stick at, and most of them advertise a "club in rear" where crap games, chuck-a-luck, and slot machines are open to all comers.*[101]

Hemingway's friend John Dos Passos adds this:

> *There was really abundant fishing on the reefs and in the Gulf Stream. A couple of Spaniards ran good little restau-*

rants well furnished with Rioja wine. Nobody seemed ever to have heard of Prohibition or game laws. The place suited Ernest to a T.

There was more there to drink than Spanish red. Hemingway soon befriended "Sloppy Joe" Russell, a companion for fishing and obtaining bootleg Scotch. Russell is said to have made more than 150 rum-running trips from Cuba to the Florida Keys in his boat *Anita*, which also served as Hemingway's primary fishing boat until he bought *Pilar* in 1934. Russell explained his tactics:

> *We loaded our whisky right in the Havana harbor and cleared our cargo in the legal way. . . . The American consul would tip off the officers and they'd be waiting for us on the other side. But we'd stick around Havana for a week and they'd get tired of waiting for us. Then we'd go across. Well, the consul finally got wise to what we were doing and got a rule passed ordering us to leave the harbor within 24 hours after clearing. After that we just didn't bother about clearing. We loaded our liquor 12 miles below Havana and came across when we pleased.*[102]

Hemingway described Russell's exploits in a letter to his cousin Bud White, January 29, 1931:

> *There is a bootlegger here with damned good fishing boat . . . we can fish tarpon in Havana harbor and drink there—go down coast to little fishing village and fish giant marlin from there—he says we can bring a load & as much*

liquor as we want back and we can dump it along in outer keys and then go out later and bring it back—you can take all you want 2–3 suitcases back with you on train with no trouble—they have no search nor bother.[103]

Even Hemingway himself tried his hand at rum-running, says Gregorio Fuentes:

During Prohibition, Hemingway went to see [Joe] Russell and told him: "I'm broke, lend me your boat." Russell and Hemingway made a deal, and the writer went to Havana and managed to get around 600 or 700 cases of cognac from Recalt's, 24 bottles to the case. The cognac cost them 40 cents a bottle, and sold in the United States at $3.50 each. . . . Hemingway smuggled the "goods" from Playa de Jaimanitas. He and Russell agreed on the day and place to meet in jurisdictional waters. They had a prearranged system of signals, using red, white, and blue lights. According to Fuentes, that was how Hemingway made enough money to go to Europe and Africa.[104]

I believe the story, but I'm a little dubious of the "600 or 700 cases of cognac" claim, simply because I can't see the thirty-four-foot *Anita* holding that much during the arduous ten-hour, ninety-mile voyage from Havana to Key West. I don't doubt Fuentes's veracity, though; as a wise man once said, it's not a lie *if you believe it*. He may have gotten that number from Hemingway, who liked to, shall we say, *embellish*. It is a good story, though.

Hot Rum Punch

1½ 750 ml bottles Barbados or lighter Jamaican rum (or use Rhum Saint
James if keeping with the theme in *A Moveable Feast*)
1 (750 ml) bottle Cognac
3 quarts boiling water
2 cups lemon juice
Brown sugar, to taste
Handful of cloves

Add all ingredients to a sturdy stockpot or slow cooker; stir occasionally, simmer on low heat for 30 minutes. Garnish each cup with
a spiral of lemon peel, careful to remove the white pith, as it contains
unwanted bitterness.

SUGGESTED READING: *The Sun Also Rises* (Chapter 11), *A Moveable Feast* ("A
Good Café on the Place St.-Michel")

Many believe punch to be the ancestor of the modern-day
cocktail. It dates back hundreds of years, to India. The
name itself derives from the Hindustani word *panch*, meaning
"five," referring to the number of ingredients in a true punch: spirit,
citrus, tea, sugar, and water. Like the Bloody Mary and sangria,
think of it as a blank canvas: you're free to improvise. The above
recipe is from Hemingway's friend Charles Baker Jr. for the Oxford
University Hot Rum Punch, which he describes as "a classic that is
simple & soothing & satisfactory, and dating back into the dim,

distant past," and "[m]ost excellent for anyone coming down with anything, due to the lemon juice."[105]

Hot rum punch appears several times in Hemingway's Paris era, which makes sense. After all, a constant theme of his memoir *A Moveable Feast* is the struggle to stay warm. He'd often escape to a nearby café, ostensibly to write but really just to warm up. In a December 23, 1921, letter to Sherwood Anderson, he writes: "And we sit outside the Dome Café, . . . and it's so damned cold outside and the brazier makes it so warm and we drink rum punch, hot, and the rhum enters into us like the Holy Spirit."[106]

This sentiment is echoed in a 1922 letter to Harriet Monroe, where he notes, "The hot rum punch and checker season has come in. It looks like a good winter. Cafés much fuller in the day time now with people that have no heat in their hotel rooms."[107]

Hemingway and Hadley, 1922. Nice day for a hot rum punch. Ernest Hemingway Photograph Collection, John F. Kennedy Presidential Library and Museum, Boston.

He also learned to make this drink by himself, as he brags in a 1921 letter to Howell Jenkins: "I brew a rum punch that'd gaol you. Living is very cheap. Hotel room is 12 francs and there are 12.61 to the paper one. A meal for two hits a male about 12–14 francs— about 50 cents apiece. Wine is 60 centimes. Good Pinard. I get rum for 14 francs a bottle. Vive la France."[108]

And so it's logical that this drink should appear in his Paris novel, *The Sun Also Rises*. Jake Barnes and Bill Gorton are spending a few days fishing in the Catalonian village of Burguete, prior to Pamplona's fiesta of San Fermín (see also Aguardiente). In Chapter 11, they're checking into a local inn. It's bloody cold—inside and out. Bill plays the piano to keep warm.

Meanwhile Jake negotiates the price of the room. Initially twelve pesetas a night seems too steep. When he learns that the price includes meals—*and wine*—it seems like a bargain. It would appear that the inn would lose money on those two. Bill suggests that they have a hot rum punch, since playing the piano isn't going to keep him warm forever. So Jake finds the proprietor and teaches her how to make a hot rum punch. Soon a girl "brought a stone pitcher, steaming, into the room. Bill came over from the piano and we drank the hot punch and listened to the wind." Bill notes that it's a wee bit light on the rum, so Jake finds a bottle in the cupboard and adds another half glass of rum to the punch.

You'll note that I suggest using Rhum Saint James, a rhum agricole from Martinique and a Hemingway favorite. As opposed to rums made from molasses, rhum agricole is made from cane juice. In a 1922 letter to Howell Jenkins, he mentions that "I'm drinking Rum St. James now with rare success. It is the genuwind 7-year old rum as smooth as a kitten's chin."[109]

He also mentions it in *A Moveable Feast*, in another scene about writing in a café on a cold Paris day. As he's working, he orders a Rhum Saint James and notices a beautiful girl sitting nearby. Still,

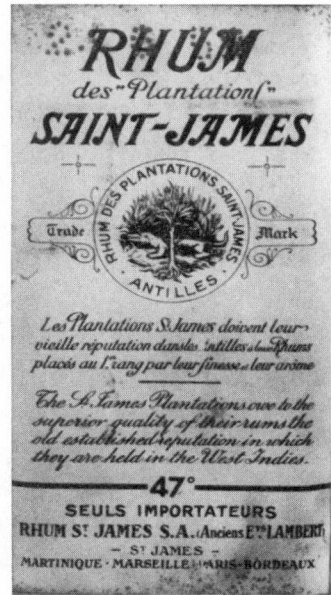

Vintage Rhum Saint James label. Courtesy Anistatia Miller and Jared Brown.

he continues to write: "But in the story the boys were drinking and this made me thirsty and I ordered a rum St. James. This tasted wonderful on the cold day and I kept on writing, feeling very well and feeling the good Martinique rum warm me all through my body and my spirit."

This is one of the few times when Hemingway admits to drinking while writing, which was against his rules. He often poked fun at one of his chief rivals, William Faulkner, famous for saying, "I usually write at night. I always keep my whiskey within reach." When asked if it were true that he mixed a pitcher of Martinis every morning before starting to write, Hemingway replied, "Jeezus Christ! . . . Have you ever heard of anyone who drank while he worked? You're thinking of Faulkner. He does sometimes—and I can tell right in the middle of a page when he's had his first one. Besides, who in hell would mix more than one martini at a time?"[110]

Sherwood Anderson

Author Sherwood Anderson was one of Hemingway's early mentors. He convinced Ernest and Hadley to move to Paris in 1921 and offered letters of introduction to the likes of Gertrude Stein, Ezra Pound, and Sylvia Beach. Hemingway later showed his gratitude by lampooning Anderson's distinctive writing style (and Anderson's recently released *Dark Laughter*) in his first novel, *The Torrents of Spring*. It was not done with malice, however; it was a move calculated to get out of his contract with Boni & Liveright, which also published Anderson. Hemingway wanted to sign up with Scribner, which had F. Scott Fitzgerald. He was betting the publisher would reject *Torrents*, not wanting to publish anything that openly mocked its top author, and would thereby be compelled to release him. The bet paid off; Boni & Liveright rejected it, he signed with Scribner, which soon published *Torrents*, followed by *The Sun Also Rises*, and Scribner was his publisher the rest of his life.

So whatever became of Anderson? In what can only be called a cocktail cautionary tale, during a cruise stopover in Panama in 1941, he apparently tossed back his Martini a little too quickly, also swallowing the olive. Unfortunately, the toothpick was still attached to the olive. It perforated his colon, and he died of peritonitis. A true cocktail casualty. Let's be careful out there, folks.

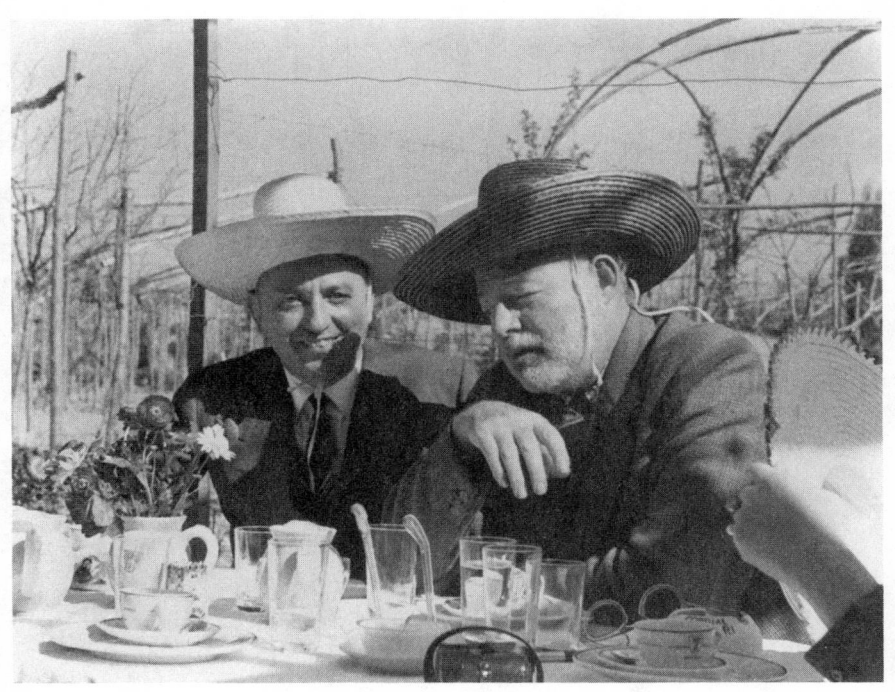

Hemingway and Giuseppe Cipriani (owner of Harry's Bar in Venice) started a warm friendship while Hemingway was writing *Across the River and Into the Trees*. When he wasn't in Venice, he stayed in Cipriani's idyllic guesthouse, the *locanda*, on the nearby island of Torcello. Here, Cipriani and Hemingway are doing a bit of drinking, so much so that it took Cipriani three days to recover from his hangover. It was apparently the first time Cipriani ever drank with a customer; it was against his rules as a bartender. Hemingway's personality, it seems, was too strong for Cipriani to refuse. Courtesy Getty Images.

The Ideal Cocktail

1 oz. grapefruit juice
⅓ oz. sweet vermouth
⅓ oz. dry vermouth
⅓ oz. London dry gin
1 tsp. Luxardo maraschino liqueur

Shake well with ice, strain into a chilled cocktail glass. Serve with a small bowl of almonds (as per the custom at the Floridita in Havana).

Can you imagine being a regular at one of the world's greatest bars, and ordering the same drink each and every time you visit? Neither can I, but that's what we'd have ourselves believe in the case of Hemingway at the Floridita, in spite of what we know about his diverse palate. No, the Floridita wasn't Cheers, and Hem wasn't Norm. So what might Papa have also had at the Floridita? According to fellow writer Robert Ruark, it was the Ideal cocktail.

In a 1963 syndicated column, Ruark reminisced about the good old days in "the sweet isle of Cuba," pre-Castro, of course, "before the revolutionists ruined it." "But it was wonderful once, dictators or not, graft or not, corruption or not. It was literally a comic-opera paradise, where the regimes were overturned regularly, and the

IDEAL

¼ Toronja.	¼ Grape Fruit.
1 Cucharadita Marrasquino.	1 Teaspoonful Marraschino.
1/3 Vermouth Torino.	1/3 Vermouth Torino.
1/3 Vermouth Seco.	1/3 Vermouth Seco.
1/3 Ginebra.	1/3 Gin.
Hielo menudo, Muy batido y colado. Sírvase con varias almendras.	Cracked ice. Shake very well and strain into cocktail glass. Serve with a few almonds.

Ideal cocktail recipe from 1937 Floridita cocktail menu. From the author's collection.

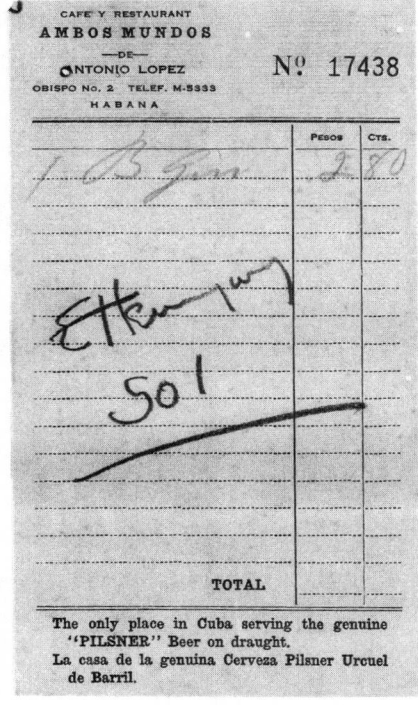

Papa's got a brand-new . . . bottle of gin. Signed hotel bill, circa 1930. Before he moved to the Finca Vigía in 1939, Hemingway would stay here during visits from Key West, always in Room 501. "Fine hotel overlooking the harbor, named Ambos Mundos, good clean room where you can work for $2.00 a day."[111] From the author's collection. *Note: Room 501 now goes by the number 511 and has been made into something of a shrine to Hemingway.*

Hemingway's favored corner of the bar at the Floridita, circa 1951. He's shown here with his close friend Toby Bruce and an unidentified woman. Photo courtesy of the Toby and Betty Bruce Collection, Key West, Florida.

overturned fled with his money to Paris or Miami or Madrid. . . . In Havana, people strolled, they did not hurry. . . . There was no racial prejudice in Cuba . . ."[112] And so it went. Yeah, Ruark could lay it on pretty thick.

In addition to his frequent paeans to Cuba, Ruark also wrote a fair bit about his memories of Hemingway. In a 1950 review (some would say *evisceration*) of *Across the River and Into the Trees*, he acknowledged that "My boyish admiration for Papa . . . was so great that once I spent two weeks looking at him in the Café Floridita in Havana, and never did screw up enough courage to step over and say hiya." On at least some of those occasions, Ruark tells us, Hemingway had himself an Ideal cocktail:

Constante, at La Floridita, ran the best restaurant and built the best drinks in the world, and there you would find Hemingway of an evening, reading his *Diario* [*Diario de la Marina*, a Cuban newspaper], looking like an old professor as he sat sipping his daiquiri or ideal—specialty of the house—next to a potted palm.[113]

The Ideal cocktail was quite popular both before and after Prohibition, and perhaps like many classics, it's due for a comeback. You'll find the Ideal in such timeless cocktail books as Hugo Ensslin's *Recipes for Mixed Drinks* (1917), *Cocktails* by "Jimmy" Late of Ciro's (1930), *The Official Mixer's Manual* by Patrick Gavin Duffy (1934), and Harry Craddock's *The Savoy Cocktail Book* (1930). It's

Further proof that Hemingway did not just drink Daiquiris at the Floridita! Vintage tourist photo, circa 1932, Hemingway and his Key West friends. Seated from left to right are Charles Thompson, possibly his wife Lorine, Ernest Hemingway, unknown gentleman, Pauline Hemingway, and Joe Russell (owner of Sloppy Joe's Key West). Photo courtesy of the Toby and Betty Bruce Collection, Key West, Florida.

more or less a Bronx cocktail with grapefruit in place of the orange juice, and more balance among the other ingredients (as well as maraschino liqueur). And while we're in the neighborhood, it's also similar to the Queens cocktail (yes, nearly every borough of New York City has a drink named for it); in the Queens, it's pineapple juice.

Because of his writing style and penchant for big game hunting, Ruark became known as "the poor-man's Hemingway," or a "Hemingway spinoff." Yet he and his wife did eventually become friends, somewhat, with the Hemingways; they accompanied Papa's entourage during a 1953 tour of the bullfights in Spain.[114] But between you and me, if Ruark's scathing review of *Across the River and Into the Trees* had been published in that newspaper Hemingway was reading while Ruark toddled over to say "hiya," I'd like to think that Papa, with a few Ideal cocktails under his belt, would have decked him. I'll even drink to that.

Irish Whiskey Sour

1½ oz. Irish whiskey
1 oz. fresh lime juice
¾ oz. simple syrup (optional)

Shake well with ice; strain into chilled cocktail glass or pour contents of shaker into a rocks glass. Garnish with lemon peel.

SUGGESTED READING: *Islands in the Stream* ("Bimini," Chapter 10)

As I explain in the chapter on the White Lady, the classic "sour" cocktail is an excellent basis for improvisation, and one that every bartender or enthusiast should master.

In this drink, Hemingway takes the classic Whiskey Sour and adds a few twists of his own. He uses Irish instead of rye or bourbon, lime instead of lemon, and goes without sugar (as was his wont).

It's featured in a great drinking scene from *Islands in the Stream* (Chapter 10 of "Bimini"), where we find Thomas Hudson, his three sons, and his friend Roger at Mr. Bobby's bar. They're having a bit of R&R after an epic battle between Hudson's son David and a giant sailfish. Plot spoiler: the fish got away. So they drown their sorrows over a few Irish whiskey sours. Roger, it seems, has been carrying his remorse "all over the island" after that lost fish. Like

Our
IRISH WHISKEY
is the
real McCoy

—as smooth as a Nylon Stocking

Vintage Irish whiskey ad. From the author's collection.

any good bartender should do in such a situation, Bobby suggests he have another whiskey sour: "I'll make you another one. Get that old remorse on the run."

You might find the drink too tart or strong without sugar, so in its place you could use a liqueur, such as Cointreau (orange) or Domaine de Canton (ginger), a syrup like orgeat or falernum, or even honey. For a bit of variety, try it with rye or even Scotch. It's all a matter of taste. *Sláinte!*

Jack Rose

2 oz. apple brandy (Calvados or Laird's applejack or apple brandy)
½ oz. fresh lime or lemon juice
¼ oz. grenadine (preferably genuine pomegranate)

Shake well with ice; strain into chilled cocktail glass. Garnish with twist of lime or lemon peel.

See also alternate recipe, below.

Perhaps fittingly for an apple drink, the Jack Rose "creation story" is the subject of some debate. One theory is quite simple: it's a rose-colored drink made from applejack. If you're thirsty, I suggest you stop reading right now and fix yourself that drink. This gets complicated.

Another view holds that it was named for, or even invented by, "Bald Jack" Rose, a Gotham gangster who copped to the 1912 assassination of gambling boss Herman "Beansy" Rosenthal. Jack Rose was granted immunity as part of the prosecution (some would say *framing*) of allegedly crooked NYPD vice detective Charles Becker, who reputedly ordered Jack Rose to make the hit. Based in part on Rose's testimony, Becker took a trip to the Sing Sing electric chair on July 30, 1915. It was a one-way ticket.

Yet another story has the drink being named for a flower, the Général Jacqueminot Rose, which in turn was named for one of Napoleon's generals, Jean-François Jacqueminot. He led the 1827

MEET JACK ROSE

(the delicious Apple Jack cocktail)

and other jazzy Apple Jack
drinks, desserts and
delightful entertaining ideas

Laird's recipe booklet, circa 1935.
Courtesy Laird's.

Rambouillet expedition, resulting in the abdication of the French king, Charles X.

Rambouillet, by the way, was the site of another expedition, in 1944, led by a war correspondent by the name of, you guessed it, Ernest Hemingway. Having covered several wars, he jokingly called himself "Ernie Hemorrhoid, the poor man's Pyle," referring to legendary correspondent Ernie Pyle. Attached to an Office of Strategic Services (predecessor to the CIA) unit with Patton's Third Army, Hemingway allegedly couldn't resist the temptation of getting into the action as the Allies pushed toward Paris. He reportedly led his own private army of French partisans in live combat. Charges were brought for violating the Geneva Convention's rules governing noncombatants, but Hemingway was later cleared by the army's inspector general. But I digress. . . .

The Jack Rose makes two appearances in the 1926 novel *The Sun Also Rises*, one of the quintessential books of the Lost Generation. The story surrounds a group of dissolute friends in postwar Paris. The Hemingway hero is Jake Barnes, an American journalist who was wounded in World War I. Jake is in love with Lady Brett Ashley, who, at varying times, loves Jake. Chapter 6 begins with Jake waiting in vain for Brett at the Hotel Crillon, where they'd agreed to meet. She never shows up, typifying his frustrated love for her. You see, Jake's war wound prevents him from, how shall I say, *consummating* his love for Brett. Yep, a pretty nasty wound.

Jake waits in the lobby of the Crillon for forty-five minutes, then, as any red-blooded male would do, he heads for the bar, where George the barman fixes him a Jack Rose. George is apparently well-known for his Jack Rose, as it makes a return appearance in Chapter 8. It seems that Jake's friend Bill Gorton has had a few on his way to Jake's flat. As they walk the streets of Paris together, it becomes obvious that Bill is "pie-eyed." Jake asks him where he's been drinking.

> "Stopped at the Crillon. George made me a couple of Jack Roses. George's a great man. Know the secret of his success? Never been daunted."
>
> "You'll be daunted after about three more pernods."

Hemingway likely had a few pie-eyed moments himself at the Crillon bar. "When I had money I went to the Crillon," he noted in his memoir, *A Moveable Feast*. Also, in the novel *The Garden of Eden*, it's in that bar where David Bourne meets his wife, Catherine.

The first recipe shown above is the commonly accepted, conventional recipe for the Jack Rose. However, submitted for your approval is a quite different recipe. It's from the classic 1922 book *Barflies and Cocktails*, written by Harry MacElhone and Wynn Holcomb. MacElhone was the owner/bartender at Harry's New York Bar in Paris.

Found within these hallowed pages is a rather different Jack Rose recipe, published around the same time that Hemingway wrote *The Sun Also Rises* (1926). Further, Hemingway happened to live in the same town (Paris) where the inimitable Mr. MacElhone tended bar, at a saloon that Hemingway was known to frequent.

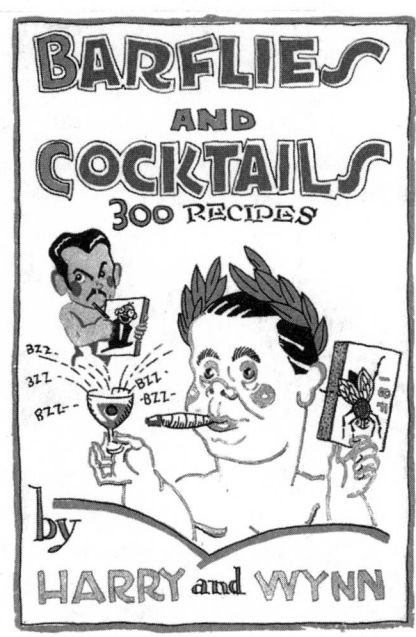

Cover of Mud Puddle Books' reproduction of *Barflies and Cocktails*. Courtesy Mud Puddle Books Inc.

So, I submit to you, ladies and gentlemen of the jury, that *this* is the Jack Rose that Jake Barnes drank while waiting for Brett Ashley on the evening in question.

HARRY MACELHONE'S 1920S PARIS RECIPE

1½ oz. applejack or Calvados

¾ oz. dry gin

¾ oz. orange juice

¾ oz. fresh lemon or lime juice

⅓ oz. French vermouth

⅓ oz. Italian vermouth

Grenadine to color (about ⅓ oz.)

Shake well with ice; strain into a chilled cocktail glass. Garnish with twist of lime or lemon peel.

Recipe adapted from *Barflies and Cocktails*, 1927 edition.

Having grown quite fond of the traditional Jack Rose recipe, I didn't want to like this drink. After all, the odd mix of ingredients reminded me of a bad B-movie, you know, *Jack Rose Meets the Bronx Cocktail*. But I made it, you know, out of a pure sense of reportorial responsibility. I just wasn't sure that the additions of gin and sweet and dry vermouth, not to mention orange juice, would work together.

I was wrong. I love this drink.

The vermouth offers an aromatic quality that reminds me of the El Presidente, that famous cocktail of Prohibition-era Cuba. The gin offers it backbone and dryness, and the orange juice balances out the tartness. The trick is to be judicious in the amount of grenadine in either recipe you choose—don't want it too sweet. They're both great drinks; it's hard to go wrong. Heck, make both.

When researching the original manuscript of *The Sun Also Rises* at the JFK Library in Boston, I was somewhat surprised to discover that in Hemingway's original, handwritten draft of this scene, he didn't mention drinking a Jack Rose. He must have added it in a later draft. We can only be thankful he did. *À votre santé!*

The "Real" Lady Brett Ashley

When published in 1926, *The Sun Also Rises* caused a bit of a stir among the Montparnasse expatriate crowd, as many of its characters were based on real people. Many of them weren't amused; bartender Jimmie Charters referred to it as "six characters in search of an author—with a gun!" So who was this Lady Brett Ashley, for whom Jake carried such a torch? It was none other than Lady Duff Twysden, described by Heming-

Photo from Pamplona café in 1925 showing Hemingway, Harold Loeb, Lady Duff Twysden, Hadley, and Pat Guthrie. Ernest Hemingway Photograph Collection, John F. Kennedy Presidential Library and Museum, Boston.

way's wife Hadley as being "a wonderfully attractive English-woman, a woman of the world with no sexual inhibitions."[115] This is made clear in the novel itself, as Hemingway describes Brett as being quite fetching, and quite the femme fatale.

Though Hemingway was somewhat smitten with her, it's not believed they ever had an affair. However, during the 1925 Pamplona fiesta, when he learned that Duff had just spent a romantic holiday with writer Harold Loeb, Hemingway fumed. His jealousy and frustration simmer through the pages of the novel, during which Brett has affairs with Robert Cohn (based on Harold Loeb), Mike Campbell, and a bullfighter named Pedro Romero, all while also in love with Jake.

So if your gal ever stands you up, or she runs off with a writer or a toreador, fix yourself a Jack Rose, and don't ever be daunted, not in public, anyway.

Jimmie Special

For two people, combine in a cocktail shaker.

1½ oz. Cognac
¾ oz. Pernod
¾ oz. Amer Picon
¾ oz. mandarin liqueur
¾ oz. sweet cherry brandy

Shake thoroughly. Drink straight or mix with soda to taste.

Amer Picon, a French aperitif bitters, is virtually unavailable in the United States, but you can use Torani Amer as a substitute.

I'll tell you about Jimmie but first I have to tell you about Gertrude. By the time Hemingway arrived in Paris in 1921, Gertrude Stein was firmly established as a literary heavyweight. She held court at her salon at 27 Rue de Fleurus, sharing a studio apartment with her companion, Alice B. Toklas. In *A Moveable Feast*, Hemingway describes the fruit liqueurs he drank there: they "tasted like the fruits they came from, concerted into a controlled fire on your tongue that warmed you and loosened it."

Stein offered advice on Hemingway's early writings. Among them was his controversial short story "Up in Michigan," which involved a young man, full of whiskey, taking a girl by force. Stein considered it *inaccrochable*, likening it to a work of art so obscene that it would be difficult to sell, and even if sold, it would be even harder to display.[116] Hemingway listened to her advice but proceeded with the story anyway.

It was during one of his visits to Stein's salon that she gave her famous assessment of Hemingway's milieu: "That's what you are. . . . All of you young people who served in the war. You are a lost generation. . . . You have no respect for anything. You drink yourselves to death."[117]

Hemingway saw fit to include the phrase "You are all a lost generation" in the prologue to his 1926 novel *The Sun Also Rises*. Yet he eventually came to discount her assessment. "But the hell with her lost-generation talk and all the dirty, easy labels," he decided in

Hemingway's baby son "Bumby," shown here in Paris with Gertrude Stein. Bumby later referred to Stein and Toklas as "two giant women gargoyles of my childhood."[118] Ernest Hemingway Photograph Collection, John F. Kennedy Presidential Library and Museum, Boston.

A Moveable Feast. As he matured as a writer and thinker, he would come to reject Stein's influence on himself and on his generation.

During the 1920s, the Montparnasse crowd might gather at such places as the Café Select, the Closerie des Lilas, the Brasserie Lipp, La Rotonde, and the Dingo American Bar. One of the most popular bartenders was a Brit named Jimmie "the Barman" Charters, a former lightweight boxer. Jimmie was behind the bar at the Dingo the day Hemingway and Fitzgerald first met. In 1937, Charters published *This Must Be the Place: Memoirs of Montparnasse*, and he asked Hemingway to write the introduction.

In doing so, Hemingway couldn't resist the opportunity to take a few jabs at Gertrude Stein. Playing off the similarities between *salon* and *saloon*, he notes: "Once a woman has opened a salon it is

Jimmie "the Barman" Charters, as shown on the cover of his autobiography.

certain that she will write her memoirs. If you go to the salon you will be in the memoirs; that is, you will be if your name ever becomes known enough so that its use, or abuse, will help the sale of the woman's book." But this shouldn't happen with a bar, he writes.

> You should expect to be able to go into a saloon or bar and pay for your drinks without appearing in the bartenders' memoirs and I was shocked and grieved to hear that Jimmie Charters was writing his. . . . If he wants to write his memoirs it is only one more step in the decline of Western civilization.[119]

While I'm sure that Jimmie was pleased as punch to have Hemingway write his introduction, I rather suspect most of this sailed right over his head.

Jimmie was a bartender, not a literary figure. But he did make great drinks, and he told some pretty good stories, and the Jimmie Special is an example of each. It not only exemplifies the creativity that was taking place in bartending at the time, but also the extent to which the American cocktail was embraced overseas. The torch was being carried as the United States suffered through Prohibition. It also exemplifies the joie de vivre that was Montparnasse during the 1920s. I'll turn it over to Jimmie to explain:

> I must tell you of a cocktail I invented while I was at the Dingo that had a powerful effect on some of the Quarterites . . . two stiff drinks of it will have some surprising effects! . . . On women this drink had the effect of causing them to undress in public, and it often kept me busy wrapping overcoats around nude ladies! But even knowing this did not prevent some of the feminine contingent from asking for the Jimmie Special. I wish I had a hundred francs for every nude or seminude lady I've wrapped up during the best Montparnasse days![120]

Apparently the wife of the Dingo's owner, a Mrs. Wilson, put the kibosh on the Jimmie Special, and Jimmie could no longer make them. "Trying to run a respectable joint here," I can envision her saying. I've made this drink twice and, for what it's worth, I observed no such effects on the females to whom I served the drink; no overcoat-wrapping for me. Having said that, I used Torani Amer, not Amer Picon; maybe that's the key.

Josie Russell

FOR A PITCHER:

4½ oz. rum

12 oz. hard apple cider

2 oz. fresh lime juice

2 tsp. sugar

Fill a pitcher with ice, add all ingredients, stir well. Serve on ice in collins or highball glasses, garnished with lime wedge or peel. Serves two to three.

As discussed in the chapter on the Vermouth Panaché, Hemingway kept a detailed log while on fishing trips, whether he was on his own boat, the *Pilar*, or on *Anita*, owned by his friend Joe "Josie" Russell. They're great fun to read.

One day in June 1933, they were out fishing on the *Anita*. The log has an entry that day, in Hemingway's unmistakable handwriting, simply captioned "Cocktail," followed by a recipe: "3 jiggers rum—1 bottle cider—lime—sugar—2 [illegible]."

I could make out the word "Cocktail" easily enough (it jumps off the page), followed by most of the rest, but after the "2" I was stumped. Two what? Cloves? Cherries? Heck, no. Was the word "siphon," as in two shots of charged water? I consulted the pros, Stephen Plotkin of the Hemingway Collection in the JFK Library in Boston, and Brewster Chamberlin of Key West, both of whom are intimately familiar with Hemingway's handwriting. Each independently agreed that the word was "spoons," as in "2 spoons of sugar."

Now that sounds like a lot of sugar, especially for Hemingway, but remember, this has four and a half ounces of rum and an entire bottle of cider, so proportionately it's not all that much sugar. I also note that no quantity of lime is given. Perhaps it's just one lime, but if Hemingway was using key limes, which are smaller, you might want to increase the amount of juice, as I've done.

The drink had no name in the *Anita*'s logbook; it just said "Cocktail." So Stephen, Brewster, and I put our heads together to come up with a name and agreed that a drink named in honor of "Josie" Russell would really hit the spot. Cocktail sleuthing can create quite a thirst, eh?

Joe "Josie Grunts" Russell

Bootlegger, rumrunner—heck, Joe Russell was no outlaw, he was just trying to make ends meet in the hardscrabble life of Depression-era Key West. In a 1933 article in *Esquire*, Hemingway described Russell, whom he nicknamed "Josie Grunts," as the man "who brought the first load of liquor that ever came into that place from Cuba."[121] True, Joe ran his share of booze across the Gulf Stream (see also Gregorio's Rx). But once Prohibition ended, and he could run his bar legit, it broke Hemingway's heart:

> When Carlos Gutierrez wrote in mid-July that the marlin were running at last, Ernest hurried down to Joe Russell's bar in Green [sic] Street to see if Joe would come along to Cuba as helmsman for the Pilar. But Joe could not come. Since the repeal of Prohibition his rumrunning business had disappeared, but Sloppy Joe's was doing well. He waved a hand towards the sailors on shore leave from the destroyers in the harbor. They were lined up three deep in front of the bar. "Not this year," he told Ernest. "I want to go just as bad as you do, Cap. But I've got to make it while I can." "I know it," said Ernest, gloomily. "But we'll lose ten fish before anybody learns how to work them."[122]

Hemingway claimed to have an even greater stake in the place. "I used to be co-owner of Sloppy Joe's. Silent owner, they call it. We had gambling in the back, and that's where the real money was."[123]

Hemingway's friendship with Russell endured until the end. In June 1941, Joe and Ernest were in Havana, and from there they'd fly up to New York to watch the Joe Louis–Billy Conn fight at Madison Square Garden, along with Key West friends Betty and Toby Bruce. But Joe required some minor surgery first, and while in recovery, he suffered a heart attack and passed away at the young age of fifty-three (some accounts say fifty-one). Ernest called Toby the next day and, choked

Joe Russell and Hemingway with a marlin, Havana, circa 1932, with Joe Jr. on the left. Ernest Hemingway Photograph Collection, John F. Kennedy Presidential Library and Museum, Boston.

with emotion, said, "I'm sorry I stood you up but Josie died yesterday."[124] In an even more poignant acknowledgment, in the *Pilar's* logbook for June 20, 1941, in Hemingway's distinctive hand, is the sole entry, "Mr. Josie died." Joe Russell is buried in the historic Key West City Cemetery.

Joe Russell was Hemingway's friend, fishing companion, and the basis for not one but two characters in *To Have and Have Not*, namely, the protagonist, Harry Morgan, and the bartender Freddy. Here's to Mr. Josie.

Maestro Collins

2 oz. London dry gin

1 oz. fresh lime juice (to taste)

1 oz. simple syrup

2 dashes Angostura bitters (optional)

2–4 oz. seltzer

Shake all ingredients *except for the seltzer* with ice, then strain into an ice-filled collins glass. Top with soda, stir, and garnish with a lime peel or wedge.

Recipe adapted from the text.

SUGGESTED READING: *With Hemingway*, by Arnold Samuelson (Chapters 1, 4, and 16); "There She Breaches! or, Moby Dick Off the Morro," *Esquire*, April 1936; and "Monologue to the Maestro—A High Seas Letter," *Esquire*, October 1935

In the spring of 1934, twenty-two-year-old Arnold Samuelson was living in Minnesota. He'd read the Hemingway story "One Trip Across," was immediately smitten, and decided he wanted to talk to the author about a career in writing. So he hitchhiked all the way to Key West. In true hobo style, the final leg of the trip was atop a railroad flatcar. Hemingway was out of town, so Arnold spent the first few nights in the Key West jail, not having enough scratch for a room.

He eventually got to meet the great author and impressed him just enough that Hemingway decided not only to mentor him as a writer, but also to hire him as a mate on his brand-new boat, *Pilar.* Arnold's memoir, *With Hemingway*, was published posthumously in 1984.

Hemingway was fond of nicknames, and Arnold soon became "Maestro," since he played the violin. "Mice" tried to be a quick study. Unfortunately, at sea, he was clumsy and often seasick. With a bit of good-natured sarcasm, Hemingway said, "Mice, you certainly must be going to be a hell of a good writer because you certainly aren't worth a damn at anything else."[125]

Hemingway playfully groused that mentoring a young writer was not what he expected to be doing at sea. In a 1935 *Esquire* article titled "Monologue to the Maestro—A High Seas Letter," he wrote, "If any more aspirant writers come on board the *Pilar* let

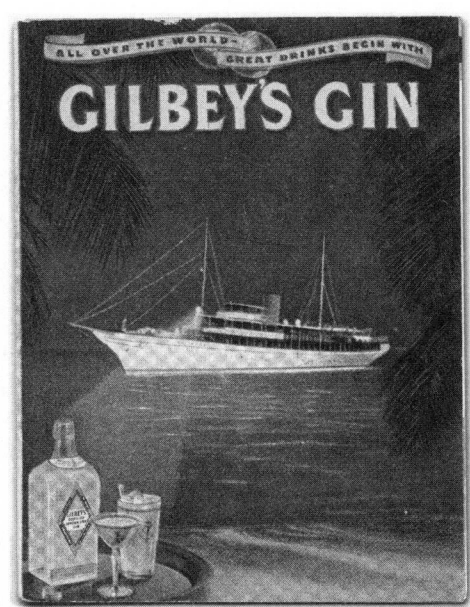

Even during Prohibition, Hemingway could buy Gilbey's in Key West for thirty dollars a case. Note the similarity between this yacht and the *Moana* (see the Rum Collins). Courtesy Ted Haigh collection.

them be females, let them be very beautiful, and let them bring champagne."[126] Maestro took it all with grace.

A day on board *Pilar* was well provisioned. According to Hemingway's kid brother Leicester, "Pauline used to pack the frosted bottles of Gilbey's Gin, plenty of key limes, sugar, and a thermos of ice water. Then they would load into the Ford roadster and be off to the docks."[127] Maestro became the onboard bartender, learning the craft from one of Hemingway's servants, Louis:

> He came to work late in the afternoons and stayed out of sight until E.H. called, "Oh, Louis!" and then would come running easily on his long legs; "A whiskey, please, one for Mister Arnold, too," E.H. would say and Louis would disappear around the corner. In an incredibly short time he would come running back with the filled glasses on a silver tray. Louis never took a drink himself but he knew how to mix them. He used a half a dozen limes and four spoonfuls of sugar in a gin cocktail, adding more limes and sugar as long as he heard no complaints.[128]

Hmmm, can we perhaps blame Louis for Hemingway's diabetes and disdain for sugar? Just sayin'. . . .

A popular opera singer by the name of John Charles Thomas soon visited Key West, and he was invited aboard *Pilar* for a drink. Samuelson poured a whiskey for himself and Hemingway, and a gin cocktail for Thomas. Thomas tasted his drink and made a face; to him it just tasted like mere lemonade. So he questioned the Maestro on its contents:

> "Can you taste any gin in this," he asked, giving me a drink from his glass.
> "No, I don't taste it."
> "That's what I thought."

Ernest, Maestro, and Pauline, July 21, 1934, Hemingway's thirty-fifth birthday, at a café in Havana. Ernest Hemingway Photograph Collection, John F. Kennedy Presidential Library and Museum, Boston.

"Maybe I forgot to put some in."

"Some bartender!" E.H. said, laughing. "He mixes a gin drink without any gin in it." . . .

I took his glass below, poured two fingers of gin in it and brought it back up.

"Ah, yes, this is much better," Thomas said. "It's really surprising what a difference a little gin will make."[129]

The drink, of course, is nothing more than a Tom Collins, but with lime juice in place of lemon. It's a refreshing summertime cooler; just be sure to put a little gin in it. And when you do, please raise a glass to the Maestro.

A Bunch of Bananas and a Bottle of Gin

Hemingway loved gin. You'll find it in no fewer than fifteen drinks in this book. Of Gordon's gin he once said: "I do not work for the Gordon's people and this is a testimonial which I offer freely and in what I hope is my right mind. This beverage is one of the sovereign antiseptics of our time. . . . Gordon's product is of approved merit and can be counted on to fortify, mollify and cauterize practically all internal or external injuries."[130]

This wasn't just talk. You see, during a 1954 safari, Hemingway and his wife Mary toured the Belgian Congo in a small plane. Unfortunately, the plane struck an old telegraph wire and was forced to crash-land. They quickly abandoned the plane, with minor injuries. They didn't sleep too well, worried about crocodiles swarming the riverbank.

The next day an old motor launch, the *Murchison*, came chugging up the river—the same boat used in filming *The African Queen*, of all things. According to Hemingway, "No hard liquor was served, but a bottle of Gordon's gin was obtainable from the Hindu in charge of the launch who sold it for what I considered and he admitted to be a rather exorbitant sum."[131] Was it perhaps one of Bogart's bottles that Hepburn didn't dump over the stern?

The *Murchison* took them to Butiaba, where a second plane awaited. Believe it or not, *this* plane crashed while taking off. Although the others were able to escape, Hemingway was trapped, and he had to use his shoulder and head as a battering ram to escape the burning craft. In addition to yet another concussion, he suffered two cracked discs, ruptured his liver and one of his kidneys, separated his shoulder, and literally cracked his head open; cerebral fluid was oozing from a spot above his ear. "He remembers an English doctor pouring gin in the crack in his skull and saying, "'Laddie, gin is as good for you on the outside as it is on the inside.'"[132] *Time* magazine carried the following:

> When his plane crashed on safari in Africa last winter and for nearly a day he was believed dead, even people who do not like his books felt a strange, personal sense of loss, and even people who never read novels were delighted when he walked out of the jungle carrying a bunch of bananas and a bottle of gin, and was quoted, possibly even correctly, as saying: "My luck, she is running very good."[133]

He would later quip to his friend A. E. Hotchner, "Would I come out with bananas?" Literally adding insult to injury, it would all be memorialized in a perfectly awful novelty song titled "A Bunch of Bananas (The Heming Way)." This 1954 atrocity was performed by Rosemary Clooney and José Ferrer. Although you can hear it online, I urge you not to, not if you ever want to enjoy listening to Rosie Clooney again. The song is so horrendous, I rather doubt I'll even be able to watch *White Christmas* this year.

Martini

From a letter Hemingway wrote in 1949, use "[j]ust enough vermouth to cover the bottom of the glass, ¾ ounce of gin, and the spanish cocktail onions very crisp and also 15 degrees below zero when they go in the glass."[134]

TRANSLATED:

1¾ oz. London dry gin (Hemingway preferred 94-proof Gordon's)

⅛ oz. French (dry) vermouth (Noilly Prat)

Stir well in a mixing glass with plenty of ice; strain into a chilled cocktail glass. Garnish with a couple of frozen Spanish cocktail onions or a chilled garlic onion. Hemingway sometimes garnished his Martini with thinly sliced onion.

The 94-proof Gordon's gin that Hemingway favored is no longer available in the United States; however, Tanqueray is similar in style and flavor.

SUGGESTED READING: *Across the River and Into the Trees* (Chapters 7, 9, and 27), *A Farewell to Arms* (Chapter 34), *The Sun Also Rises* (Chapter 19), *The Garden of Eden* (Chapters 11, 13, 14, 15, 16, 18, and 29), *Islands in the Stream* ("Bimini," Chapters 5 and 12), *Ernest Hemingway: Selected Letters*

This is going to be a long chapter—go fix yourself a drink. Hemingway certainly loved a good Martini. He featured it in no fewer than five of his novels, and he mentioned it often in

1930s Gordon's gin ad.
Courtesy Gordon's Gin.

his letters. He was precise about how it should be made, very cold and very dry. He not only suggested the manner in which ice cubes should be made, but also that the Spanish onions be frozen. He also specified Gordon's gin and Noilly Prat vermouth.

We first see the Martini in bartending books of the 1880s, such as Harry Johnson's *New and Improved Bartender's Manual,* as well as another (possibly a prototype) drink known as the Martinez. Under either name, the drink started out as a rather sweet drink, made with Old Tom gin and Italian (sweet) vermouth. Over the course of the twentieth century, the drink became decidedly drier, with the use of London-style gin and French (dry) vermouth. Accordingly, this drink became known as the "dry Martini."

Then a funny thing happened. Luminaries such as Dorothy Parker, Winston Churchill, and Hemingway himself began popularizing the idea that the drier their dry Martini, the better. Indeed, we're told that Parker merely *whispered* the word "vermouth" over the glass, while Churchill only glanced at the vermouth bottle across the room (or in the direction of France) while he poured his measure of gin. In the 1940s cocktail impresario David Embury espoused a 7-to-1 ratio of gin to vermouth and, while doing so, saw fit to lampoon author Bernard DeVoto, who had the audacity to tout a 3.7-to-1 formula. So, whereas "dry Martini" initially meant "using *dry* gin and *dry* vermouth," it became stylish to make your dry Martini drier yet, by using less and less vermouth.

THE MONGTOMERY MARTINI

Hemingway's Montgomery Martini was perhaps the driest of the dry. It debuted in *Across the River and Into the Trees* and is named after a top Allied commander in World War II, British field marshal Bernard Montgomery.

Hemingway held little affection for "Monty," saying he was too cautious in battle, that he required a *15-to-1* troop superiority before committing them in battle. The Montgomery Martini is überdry, with a 15-to-1 ratio of gin to vermouth, an obvious dig at Monty's *commitment issues.*

In this 1950 novel, we have army colonel Richard Cantwell contending with his deteriorating health, advancing age, and peacetime reduction in rank. In short, he's in crisis, and he turns to his young lover, Renata (an Italian countess), and the Martini, for solace. He prefers his Martinis *"Secco, molto secco e doppio"*—dry, very dry and double. In Chapter 9, at Harry's Bar, he specifies the degree of dryness, and a cocktail name is born.

"Waiter," the Colonel called; then asked, "Do you want a dry Martini, too?"

"Yes," she said, "I'd love one."

"Two very dry Martinis," the Colonel said. "Montgomerys. Fifteen to one." . . .

The Martinis were icy cold and true Montgomerys, and, after touching the edges, they felt them glow happily all through their upper bodies.

Later in this scene, Cantwell is more discreet while ordering another round, not calling them Montgomerys because two Britishers are at the next table. Later, Renata asks if they should have another, and since the British are gone, Cantwell assents.

"They make me feel very good," says Renata, to which Cantwell replies, "They have a certain effect on me, too, the way Cipriani makes them," referring to Giuseppe Cipriani, owner of Harry's Bar (see the Campari & Gin).

In one of the closing chapters, Cantwell and Renata have a final Martini together at Harry's. It's a bittersweet evening, as they both know that they'll soon be parting. Upon taking a sip of her drink, Renata feels "its warmth and its momentary destruction of sorrow."

Around the time of *Across the River and Into the Trees*, Hemingway was the subject of a *Life* magazine character essay by Malcolm Cowley, "Portrait of Mister Papa." Cowley played up the Hemingway-as-Martini-drinker motif. Hemingway was not amused: "He has me in World War II as a martini addict with a canteen of gin on one hip and a canteen of vermouth on the other—mixed fifty-fifty, I presume. Can you imagine me wasting a whole canteen on vermouth?"[135]

Perhaps Hemingway's most notable wartime Martini story was when he allegedly "liberated" the Hotel Ritz in Paris. Hemingway was a war correspondent for *Collier's*, but sometimes he "forgot" his noncombatant role and engaged in actual fighting. He became attached to a unit, led by Colonel David Bruce of the Office of Strategic Services, which attracted a collection of French partisan "irregulars." Hemingway assumed a leadership role, preferring to be called "Captain" and telling the men he'd have a higher rank if he weren't illiterate (!).[136] By August 24, 1944, they'd advanced all the way to the outskirts of Paris, against sporadic German resistance. Once inside the city, Hemingway and his men headed straight for the Travellers Club, which they immediately "liberated." After a Champagne toast, they continued on to the Ritz:

> They . . . requested and were given lodging in the hotel, and quarters were found nearby for the "Private Army." When asked what they needed, they answered that they would like to have fifty martini cocktails. The bartender could not be found and the cocktails were mediocre. But Ernest was finally in nominal possession of the Ritz.[137]

This story is corroborated by, of all people, Monty's biographer Alan Moorehead. In "The Liberation of Paris" chapter of his book *Eclipse*, he notes:

> It was a little galling to find Ernest Hemingway sitting in the dining-room over a bottle of Heidsieck. At that time he was acting as the commander of a company of maquis who had fought their way in through Versailles. He had liberated the Ritz just an hour before.[138]

Upon reading this, Hemingway set the record straight: "Actually the wine was Perrier-Jouet and it was not Versailles but Rambouillet."[139] So noted, Mister—er, *Captain* Hemingway.

THEY MADE ME FEEL CIVILIZED

Martini experts Anistatia Miller and Jared Brown have characterized the Martini as "the quintessential American cocktail, the crowning jewel of civilized decadence." The Bard of Baltimore, H. L. Mencken, observed that the Martini was "the only American invention as perfect as the sonnet." Hemingway's depiction of the drink in *A Farewell to Arms* fits right in. In the novel, Frederic Henry is an American in the Italian ambulance corps during World War I. He has fallen in love with a nurse, Catherine Barkley, who is carrying his child. Frederic deserts from his unit, and he and Catherine flee to Switzerland, where they'll have their child and escape from the horrors of war.

In Chapter 34, Frederic has arrived in the northern Italian town of Stresa, where Catherine awaits him. He feels out of place wearing borrowed civilian clothes, but when he enjoys a Martini at the hotel, it provides him with a sense of self-assurance and helps him tune out the war, to leave it far behind him:

> I drank a couple more martinis. I had never tasted anything so cool and clean. They made me feel civilized. . . . The barman asked me some question. "Don't talk about the war," I said. The war was a long way away. Maybe there wasn't any war. There was no war here.

Similarly, in *The Sun Also Rises*, Hemingway uses the Martini as a way to transition back to civilization in the wake of the bacchanalia of Pamplona's fiesta. In Chapter 19, we find Jake Barnes and Brett having a Martini in Madrid. Awaiting their train back to Paris, they head for the bar of the Palace Hotel, where they sit on bar stools and have Martinis. After all the debauchery of Pamplona, the bar offers a safe haven. "It's funny what a wonderful gentility you get in the bar of a big hotel," Jake observes. "No matter how vulgar a hotel is, the bar is always nice."

In *The Garden of Eden*, Hemingway explores a number of unconventional themes, including cross-gender role-playing and open marriage, as writer David Bourne and his newlywed wife, Catherine, have a ménage à trois with a beautiful Italian girl named Marita. The Martini is featured prominently in this novel; gin and vermouth verily drip from its pages. In Chapter 11, David, Catherine, and Marita are getting to know each other over a few. In fact, it's a bit of an initiation for Marita, her first Martini:

> "It tastes very good but terribly strong."
>
> "They are strong," David said. "But there's a strong wind today and we drink according to the wind."

Before long the trio are doing everything together, spending their days at the beach and their evenings together at the bar. The Martini plays a strong supporting role in their getting to know each other.

By Chapter 13, Catherine is beginning to show signs of a mental breakdown. David makes her a Martini, thinking it might cheer her up, but she pours it out on the bar, then eats the olive. "There isn't any us," she says. "Not anymore." He makes her a second Martini, which she again pours out. She finally drinks the third, and her mood improves. "You just lose something and it's gone that's all. All we lose was all that we had. But we get some more. There's no problem is there?" she says.

In Chapter 14, David has spent the morning writing, then the trio go to the beach. After a decadent lunch washed down with plenty of Bollinger Champagne, Catherine is worn out and takes a siesta, sleeping away the afternoon. David and Marita sit at the bar having a drink. He begins to question his own behavior, wondering how he ended up in a ménage à trois. David makes them both a Martini, and when Marita disappears to go see how Catherine is doing, David decides to drink her Martini. As he does so, he feels a "clear and undeniable" sense of pleasure drinking her drink, "because it was hers." But he recognizes the situation he's put himself in, in love with two women, and he's not sure he likes it.

Toward the end of the novel, Catherine burns the stories that David has been writing for weeks. She views them as "worthless" and feels she's doing him a favor by destroying them. Marita tries to console him, telling him that he can write them over again. He tries, but initially fails. Like any good mistress should do in a situation like this, Marita suggests he have a drink, and David, naturally, mixes them Martinis, "icy cold and dry."

In the novel's closing chapter, Catherine has departed, and David, miraculously, is able to rewrite the stories she destroyed.

Islands in the Stream also contains a few choice Martini scenes. The first part surrounds a painter, Thomas Hudson, who lives and works in Bimini. He's eagerly awaiting a summertime visit by his three adolescent sons. In Chapter 5, Hudson has spent the morning working. Now that his author friend Roger has arrived, he's knocking off for the day. They then engage in a fairly comical discussion of whether or not it's okay to have "a quick one," even though it's not yet noon. They rationalize it away thusly: Tom's finished working, and Roger is on vacation, so what the hell, let's have a Martini, eh? But rules are rules, and Tom has a rule against drinking before noon. Roger piously pretends to agree: "I've been keeping that rule too. It's an awful nuisance some mornings when a drink would make you feel all right." So Tom makes the executive decision, and they prepare Martinis.

"Joe," Roger called. "Bring the shaker and rig for martinis."

"Yes *sir*. I got her rigged now."

"What did you rig so early for? Do you think we are rummies?"

"No sir, Mr. Roger. I figured that was what you were saving that empty stomach for."

The original manuscript from *Islands* has a slightly different version of this scene (for example, Hudson's name was George). This time it's Roger making the Martinis, and he asks if a 6-to-1 ratio is okay, or if it should be drier (!). The houseboy offers to make them, claiming that his are the world's driest, explaining that he "weaves" the vermouth around in the glass the same way you'd do a clove of garlic in a salad bowl. He does this just "to moisten the sides equally and then add the gin." But Roger is the one making the Martinis, and his are "awfully good." Indeed, "Roger made admirable martinis that you felt take hold right under your arms."[140]

Later in the scene, we see Hemingway's obsession with coldness, when Roger insists that their second Martini be made in a freshly chilled glass. "How cold the glass is is the trick. We really ought to chill them with dry ice. The drink too. I'll get it worked out someday," Roger says. A man before his time, I'd say.

Indeed, Hemingway's Martinis were as legendary in real life as they were in his prose. One afternoon in 1948, the Hemingways were invited to a party hosted by a neighbor, Frankie Steinhart. The guest of honor was the Duke of Windsor, the former Edward VIII, king of England, perhaps better known for having abdicated the throne to marry Wallis Simpson. Hemingway had fended off prior invitations, that is, until the duke himself called. Put on the spot, Hemingway relented, but brought his houseboy Rene along, insisting no one made a Martini quite like him. They packed up thinly sliced onions, olives, Gordon's gin, and dry vermouth, and set off on foot for Steinhart's.

You just can't beat Martinis alfresco. Spencer Tracy, Hemingway, and others on the patio of the Finca Vigía, 1956, during the filming of *The Old Man and the Sea*. Note the ever-present Gordon's and Noilly Prat. Ernest Hemingway Photograph Collection, John F. Kennedy Presidential Library and Museum, Boston.

The party was an afternoon black-tie affair, but Hemingway was determined to keep it casual. When he and Rene arrived, a waiter tried to offer them each a jacket, but quickly realized it was a lost cause. Hemingway assumed command, requesting ice, a mixer, and a place to make drinks. Rene began to make the Martinis, very dry, very strong, and garnished with olives or thinly sliced onions. Soon everyone who was anyone was over at Hemingway's make-shift Martini bar, including the Duke of Windsor, who soon shed his jacket, loosened his tie, and rolled up his shirtsleeves. Papa's floating Martini bar had stolen the show.[141]

Hemingway became pals with the duke and duchess, and not only took them to the Floridita but hosted them at the Finca Vigía.

According to Leonard Lyons of the *Miami News*, "Hemingway quickly solved the problem of whether the Duchess should be addressed as 'Your Highness' or 'Your Royal Highness,' by addressing her as 'Wallie.'"[142]

MARTINIS, DRY AND *COLD*

A 1947 letter Hemingway wrote from his home near Havana to his publisher, Charles Scribner, informs us that he not only liked his Martinis dry, he liked them *cold*: "We have real Gordon's Gin at 50 bucks a case and real Noilly Prat and have found a way of making ice in the deep-freeze in tennis ball tubes that comes out 15 degrees below zero and with the glasses frozen too makes the coldest martini in the world."[143] Indeed, not only were the Martinis chilled with those giant ice cubes, he also froze his Spanish cocktail onions so they'd help keep the drink as cold as possible.

In a letter to folks back in Key West, he noted that with this method of making ice, the "whole drink comes out so cold you can't hold it in your hand. It sticks to the fingers."[144] Now *that* sounds like a cold Martini. And if you want to freeze your Spanish onions à la Hemingway, place them in a zippered plastic bag in the freezer. Also, although Hemingway never mentioned them, try a dash of orange bitters in your Martini, as the drink was made in the days before the Great War. *Salut!*

Hemingway and his third wife, Martha Gellhorn, in happier times at the Stork, circa 1940. Courtesy Stork Club Enterprises LLC, www.storkclub.com.

The Mint Julep

2–4 oz. bourbon whiskey
Crushed ice
Simple syrup, to taste
4–5 mint leaves, mint sprig for garnish

In a silver julep goblet, muddle the mint leaves with simple syrup. Crush some ice with a wooden mallet in a Lewis bag, or a tightly woven dish towel (not terry cloth, as ice will cling to it too much). You want it dry, almost powdery. Pack ice into goblet, then add your whiskey. Insert a spoon and swizzle it awhile, garnish it with the mint sprig.

From his late twenties through the rest of his life, Hemingway was drawn to the mountains of Wyoming, Montana, and Idaho. He went there to write, to hunt and fish, for the climate, to just escape. Hemingway's son Patrick understood the allure of the West for Papa. "You have to appreciate what a trip to Idaho meant to my father. He had spent all those years, first in Key West, then in Cuba, where the fall weather was hot and muggy, and there was no respite from the summer they had just endured. Then to come out to Sun Valley and into that cool, clean, crisp, clear air, with the deep blue skies, the good hunting, the good friends he liked and trusted—that was a wonderful contrast for him."[45]

One of those friends was a fellow named Taylor "Bear Tracks"

Williams, the head guide at the Sun Valley Resort. So respectful of his skills with a rifle, Hemingway referred to him as "the old Kentucky Colonel who will kill you dead at 300 yards with a borrowed rifle."[146] Further, "we call him Colonel because he is from Kentucky but everybody thinks he is a British Col. because he looks like one who has been in India too long and is also deaf."[147]

Like any "old Kentucky colonel," Taylor knew his bourbon whiskey. "Taylor had lived in Idaho for years but he was a Kentuckian," said a friend, Dorice Taylor. "His first personal project on taking a job at Sun Valley as a guide was to plant a mint bed. Taylor didn't 'make' a mint julep, he 'built' a julep. Even if you were on your fourth—or fifth—Taylor didn't yield to the temptation to sweeten your old drink with another hoot of bourbon. He washed and polished the glass and started from scratch. Hemingway appreciated Taylor's sportsmanship and juleps."[148] According to Hemingway's friend Tillie Arnold, "[h]e always had a mint bed some place. We never did find out exactly where it was. He said that the mint would be better if it was grown on the grave of a Confederate soldier."[149] Tillie's husband, Lloyd Arnold, wasn't so sure that Williams "hadn't lifted one complete and transplanted it in Idaho." In any event, upon sampling his first Taylor Williams Mint Julep, Hemingway exclaimed, "Christ! This is good, how long before a man can't get up and walk out by himself?"[150]

As noted above, the ol' Colonel kept the location of his mint bed a secret, and I hold no hope of ever finding it all these many years later. I've found, however, something nearly as good, "up in Michigan."

The Hemingway short story "Summer People" is yet another of the great, semiautobiographical Nick Adams stories, set in the Michigan woods of Hemingway's youth. His family spent their summers near Petoskey, at their cottage Windemere, on Lake Walloon. "Summer People" is set in the town of Horton Bay, named

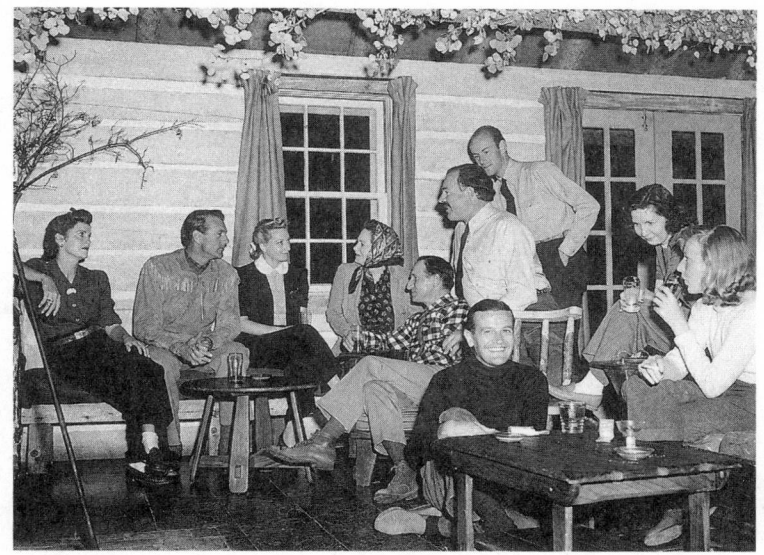

Oh, to have been a fly on the wall, a welcome party for Mr. and Mrs. Gary Cooper, Trail Creek Cabin, Sun Valley, Idaho, October 1940. From left to right, Rocky and Gary Cooper, Mrs. Winston McCrea, Dorothy Parker, "Colonel" Taylor Williams, Ernest Hemingway, Winston McCrea, Tillie Arnold, Martha Gellhorn, and Alan Campbell (Parker's husband, in foreground, facing camera). Photo by Lloyd Arnold. Courtesy William Smallwood.

for an inlet of nearby Lake Charlevoix. The story begins in typical Hemingway fashion, with a description of the landscape, noting that "halfway down the gravel road from" the town of Horton Bay was a spring on the side of the road, and the water came out of the spring, "and flowing away through the close growing mint into the swamp." Nick is alone, and he wishes he could immerse himself into the spring, as it was a very hot night. "I bet that would fix me," he concludes.

In October of 2013, while presenting at the Michigan Hemingway Society's annual conference, I visited Horton Bay, and was fortunate enough to talk with Jim Hartwell, proprietor of the

Hartwell & Co. Bookshop, part of the Red Fox Inn. Jim's grandfather Vollie Fox is said to have tutored the young Hemingway on trout fishing in Horton Creek. Jim directed me to the very spring mentioned in the story, "halfway down the" now-paved road toward the lake. Sure enough, mint still grows around the spring. I took a few cuttings, and now I have some of that very mint growing at my home. Kinda neat, in an admittedly geeky way.

Sadly, Jim passed away in March of 2015, so the next time I fix a Hemingway Mint Julep, I'll raise a glass to him.

Hemingway mentions this same spring at the beginning of "The Last Good Country." The story begins with Nick Adams "watching the bottom of the spring where the sand rose in small spurts with the bubbling water. There was a tin cup on a forked stick that was stuck in the gravel by the spring and Nick Adams looked

Hemingway's "Summer People" friends. Left to right, Carl "Odgar" Edgar, Katy "Stut" Smith, his sister Marcelline Hemingway, Bill Horne, Ernest Hemingway, and Charles Hopkins, circa 1919. Ernest Hemingway Photograph Collection, John F. Kennedy Presidential Library and Museum, Boston.

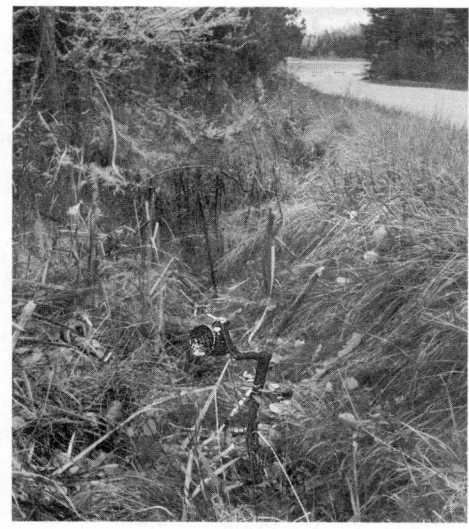

The spring at Horton Bay, with the "close growing mint" surrounding the "forked stick." The tin cup has been replaced by a blue enameled model. In the distance is Lake Charlevoix. Courtesy Christopher Struble, president of the Michigan Hemingway Society.

at it and the water rising and then flowing clear in its gravel bed beside the road." Nick "could see both ways on the road and he looked up the hill and then down to the dock and the lake, the wooded point across the bay and the open lake beyond . . ." If you visit today, you'll see a cup hanging there on a forked stick, so if you want a little branch water for your bourbon, or if you want to mix yourself a Mint Julep at Horton Bay, you're halfway there.

Bourbon Renewal

"Good whiskey was very pleasant. It was one of the pleasant parts of life." So noted protagonist Frederic Henry in Hemingway's 1929 classic, *A Farewell to Arms.* No doubt Hemingway loved his whiskey. But as I note later in the Whiskey & Soda chapter, I've never found a reference to bourbon among his prose; when Hemingway wrote about a specific whiskey, it was typically Scotch. Yet, here in the Great American West, we find him enjoying a Mint Julep with Kentucky's finest, and I've found another good bourbon story, below. Who knows, maybe bourbon was his local drink of choice; to borrow a line from "Get a Seeing-Eyed Dog," "it's our drink for out here."

In the summer of 1930, he and Pauline spent a couple of months at the L-Bar-T Ranch in northwestern Wyoming. One day, while hunting for a grizzly bear that had been terrorizing local cattle, Hemingway was riding a horse named Goofy (I'm not making this up). Goofy got spooked by something and bolted, dashing headlong into a thick forest. Hemingway remained on the horse long enough to have his face severely lacerated by tree branches. He was bleeding profusely, and first aid did no good. So Hemingway and hunting companion Ivan Wallace rode on to a nearby ranger station, where they rented a dilapidated old car, driven by the ranger's teenage daughter.

They drove to the nearest town, Cody, Wyoming, where a Dr. Trueblood (a former veterinarian) stitched up Hemingway's face. According to Wallace, "The doctor wanted to put him to sleep, but Hemingway wouldn't hear of it. 'All I want is some whisky,' he kept saying, 'Just give me some whisky.'"[151] So, like any good Prohibition-era sawbones worth his salt, Dr. Trueblood promptly prescribed a bottle of Old Oscar Pepper Bourbon Whiskey, which, shall we say, helped numb the pain, while Dr. Trueblood stitched up the gaping wound using (again, no joke) a long strand of horsehair. On the long drive back to the ranch, Hemingway and Wallace took a shot of bourbon each time their teenage driver stopped to open and close the livestock gates. Both of them slept most of the following day away, thanks to that Old Oscar Pepper Bourbon.

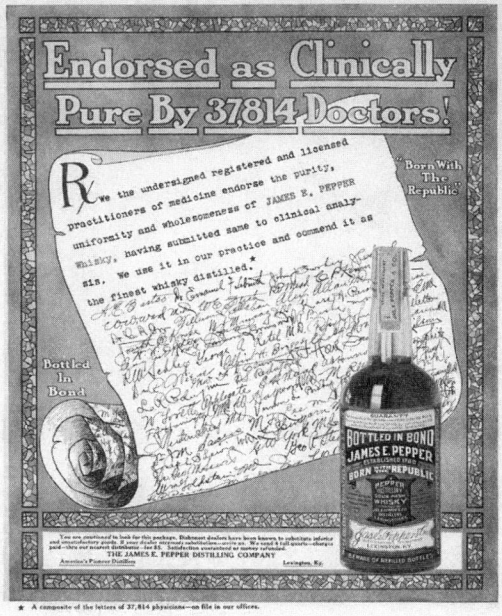

Just what the doctor ordered? Vintage Pepper Whisky ad. Courtesy Georgetown Trading Company, current distillers of James Pepper Bourbon Whiskey.

Later that day, Hemingway offered to buy old Goofy. When the ranch owner offered a more reliable horse, Hemingway muttered through his bandages, "I don't want to ride him, I want to shoot him for bear bait."[152] Fear not, dear reader, the transaction never went through. Hemingway's wounds eventually healed, and ol' Goofy would live to ride another day.

Mojito

2 oz. white rum
Juice of 1 lime
1 tsp. sugar (or ¾ oz. simple syrup)
1–2 oz. seltzer
5 mint leaves

Shake all ingredients (except for seltzer) well with ice, strain into an ice-filled collins glass, then pour seltzer into shaker to rinse ice (and chill seltzer) and strain into glass. Stir; garnish with mint sprig.

Recipe adapted from *Sloppy Joe's Bar Cocktails Manual*, 1939.

As they say, you can't prove a negative; how can you possibly prove that something *didn't* happen? You might ask, what on earth does this have to do with Hemingway? Well, it concerns the Mojito, and all the claims you'll see about it being Hemingway's *favorite* drink. Although I can't prove it, I simply don't believe that Hemingway was much of a Mojito drinker, notwithstanding numerous claims to the contrary. But I can't prove it.

Numerous claims? Well, there's a little joint in Havana called La Bodeguita del Medio. Behind the bar is a framed piece of butcher paper with writing on it, allegedly Hemingway's. It reads, "My Mojito in La Bodeguita My Daiquiri in El Floridita." That simple little inscription has not only launched a thousand claims

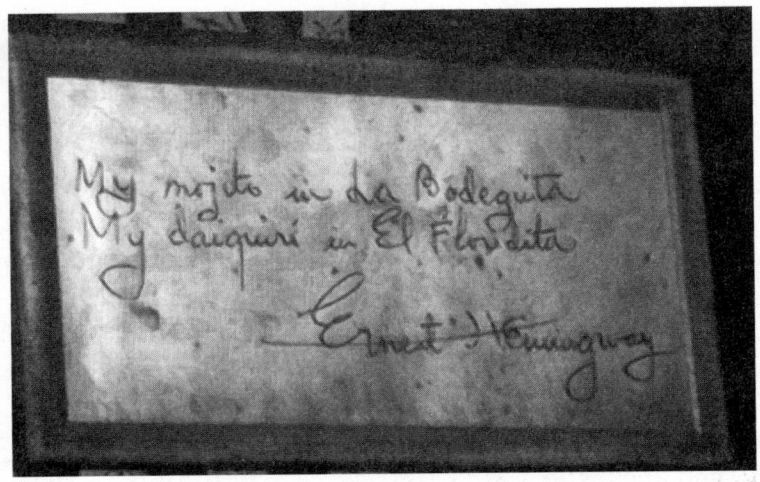

Courtesy Tony Abou-Ganim, www.modernmixology.com.

that "Hemingway's favorite drink was the Mojito," but it's also made La Bodeguita quite a lot of money from visiting tourists. If I had a dollar for every book or website that claimed the Mojito to be his *favorite* drink, or the drink "most associated with" him, well . . .

Why so skeptical in the first place? With nearly every other drink in this book, I can place the particular drink either into Hemingway's hands, from biographies, memoirs, or letters, or into his characters' hands, from his prose. Heck, if Hemingway hadn't been so fond of writing about what he drank, well, I wouldn't have written this book, now would I? If he drank it, he generally wrote about it *somewhere*. Not so with the Mojito. In fact, I've not yet encountered a single reference to either the drink or the Bodeguita, in all my twenty-some years of research. Let me qualify that: I did find one. Indeed, José Andres Garate, a close friend during the 1940s and '50s, said that he "drank with Papa at the Floridita many times and ate oysters with him at Ambos Mundos Hotel." When asked about the Mojito story, he replied, "I've never heard of La Bodequita [*sic*] del Medio."[153]

Further, there are countless photos of Hemingway at other Havana watering holes, such as the Floridita, Sloppy Joe's, the Club Puerto Antonio, and at other places worldwide, like Harry's Bar and the Stork Club. Any photos of Hem in the Bodeguita? Ixnay.

Hemingway simply didn't like sweet drinks, and the Mojito (which usually packs at least an ounce of simple syrup) is a sweet drink. In his later years, with concerns about diabetes, he typically avoided sugar. In *Islands in the Stream*, he drank his "double frozens without sugar. If you drank that many with sugar it would make you sick." In fact, you just don't see too many sweet drinks in his prose. True, the Jack Rose comes to mind, but that was from 1926's *The Sun Also Rises*. Hemingway was twenty-seven, not yet worried about sugar. By the mid-1930s, however, we're seeing his penchant for sugar-free drinks, such as his "E. Henmiway" Special (a Daiquiri with maraschino liqueur in place of the sugar) and Death in the Gulf Stream. ("No sugar. No fancying.") He once complained to A. E. Hotchner that one of the reasons he didn't like dining at other people's homes was that he couldn't trust the food and drink. On one occasion his host served sweet Champagne, which he *had* to drink to be polite, but it took a week to get it out of his system.[154]

I'm not alone in my skepticism. Hemingway scholar Matthew J. Bruccoli observed, "I do not have any evidence that Hemingway ever drank that particular cocktail," though "it is a safe generalization that Hemingway tried every cocktail ever mixed."[155] In *The Hemingway Cookbook*, Craig Boreth discusses it under the heading "The Myth of the Mojito." Further, I've asked noted Hemingway historian Brewster Chamberlin for his views on the actual framed document. The archivist for the Key West Art and Historical Society, he has developed an extensive Hemingway chronology, requiring many hours poring over his handwritten fishing logs. So he's quite familiar with Papa's handwriting. Says Brewster: "I have carefully examined the handwritten note attributed to Hemingway and I am convinced that he did not in fact write it. The handwriting is not his."[156] Indeed, several books have asserted that the whole thing was a publicity stunt, cleverly concocted by Cuban writer Fernando Campoamor, along with the bar's owner. According to Campoamor, they hired a calligrapher to forge Hemingway's handwriting, and "[t]he little joke grew into a big lie."[157] And a great many pesos, it seems.

Forgery? Publicity stunt? Did Hemingway actually sign it just to be nice, to do the owner a favor, or to settle a bar tab? Who knows? Who cares? I'd just like to see the whole "Hemingway's favorite drink" rubbish put to rest or, at least, the *favorite* part. Mind you, I have nothing against the Mojito, it's a perfectly lovely drink when made correctly, with fresh lime juice, not lemon-lime soda, and with just a trace of mint, not muddled clumps like Sargasso seaweed. I make one for my wife now and then with mint from our herb garden. I just don't think it was among Hemingway's favorite drinks, so I therefore offer it to you, dear reader, with a rather strong caveat. Here's looking up your address.

Mountain Stream Scotch

3 oz. blended Scotch
1–2 oz. water

Add ingredients to a heavy-bottomed Old Fashioned or rocks glass. Place in freezer at least an hour. Sip and enjoy.

After Ernest and Pauline split up in 1939, Ernest moved to Havana with Martha Gellhorn, while Pauline remained in Key West. After Pauline's death in 1951, it fell to Hemingway to manage the house. In 1955 he came to Key West to meet with a rental agent and took up temporary residence in the two-story pool house. Here, he unveiled a new drink to his friend A. E. Hotchner:

"Hotchner," he said with conspiratorial earnestness, "I have stumbled across a new invention which may make us dependently wealthy! Regard!" He took two glasses, put a couple of jiggers of Scotch in each, added water and placed the glasses in the freezing compartment of the refrigerator. "While we are waiting for the *denouement*, I will show you the joint."

Later, Hemingway deemed that enough time had passed to unveil his new "invention":

"Past meridian," he said. "We can break out the serious drinks." He took the two glasses of Scotch from the freezer and replaced them with two others. The water had frozen around the Scotch, and when you tilted the glass, the Scotch cut a rivulet through the ice to reach your mouth, ice-cold and giving the illusion that you were drinking out of a mountain stream that had suddenly turned to Scotch. I complimented Ernest on his invention.[158]

This is yet another instance of Hemingway's penchant for cold drinks really being *cold*. Witness his preparation of the Martini, with onions, glasses, and tennis-ball-can ice cubes, all frozen at fifteen degrees below zero (!). There's also a great scene in Chapter 12 of *The Sun Also Rises*, where Jake and Bill chill their bottles of wine in a cold spring, and when Bill drinks it, he exclaims, "Whew! That makes my eyes ache," and Jake notes, "The cold helps it." I have to say that while I'm not much of a Scotch drinker, I've tried this with rye whiskey, and it's delightful.

Negroni

1 oz. dry gin

1 oz. Campari

1 oz. Italian (sweet) vermouth

Orange wedge or twist as garnish

On the rocks: Add all ingredients except garnish to an Old Fashioned glass filled with ice. Stir.

Up: Stir all ingredients except garnish well in a mixing glass; strain into a chilled cocktail glass.

SUGGESTED READING: *Across the River and Into the Trees* (Chapter 6), "The Good Lion"

This classic drink is said to have been based on the Americano, so I refer you to that chapter as background. Apparently that drink wasn't strong enough for the likes of an Italian nobleman by the name of Count Camillo Negroni, so the story goes. He was a habitué of the Bar Casoni in Florence. He asked the bartender, Fosco Scarselli, to liven up his Americano with a measure of gin in place of the seltzer. And thus was born the Negroni.

The Negroni is mentioned briefly in the 1951 short story "The Good Lion." This lion was more sophisticated than the others, choosing to eat pasta and scampi rather than, say, Hindu traders or cattle. Further, instead of drinking blood, the good lion opted for a Negroni or an Americano, which he liked to drink at Harry's Bar in Venice. At one point in the story, as he's heading for Harry's, his father tells him, "Remember me to Cipriani and tell him I will be in some day soon to see about my bill." But by the time the good lion arrives at Harry's Bar, he's changed his tune, and he orders a Hindu trader sandwich and a "very dry martini, with Gordon's gin." Hemingway intended "The Good Lion" as a children's story. For what it's worth, it never occurred to me to read it to my kids, even when they were naughty.

In *Across the River and Into the Trees*, the Negroni makes an appearance, or is it the Americano? Indeed, Hemingway appears to

Hemingway in Cortina, Italy, circa 1949, perhaps fixing a Negroni. Courtesy Getty Images.

confuse the two drinks and also somewhat botches the recipe. But these are forgivable offenses both.

The Negroni, like the Americano, is an excellent introduction to aperitif bitters, in this case Campari, but also others such as Fernet-Branca, Averna, Aperol, Cynar, Luxardo Bitter, Gran Classico, Amer Picon, and other such products (yes, even Jägermeister). And, as the recipe notes, the Negroni can be enjoyed on the rocks or straight up. Many people prefer the former, as the drink will mellow somewhat as the ice melts. *Salute!*

The Trouble with Harry's

One of Hemingway's favorite watering holes was Harry's Bar in Venice, featured prominently in his 1950 novel *Across the River and Into the Trees*. Other celebrities loved Harry's, such as Truman Capote and Orson Welles. Hemingway and Welles began an odd sort of friendship in 1937, during the production of the documentary film *The Spanish Earth*. Hemingway had written the text, which Welles was hired to narrate, and Welles questioned him about the commentary. As Welles wrote, it didn't go well, with Hemingway challenging Welles about what he could possibly know about men at war. Welles responded by making effeminate gestures and saying "Mister Hemingway, how strong you are and how big you are!" and so forth. The two of them eventually ended up picking up chairs and scuffling right there on the stage. According to Welles: "It was something marvelous: two guys like us in front of these images representing people in the act of struggling and dying. . . ." However, they ended "by toasting each other over a bottle of whiskey."[159]

Thus began a long, odd, on-again, off-again friendship between Welles and Hemingway, punctuated by Welles's incessant teasing of Hemingway. Welles had his moments at Harry's Bar, as well. According to Arrigo Cipriani, he was so disorganized he'd often forget to pay his check and had to be caught at the train station. Further:

He was as big as an armoire, and he always had an appetite to match when he walked through the door of Harry's Bar. And an even bigger thirst. He immediately ate two plates of shrimp sandwiches and washed them down with two bottles of iced Dom Perignon. And then he would lean back in his chair and look around with a contented air. He was a lion with the whole world.[160]

Having read this, I cannot help but think that "The Good Lion" might have been based in part on Welles. Perhaps this caricature was Hemingway's very veiled way of returning the needling that Welles inflicted on him. After all, Hemingway likely saw Welles as being a bit, shall we say, *affected*, and both the lion and Welles exude this sort of haughty and urbane air. Then there's the matter of forgetting to pay the tab at Harry's Bar, and you also have both the lion and Welles as great consumers of shrimp. Further, Welles did love his Negronis, too, noting in 1947 that "The bitters are excellent for your liver, the gin is bad for you. They balance each other."[161] You can't argue with the man.

Truman Capote also adored Harry's. According to his friend Donald Windham, Capote "had dinner their [*sic*] nearly every night. 'For him Venice was Harry's Bar,'" and he refused to have a Martini anywhere else.[162]

Since both Hemingway and Capote loved Martinis, both loved Harry's, and both (as it happens) loved the Hotel Monteleone in New Orleans (Capote claimed to have been born there), you'd naturally assume they were fast friends. Well, perhaps not. "I hated him," Capote told an interviewer:

He was always writing little things about me, when I was very, very young. I was about eighteen or nineteen when I thought: "My God, here's this man fifty years old, this famous man. What the hell does he always want to be knocking me in the teeth about?" . . . *And then, when Nelson Algren's book* The Man with the Golden Arm *came out, Hemingway gave him a quote which the publisher used and the quote said: "All you Truman Capote fans get your hats and coats and leave the room. Here comes a real writer." Well, I thought that, really, I mean, it's really too much. When my* Breakfast at Tiffany's *came out he wrote me a little note telling me how good it was, or how much he liked it. And I thought: "There's more of your hypocrisy for you."*[163]

Oh well, so much for that theory. Anyway, here's hoping there's a Harry's Bar in your life.

Ojen Special

1½ oz. Ojen (if available, or use Anis del Mono)
2–3 dashes Peychaud's bitters
1 tsp. sugar, or a dash of simple syrup
2–3 oz. seltzer

Add all ingredients to a mixing glass filled with ice. Stir well; strain into chilled cocktail glass.

SUGGESTED READING: *To Have and Have Not* (Chapters 21 and 22)

Often referred to as "Spanish absinthe," Ojen is a slightly sweeter style of anisette, the wormwood-free, anise-flavored liqueur. It originated in the southern Spanish town of Ojen (pronounced *oh-hen*) in the nineteenth century and was made for many years by the Manuel Fernandez company of Jerez. Sadly, production ceased in the 1980s.

Your best shot at finding an old bottle might be in New Orleans, as a merchant there (Martin Wine Cellar) purchased several hundred cases and sold the last of it in 2009. The Crescent City has historically had a taste for anise-flavored drinks, including absinthe, Herbsaint, and Green Opal. In fact, the Ojen cocktail was one of the official drinks of Mardi Gras, particularly for the Krewe of Rex.

Nowadays, Orleanians with a taste for Ojen have embraced another of Hemingway's preferred anisettes, Anis del Mono. Indeed,

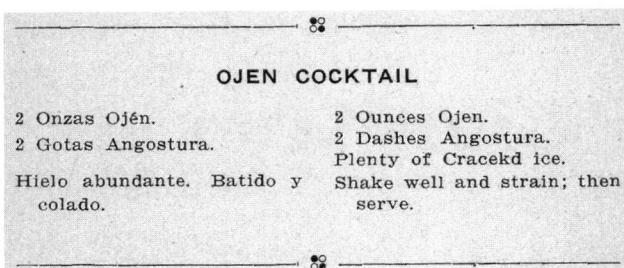

Even closer to Key West than New Orleans, we see the Ojen cocktail in Havana, on the Floridita's 1937 menu. From the author's collection.

in his 1937 book *Famous New Orleans Drinks and How to Mix 'Em*, Stanley Clisby Arthur refers to Anis del Mono as being among the "old and odd names for Ojen in New Orleans." It's not exactly the same, but it's a worthy substitute.

The 1937 novel *To Have and Have Not* centers around the denizens of 1930s Key West, both the working-class Conchs barely scraping by in what Hemingway called "the Saint Tropez of the Poor," and those more fortunate, at least, financially. Hemingway has his character Richard Gordon drinking an Ojen Special, which I'm guessing is an Ojen cocktail.

An essential ingredient in this drink is Peychaud's bitters, a New Orleans original and invented in the 1850s by pharmacist Antoine Amédée Peychaud, who happens to be a cousin of yours truly. Peychaud's pairs nicely with another classic cocktail with a slight licorice taste, that being the Sazerac cocktail. Peychaud's bitters are available online through the Sazerac Company.

The Ojen Special appears in Chapter 22 of *To Have and Have Not*. In the preceding chapter, we find author Richard Gordon having an argument with his wife, who is ready to leave him. She knows he's having a fling with Helene Bradley, who is known for collecting not only books but their authors. Meanwhile, Gordon's wife is contemplating an affair of her own with Professor Mac-Walsey, might even marry him, in fact. Gordon is crushed. Later that day, while he's making love to Helene Bradley, her husband walks in on them. No, it hasn't been the best of days, all in all.

In Chapter 22, Gordon is drowning his sorrows. He finds his way to a dive bar, the Lilac Time. The owner of the joint offers to fix Gordon a drink, and fix him "up hokay" in the process. He offers him an Ojen Special, made from "Spanish absinthe," which he claims will make him feel so good he'll want to fight anyone in the bar. But after three of them, Gordon doesn't feel any better: "the opaque, sweetish, cold, licorice-tasting drink did not make him feel any different." He asks for straight whiskey, but the bartender warns him to be careful what he drinks after the Ojen. Gordon downs a whiskey anyway. It doesn't provide the solace he's looking for.

> The whiskey warmed his tongue and the back of his throat, but it did not change his ideas any, and suddenly, looking at himself in the mirror behind the bar, he knew that drinking was never going to do any good to him now. Whatever he had now he had, and it was from now on, and if he drank himself unconscious when he woke up it would be there.

Note the bartender's advice to be careful what you drink after you've had an Ojen cocktail. Indeed, in Spain there is an old expression, *una copita de ojen*—perhaps it's best to have only one cup of Ojen.

The Two Sloppy Joe's

A fair amount of the action in *To Have and Have Not* takes place in bars. In addition to the character of Harry Morgan, the bartender Freddy and Freddy's Bar are also based on Hemingway's good friend Joe Russell and his bar, the infamous Sloppy Joe's. But remember, there were two bars called Sloppy Joe's in Hemingway's world, one in Havana and one in Key West. They weren't related, and only the Key West location remains.

Sloppy Joe's Havana

According to the bar's 1939 promotional booklet, José Abeal y Otero came to Cuba from Spain in 1904 and became a bartender. After stints in New Orleans and Miami, he returned to Havana in 1918 and soon opened a place at the corner of Zulueta and Animas Streets. Friends visiting from the States no-

Vintage Sloppy Joe's postcard, and cover of the 1939 Sloppy Joe's Bar guide. From the author's collection.

ticed "the poor appearance and filthy condition of the place" and christened it "Sloppy Joe's." That's the "official version," anyway.

When Prohibition began in 1920, Havana became a favorite destination for thirsty Americans. Sloppy Joe's became one of the "must-see" attractions, sort of what Pat O'Brien's is to New Orleans. Among the celebrities who visited were John Wayne, Clark Gable, Spencer Tracy, Frank Sinatra, and of course, Ernest Hemingway.

Sloppy Joe's became famous for a number of drinks, notably the Sloppy Joe's Cocktail and the Mojito. Sadly, it folded after Castro took power. There is talk of resurrecting it, but I'm not aware of that happening yet.

Sloppy Joe's Key West

The Key West Sloppy Joe's was owned by Hemingway's friend Joe Russell, whom Hemingway nicknamed "Josie Grunts." His wasn't the only speakeasy in town; the Garden of Roses and Sweeney's Bar were popular joints during Prohibition. Russell's first bar was on Front Street, and he soon took over an existing speakeasy called the Blind Pig, at 428 Greene Street. Beginning in 1928, Hemingway began coming to Key West to visit (he eventually moved there in 1931), and he relied on Russell as a charter boat skipper and a source of bootleg booze.

Legend tells us that it was Hemingway who suggested to Russell that he rename the Blind Pig "Sloppy Joe's," after the infamous saloon ninety miles south in Havana. As much as I enjoy debunking myths, I might have to concede on this one. The danged claim might just be true. But Russell must have been aware of the Cuban one; after all, he was one of the people who introduced Hemingway to marlin fishing off Havana.

Speaking of introductions, it was at the Greene Street location of Sloppy Joe's that Hemingway met his third wife, Martha Gellhorn. He was there, having a few drinks, when the visiting Martha and her mother strolled in. He was dressed like a bum, sporting an old T-shirt and "odiferous Basque shorts." Martha was quite fetching, and the sight of Hemingway with this lovely blonde struck Skinner, the bartender, as resembling "beauty and the beast." Nevertheless, Hemingway turned on the old charm, and the three of them spent the afternoon drinking frozen Daiquiris. Hemingway ended up missing a dinner party back at the house, much to the consternation of his wife Pauline. This was only the beginning of her travails, of course, as Martha would eventually come to replace poor Pauline.[164]

Russell soon expanded the Greene Street bar, adding a dance hall called the Silver Slipper (which Waldo Peirce memorialized in a classic 1936 painting of the same name, depicting Hemingway, where else, at the bar).[165] Joe ran Sloppy Joe's at that Greene Street location until 1937, when his landlord had the audacity to raise the rent 25 percent! That is, from three dollars a week to four dollars. Still, that was a lot of scratch in 1937. Joe found a new location at the corner of Greene and Duval. But the lease agreement said that anything he'd placed on the walls, such as Hemingway's fishing trophies, Waldo Peirce's paintings, or anything else, had to remain behind. So Joe figured out a plan: he let the lease expire, thinking that when it was midnight, he would no longer be bound by it. He recruited movers, promising them drinks at the new bar, to show up *after* midnight:

"Every drunk in town just happened by," Josie's son-in-law, Bill Cates, told Hemingway when he returned from Spain, *"and they carried the whole damn place down the street where they got set up for a night of free drinks."* *"Only in Key West,"* replied Ernest. *"Only in Key West."*[166]

The Greene Street location eventually became Captain Tony's, which it remains to this day. So if you're confused by Captain Tony's claims of being "the original Sloppy Joe's," in a way, at least in Key West, it is. It was here that Hemingway spent most of his Key West barroom time, and the Freddy's Bar scenes from *To Have and Have Not* happened here. By the time Sloppy Joe's moved to its present Duval Street location, Hemingway was occupied with the Spanish Civil War, and he moved to Cuba shortly thereafter. But because of his friendship with Joe Russell, when Hemingway was in Key West after 1937, it's likely that he was doing his drinking at the current location on Duval.

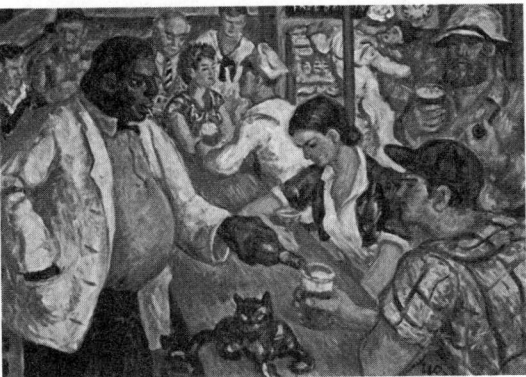

Waldo Peirce's 1936 watercolor, *Ernest Hemingway at Sloppy Joe's, Key West, Florida*. Peirce is shown on the right with pipe and a beer, while Skinner is serving Hemingway at the bar. Courtesy Karin Peirce.

Pauline Hemingway's Rum Scoundrel

1½ oz. white rum
½ oz. fresh lime juice
¾ tsp. brown sugar

Add ice to shaker, "hand shake 75 times."* Strain into chilled cocktail glass.

* According to the handwritten recipe from Betty Bruce's collection.

I f the world now knows Hadley Richardson as "the Paris Wife," we can safely call second wife, Pauline Pfeiffer, "the Key West Wife."[167] Her marriage to Hemingway (1927–40) spanned his tenure in what Hemingway affectionately referred to as "the Saint Tropez of the Poor."[168] Here, she raised their two sons, Patrick and Gregory.

This recipe was given to me by Benjamin "Dink" Bruce, son of Hemingway's right-hand man, T. Otto "Toby" Bruce, and a hell of a guy. More on the Bruces is found in the chapter titled Cayo Hueso La Floridita.

This delightfully simple little libation is Pauline's take on the Rum Scoundrel, which was a popular drink at the world-famous

Stork Club, on East Fifty-Third Street in Manhattan. Said to have been invented by bartender Julius Corsani, it's more or less a Daiquiri with a sugared rim, and Pauline's is more or less a Rum Scoundrel, but with *brown* sugar. The old adage about standing on the shoulders of giants will take you a long way in the land of cocktails.

The Stork Club, New York City

The Stork Club was a magnet for celebrities, and Hemingway was not immune to its pull. He often came to New York on business, or after completing a book, which left him emotionally and physically spent. "When I hit New York," he said to Earl Wilson, "it is like someone coming off a long cattle drive hitting Dodge City in the old days."[169] He'd go to the '21' Club, Toots Shor's, Costello's, or the Stork, where he became friends with its colorful owner, Sherman Billingsley.

An unabashed self-promoter, Billingsley loved his celebrity clientele, even if he wasn't entirely sure who they were. When Carl Sandburg visited, Billingsley asked, "What does he do?" When told he was an author, Billingsley said, "Tell him to stick in 'Stork Club' once in a while."[170]

Stork Club matchbook. From the author's collection.

Hemingway got the memo, seeing fit to mention the Stork now and again, including one notable passage in Luis Quintanilla's 1938 book *All the Brave*, on the hardships of war-torn Spain:

> *When you have sat at a table and been served a plate of water soup, a single fried egg and one orange after you*

*have been working fourteen hours, you have no desire to
be anywhere but where you were, nor to be doing anything
but your work, but you would think, "Boy, I'll bet you could
get quite a meal at The Stork tonight." Hunger is a marvelous sauce and danger of death is quite a strong wine. You
keep The Stork, though, as a symbol of how well you would
like to eat.*

The Stork also found its way into *Islands in the Stream*, during a conversation between Tom Hudson and his friend Roger
Davis, on the many ways Roger had broken up with girlfriends.
One such occasion at the '21' Club, it seems, had Roger politely
excusing himself from his date, paying a visit to the men's
room, and never coming back to the table, or the girl. He

Shown in picture, Hemingway, Sherman Billingsley, and novelist John
O'Hara, circa 1936. Courtesy Sherman Billingsley's Stork Club.

planned to "leave the other one at the Stork, which was the place she really loved, but he was afraid Mr. Billingsley might not like it and he needed to borrow some money from Mr. Billingsley."

Speaking of money, there was the night at the Stork in 1940 that Hemingway tried to cash a check he'd just received for the film rights to *For Whom the Bell Tolls*. It was for a mere hundred grand. Billingsley asked Hemingway if he could just wait until closing time, they should have the cash on hand. He did and they did.

To return the favor, Hemingway helped Billingsley with a legal matter. Constantly fighting Stork Club copycats, Billingsley learned that his nephew Glenn (an illegitimate child of his brother Logan) had had the audacity to open a new Stork Club in Key West. So Billingsley called Hemingway, asking if he could recommend good local counsel. "I'll be your lawyer," Hemingway replied. About an hour later, Hemingway reported back to his "client," "The Key West Stork Club has changed its name to Billingsley's Cooked Goose."[171]

As a final note, if the name Billingsley rings a bell, Glenn's wife was none other than Barbara Billingsley, the TV mom of Beaver Cleaver. Gee, Wally, Glenn sounds a bit more like Eddie Haskell to me.

Pernod Cocktail

2 oz. Pernod
½ oz. water
1 dash Angostura bitters
¼ tsp. sugar

Shake well with ice; strain into a chilled cocktail glass.

SUGGESTED READING: *The Sun Also Rises* (Chapters 3 and 8); see also Absinthe

Traditional Pernod is an anise-flavored liqueur, joining Anis del Mono and Ojen in the realm of Hemingway anisettes. To understand Pernod I suggest you start with absinthe since, for the bulk of the last century, Pernod was more or less wormwood-free absinthe. Now that true absinthe is again legal, Pernod Ricard makes its "traditional" Pernod as well as an "Absinthe Supérieure."

When Hemingway speaks of Pernod in his works, one is often not sure if it was the absinthe substitute or the real thing, or the real thing hidden in a "regular" Pernod bottle, as occurs in *The Garden of Eden* and "The Strange Country." Oh, what a tangled web we weave. . . . In *The Sun Also Rises*, though, it's not absinthe.

In Chapter 3, Jake Barnes is out for a night on the town in Paris. It's a warm evening, and he's sitting on the terrace of the Napolitain. He catches the eye of a passing *poule*, a polite term for a prostitute, and she sits down with him. She orders a Pernod, which

Jake teasingly refers to as "not good for little girls." She brushes off the comment and orders it anyway, and Jake joins her. Hemingway describes Pernod as "greenish imitation absinthe. When you add water, it turns milky. It tastes like licorice and it has a good uplift, but it drops you just as far." Jake and the girl drink their Pernod, and the girl, perhaps reminiscent of Edgar Degas' 1876 painting *L'Absinthe*, looks "sullen."

So he takes her to dinner. Before he knows it, he's been caught up in a group of friends who are going dancing, and his *poule*, Georgette, tags along. By this point, he's lost all interest in the girl and the evening and is pretty much going through the motions. Soon Brett shows up with an entourage of effeminate young men, and one of them decides to dance with Georgette. The men make him angry, and Jake has had enough. He ducks out to the bar next door for a beer, followed by a Cognac, neither of which he enjoys. It is not Jake's night, indeed. Perhaps the Pernod has dropped him just as far, but knowing what we know about Jake, you can't blame it all on the Pernod.

In Chapter 8, Jake and Bill are on an evening walk through Paris on their way to dinner. They've decided to eat on the Île St.-Louis, where they go to Madame LeComte's. In real life, it's known as Au Rendez-Vous de la Marine, and is still there, located at 33 Quai d'Anjou. But along the way they stop for a drink, likely a Pernod. Jake notes that Bill is "about a hundred and forty-four" drinks ahead of him.

In cocktails, Pernod is often used much like salt, in small amounts as a flavor enhancer. In fact, it was a favorite "secret ingredient" of Donn Beach, owner of the iconic Polynesian-styled restaurant chain Donn the Beachcomber, which, along with Trader Vic's, epitomized the tiki boom of the latter half of the twentieth century. According to tiki expert Jeff "Beachbum" Berry, "Donn would add a dash Angostura and a dash Pernod to almost all of his drinks that contained dark rum. The bitters/anise combo apparently amplified and dimensionalized the molassesy flavor."[172] In fact, many craft bartenders keep a dasher bottle handy for just this purpose. Well, dear reader, you're now equipped for an evening in Paris, and you're in on the secret to a great tiki drink. Enjoy.

Physician, Heal Thyself

1¾ oz. Scotch

1¾ oz. Sherry (such as Jerez or Manzanilla)

1¾ oz. Champagne

Serve on the rocks in a highball or collins glass.

Recipe adapted from the diagram.

B y the late 1950s, Hemingway's health was deteriorating. Multiple concussions, the lingering effects of two plane crashes, and nearly sixty years of a reckless lifestyle had taken their toll. Hemingway was under strict doctor's orders to cut back on his drinking, as well. Although it seems like a recipe for trouble by today's standards, he was allowed a liter of wine per day, and perhaps one cocktail. Often that one drink would be Scotch with half a lime squeezed in (see Scotch & Lime Juice), but maybe he'd enjoy this drink instead.

You see, while researching a file folder marked "Medical Records—1958" in the Hemingway Collection of the JFK Library in Boston, Marti Verso-Smallidge of the JFK staff discovered this diagram for me, bless her heart.

Perhaps it was misfiled, or Hemingway was telling his doctor about a new drink he'd concocted. All other details of this gem

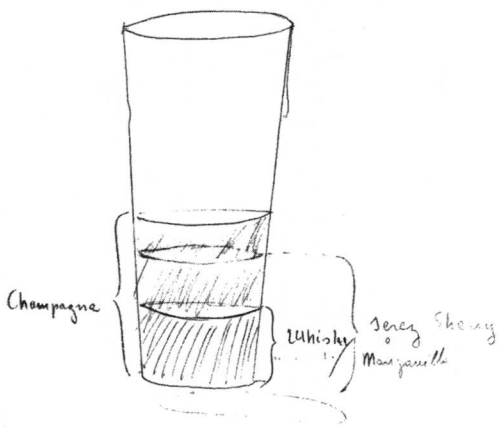

Drink diagram found in Hemingway's medical files. Ernest Hemingway Photograph Collection, John F. Kennedy Presidential Library and Museum, Boston.

remain a mystery, but I offer it to you, dear reader, with a name of my own creation, the Physician, Heal Thyself cocktail.

As is the case with much of Hemingway's writings, even scribbling such as this, you can't always tell what he means by "whiskey." But here, Hemingway specifically spells it "whisky," which suggests to me that he means "Scotch," since bourbon, rye, and Irish are usually spelled "whiskey." And while this wouldn't be the first thing I'd think to make for myself, I have to say it is a complex and interesting drink, and I did enjoy it. The whisky provides an authoritative backbone, complemented by the Sherry and enlivened by the effervescence of the Champagne. Sherry is a born flavor enhancer, especially in cuisine; witness its role in turtle or she-crab soup, both classics. This drink is also good with either a good small-batch bourbon or a spicy rye. A blended whiskey is fine, but a smoky, peaty single-malt Scotch really makes the drink sing.

Pink Gin (Gin & Bitters or Gin & Angostura)

1½–2 oz. London dry or Old Tom gin

4–5 dashes Angostura bitters

Up: "Rinse" (coat the insides of) a chilled cocktail glass with the bitters. Add gin and ice to a mixing glass, stir well, then strain into the bitters-rinsed glass.

On the rocks: Fill an Old Fashioned glass with several large ice cubes; add gin and bitters. Stir and serve.

SUGGESTED READING: "The Butterfly and the Tank," *The Fifth Column* (Act 2, scene 2), *Under Kilimanjaro* (Chapters 14, 15, 19, 32, 35, and 40)

This is one of the world's most basic drinks, having just two ingredients. Perhaps due to its simplicity and the availability of its parts, the drink is well traveled. Wherever the sun might set in the British Empire, from Gibraltar to Egypt to Hong Kong and New Zealand, you were bound to find its subjects raising a glass. In Java, they sometimes added a couple of dashes of absinthe, calling it the Gin Pahit (pronounced "pie-eat").

Hemingway covered the Spanish Civil War in 1937–38, and from that experience he wrote *For Whom the Bell Tolls*, the play *The*

Fifth Column, and the short stories "Night Before Battle," "Under the Ridge," "The Denunciation," and "The Butterfly and the Tank." In several of these works, the action takes place in Chicote's and the Hotel Florida, where Hemingway spent much of his time in real life, as well.

"The Butterfly and the Tank" is the story of a rainy afternoon spent at Chicote's. The protagonist stops by the bar for a quick drink after work. The war is taking its toll on the locals; everyone is on edge. Nevertheless, Chicote's is a lively joint that rainy afternoon, and the protagonist orders a "gin and Angostura and put it down against the rain."

He ends up stuck at a table with a man he knows, plus two other people he doesn't. He feels a bit out of place at the table and begins to wish he hadn't stopped in for a drink, since at home he could change into dry clothes, have a drink reclined on the bed, and not have to look at these characters.

Amid all the gaiety at Chicote's a man starts spraying people with a flit gun. A flit gun is what you'd use to spray bug killer in the days before aerosol. The flit gun man's act gets old pretty quickly, and before you know it the man gets tossed out, along with his flit gun. But he makes the fatal mistake of coming back in. After his next attack, someone shoots him dead, and the killer and his accomplices skedaddle. The police arrive, lock everyone in, and conduct a lengthy investigation that results in nothing.

The following day, the protagonist discusses the incident with Chicote's manager over a gin and Schweppes Indian tonic water with quinine. The manager encourages him to write the story, engaging in what Hemingway calls "Spanish metaphysics" while analyzing it all. The flit gun man was simply trying to be entertaining and break the wartime tension, he says. He'd bought the flit gun to use as a prank at a wedding, and filled it with eau de cologne, not pesticide. He got swept up in the boisterous atmosphere of Chicote's that afternoon and paid for his gaiety with his life. A tense, war-torn city was just not the place for his antics, it seems. The manager prosaically describes the clash as resembling a butterfly confronting a tank.

Like a good dry Martini, it is essential that this drink be served ice-cold, and I would recommend not making too big a drink; otherwise it will become warm too quickly. You might even insert a bit of "flair" into your bartending, spinning the glass while doing the Angostura rinse. Now that I think of it, a flit gun filled with Angostura would be just the thing.

Chicote's Bar

Chicote's Bar was one of Hemingway's all-time favorite watering holes. During the Spanish Civil War, it offered a respite from the incessant shelling during Franco's siege of Madrid. Hemingway devotes no fewer than the first six paragraphs of "The Denunciation" (see the Gin & Tonic) in extolling its virtues, praising the bartender (he compares him to George at the Paris Ritz), the clientele ("the good guys went to Chicote's"), the atmosphere ("It was the best bar in Spain," and among the world's best), and the drinks ("wonderful"). Among the reams of correspondence in the Hemingway Collection of the JFK Library in Boston is a note Hemingway sent to Chicote in 1933. Translated, it says, "To the great bartender Pedro Chicote, as a memory of a pair of banderillas in San Sebastian." This may refer to a bullfight they attended, or perhaps it's a veiled reference to two cocktails Chicote made for Hemingway at Chicote's San Sebastian location. Apparently, when the Spanish Civil War broke out in 1936 and Madrid came under heavy siege and bombardment from Franco's forces, Chicote remained at the San Sebastian branch, while his loyal staff remained to run the Madrid bar.

Now known as Museo Chicote, it's is still there, at No. 12 Calle Gran Via in Madrid. It retains the original décor from the old days, faithful to how it looked back when Hemingway was a patron. However, the sound of Franco's artillery has been replaced by the incessant thunder from DJs, as it becomes a dance club after dark. If you stop by, please have a Gin & Tonic or a Pink Gin for me.

Pisco Sour

2 oz. pisco

¾ oz. fresh lime juice

1 oz. egg white (use pasteurized egg whites if you're uneasy about raw eggs)

1 oz. simple syrup (to taste)

1–2 dashes Angostura bitters

Before adding bitters, shake all other ingredients with ice very well, to emulsify the egg white, then strain into a chilled cocktail glass. Express your inner artiste by dashing bitters atop the foam.

This is yet another variation on the classic sour cocktail; one could say it's a White Lady, with pisco in place of the gin. Pisco is an unaged grape brandy made in Chile and Peru. The Pisco Sour is the national cocktail of Peru, which also claims to be its birthplace. Be careful how you mention this little tidbit around, oh, I don't know, a *Chilean*, as the fine people of Chile are pretty proprietary over the drink themselves. There are two commonly accepted versions of its origin.

One story tells us that the Pisco Sour was invented around 1920 by the owner of the Morris Bar in Lima, a Yank by the name of Victor "Gringo" Morris. Raised a Mormon in Salt Lake City, Morris came to Lima in 1904 to work on the new railroad. He opened the Morris Bar in 1916, where he served his own local variation on the Whiskey Sour. Business was less than brisk, however.

Morris died in 1929; the bar, thereafter. Fortunately, several of Morris's barmen found work, at the elegant Hotel Maury, and from there the drink flourished throughout Lima. Peru celebrates a National Pisco Sour Day the first weekend of February each year.

The other version tells of an English steward, Elliot Stubb, who came to South America on board the good ship *Sunshine*. He disembarked in Iquique in 1872, which at the time was in Chile but is now in Peru. He opened a bar and invented a drink that would become the Pisco Sour, though some say he invented the Whiskey Sour.

In any event, Hemingway traveled to Peru in 1956 to film some scenes for the movie *The Old Man and the Sea*, which starred Spencer Tracy in the role of Santiago. Although the film was based and

Hemingway at the bar of the Cabo Blanco Fishing Club, April 1956. Courtesy José Schiaffino.

partially filmed in Cuba, it was believed that the odds of catching a giant marlin were better in the waters off Cabo Blanco, so off they went to Peru. Hemingway generally enjoyed traveling and fishing new waters, but he came to view the trip as an expensive waste. He stood to receive a share of the film's profits, so the more money being spent chasing fish, the less there'd be afterward. They spent a lot.

According to legend, Hemingway not only drank the Pisco Sour while he was in Cabo Blanco, he "set the record" for the number he knocked back. The Cabo Blanco Fishing Club's owner, Alfred C. Glassell Jr., noted, "He was a damned good fisherman. . . . Hemingway did a lot of drinking, he was a big drinker. That's one of the reasons we were glad to get him down to the club. His bar bill kept us operating for a year. As the owner of the club I *had* to say I was very happy about that."[173]

Just as the drink's origin is subject to debate, so is the question of whether Hemingway actually drank Pisco Sours while in Peru, as much of the "evidence" is anecdotal. Comes with the territory, I guess. To quote the great David Wondrich, "Mythology trumps mixology, just about every time." We do know that Hemingway was given a bottle of pisco by two journalists from Lima, Manuel Jesús Orbegozo and Jorge Donayre.

Inscribed on the bottle were the closing lines of the poem "Brindis," by the great Peruvian poet Domingo Martínez Luján. Luján and Hemingway both shared a love for the fruit of the vine. The poem ends with the haunting lines, *Mientras lloren las viñas, / yo beberé sus lágrimas*, which means "When the vineyards weep, / I will drink their tears." Touched by both their gesture and this profound poem, Hemingway was moved to reply, "I will drink these tears and then save the bottle as a remembrance."[174]

Notwithstanding my skepticism over other Hemingway legends, I tend to believe that he did partake of this drink while in

April 1956, Hemingway presented with a bottle of pisco by Peruvian journalists Manuel Jesús Orbegozo and Jorge Donayre. Courtesy José Schiaffino.

Peru. Although his description of pisco is a bit off, biographer Carlos Baker wrote that "Ernest sampled the good Peruvian wines and drank a drink called pisco, which was like tequila fortified with vodka."[175] I also note that a Baker more knowledgeable on the subject of drink, Charles Baker Jr., wrote of the charms of the Pisco Sour in his 1951 book *The South American Gentleman's Companion* and, as he was a pal of Hemingway, I might conjecture that Baker would have sent him a copy. Baker characteristically described "the finishing touch put-on by the talented bar-maestro at the wonderful and luxurious Lima Country Club, before they served them to your pastor and Limenian good friends on our suite balcony overlooking the polo fields and possibly the handomest swimming pool you'll find in the world." Vintage Charles Baker, indeed.

Further, during a 2001 interview, eighty-four-year-old fisherman Virgilio Querevalu noted that Hemingway "enjoyed Pisco and at the age of 57 he lived his life full of happiness. He liked 'cumbia' and 'chachacha' [*sic*] and most nights he will dance with Mary, his wife at that time, as well as with other young local ladies. Happily his last wife showed some tolerance of Hemingway's affairs."[176] Now that sounds to me like he had a few Pisco Sours, eh? I'll leave this question for you to ponder, dear reader.

Fortunately, we're in the midst of a pisco renaissance, with production techniques rising, along with its public image. To that extent, it is sharing the prosperity enjoyed by its fellow Latin American cousins cachaça, tequila, and mezcal, which have heretofore been saddled with a negative, "drink of the masses" reputation.

For more information, I highly recommend *El origen del Pisco Sour* and *Cabo Blanco Fishing Club*, both by José Schiaffino.[177]

Rum Collins

2 oz. rum

1 oz. fresh lemon or lime juice

1 tsp. sugar (though Hemingway likely went without)

4 oz. seltzer

Add all ingredients to a tall collins glass filled with ice. Stir well. Garnish with a lemon or lime wedge. Stir and serve.

For more about this style of drink, see the Tom Collins. This is an excellent refresher, perfect for hot summer days. You can use a lighter rum, a darker aged rum, or a combination of both. Add a splash of Angostura or Fee Brothers aromatic bitters for an extra bit of spice.

After several years of chartering fishing boats in Key West, such as Joe Russell's *Anita*, in the spring of 1934 Hemingway purchased a sleek thirty-eight-foot cruiser from the Wheeler Shipyard in Brooklyn and outfitted her for the Gulf Stream. He christened her *Pilar*, in part for the shrine and feria in Zaragoza, Spain, and partly to honor his wife Pauline; it was one of her pet names when they fell in love in Paris in 1926. She bore him two sons, Patrick and Gregory, but always wanted to give him "a little Pilar."

By the spring of 1935, Hemingway was ready to take *Pilar* over to the Bahamian isle of Bimini, nestled on the east side of the Gulf Stream just forty-five miles out from Miami. He'd heard that it was a fisherman's paradise, where the marlin and tuna were legendary. On April 7, he and a group of friends (including John Dos Passos and Mike Strater) left Key West for Bimini.

They decided to fish along the way, and in short order Strater had hooked into a dolphin fish, while Hemingway and Dos had sharks on their lines. Hemingway gaffed the shark with one hand, while trying to shoot it with his Colt pistol with the other. Suddenly, the thrashing shark caused the gaff to break. Part of it struck Hemingway's pistol hand, the gun went off, and a bullet fragment went through one of Hemingway's legs and into another (!). Humiliated, he turned back to Key West to seek medical treatment. The wounds were slight, and he carried the fragment in his leg the rest of his days.

The incident caused him to hate sharks all the more. Far too many prized fish were mauled by sharks before they could be boated. After they finally reached Bimini a few weeks later, Hemingway hooked into a trophy tuna, and an epic battle raged throughout the afternoon between Papa and the big fish. Soon a party of spectator boats circled *Pilar*, including the *Moana*, owned by multimillionaire William B. Leeds. It was now dark, and a storm was approaching. Finally, it looked as if Hemingway had won, and he was reeling in the great fish. But then the sharks came. As told by John Dos Passos:

> In the light of the searchlight, we could see the sharks streaking in across the dark water. Like torpedos. Like speedboats. One struck. Another. Another. The water was murky with blood. By the time we hauled in the tuna over the stern, there was nothing

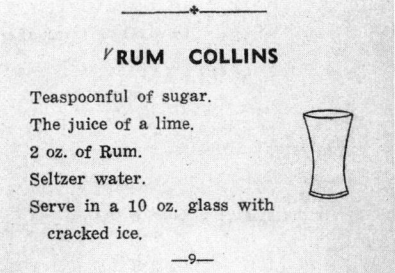

ᵛRUM COLLINS

Teaspoonful of sugar.
The juice of a lime.
2 oz. of Rum.
Seltzer water.
Serve in a 10 oz. glass with
cracked ice.

—9—

Rum Collins recipe, from Sloppy Joe's 1939 cocktail manual. From the author's collection.

left but his head and his backbone and his tail. For once, Hemingway didn't curse—not aloud anyway. He just muttered a few unheard remarks to himself, stowed his gear and joined his friends aboard Leeds' yacht for drinks, just as the threatened squall attacked.[178]

"Now, if I'd had that machine gun," Hemingway said to Leeds, "I could have taken care of those goddam sharks." See, the evening before, Hemingway had been over on Leeds's boat, having a few Rum Collinses, all the while coveting Leeds's Thompson submachine gun. He tried everything, offered to buy it for one thousand dollars, roll dice for it, target shoot for it, every kind of challenge, but Leeds said no. But somehow that night, after losing that huge tuna, he managed to wheedle it away from Leeds. Hemingway now had a new weapon in his arsenal to fight the hated sharks. Fast-forward twenty years and, as much as I think ol' Santiago would have appreciated having that kind of firepower to deal with sharks, I hardly think they'd award a Nobel Prize to *The Old Man and the Thompson Gun.*

So whether you're deep-sea fishing or just grilling tuna or black-tip shark in the backyard, the Rum Collins is a perfect summertime cooler. It's also a great way to enjoy the complex and varied flavors of rum in a relatively low-alcohol drink. Just be sure to use freshly squeezed lime juice, as always.

William B. Leeds and His *Moana*

Hemingway and son Jack (aka Bumby), circa 1935, possibly aboard *Moana*. Ernest Hemingway Photograph Collection, John F. Kennedy Presidential Library and Museum, Boston.

Tin plate tycoon William B. Leeds was certainly one of the "haves" among Hemingway's acquaintances. He was a regular on the Gulf Stream yachtie circuit, from Bimini to Miami to Havana to Key West. Hemingway didn't just drink Rum Collinses on Leeds's boat; in a 1939 letter written to his second son, Patrick, he tells of a recent evening spent on the *Moana*: "We stayed up late and I drank a few highly frozen Daiquiris just to see what their effect would be (it was moderately terrific and made me feel a friend of all mankind)."[179]

In addition to serving as the venue for a couple of Hemingway drinking stories, the *Moana* had quite a history of its own. It was built in 1931 at the Bath Iron Works in Maine and christened the *Caroline*. After Leeds bought it, he renamed her *Moana*. In the summer of 1937, Leeds considered outfitting her as a hospital ship to be stationed in the Galápagos Islands, where medical services were lacking. Although that plan never came to pass, in 1941 Leeds sold the *Moana* to the U.S. Navy, which refitted her to become a PT boat tender, the USS *Hilo*. She had an illustrious war record and earned four battle stars during campaigns across the South Pacific.

Bill Leeds's yacht the *Moana*. Just for kicks, compare this photo to the Gilbey's gin ad in the Maestro Collins chapter. Courtesy General Dynamics, Bath Iron Works.

Rum Swizzle

1½ oz. rum

¼ oz. fresh lemon juice

½ oz. fresh lime juice

1 tsp. sugar (or a syrup, such as orgeat or falernum, to taste)

Large dash Angostura bitters

2 oz. seltzer

Add ingredients to a collins glass filled with crushed ice. Use swizzle stick to agitate it, working it between two palms. Serve with straws.

Recipe adapted from *The Rum Connoisseur*, Ronrico Corporation, 1941.

SUGGESTED READING: *Islands in the Stream* ("Bimini," Chapter 11)

There are several variations on this classic rum drink, which, at its heart, is not unlike a taller cousin of your basic Daiquiri: rum, lime juice, and a sweetener. Sad to say, you don't see many swizzles on menus these days (though it is making a comeback), but it was very popular between the world wars.

Funny how an implement can outlive the thing for which it was invented; you've heard of a swizzle stick, right? Similar to the method of jiggling a spoon in a mint julep to chill it, so would you use a swizzle stick to, well, you know. But a true swizzle stick isn't just a stirring stick; it's made from the branch of a tree or bush, cut from the point where smaller branches extend out from the main. It's essentially a crude blender, and when held in one's palms and worked back and forth, it agitates, or *swizzles*, the drink.

And there are about as many varieties of Rum Swizzles as there are types of rum.

We find this classic drink in *Islands in the Stream*, the story of artist Thomas Hudson and his life in Bimini and Cuba. In the "Bimini" part, his three sons come to the island for a summertime visit, where they spend days swimming and fishing the Gulf Stream. In Chapter 11, they've cooked up a scheme where Hudson, his friend Roger Davis, and the three minor children will all pretend they're complete rummies, the whole lot of 'em. Apparently they'll perform their little one-act play on the unwitting passengers of a yacht that's just come into the harbor.

Even Mr. Bobby plays along; after all, his bar is the stage. Bobby has a gin bottle filled with water for Andy, and a rum bottle with tea for Davis and Hudson. When the scene begins, the yachties are there at the bar already, drinking Rum Swizzles. They're described as a nice-looking, polite group of people who make room at the bar for the Hudson party. Of course, they'll pay dearly for their kindness!

As part of his character, Mr. Bobby (who's drinking *real* rum, by the way) makes no bones about his disdain for Hudson and his adoration for little Andy. When Hudson asks for a shot of rum, Mr. Bobby will begrudgingly give it to him or he might insist on Hudson waiting twenty minutes before his next shot. But with David and Andy, who are probably fourteen and twelve, he's far more hospitable, filling their glasses whenever they ask.

Then Roger pipes up, directing Bobby, "Give the little rat a drink," referring to Andy. Andy in turn orders gin, to the shock and discomfort of the nice people from the yacht. Their discomfort at what they're witnessing is so strong it's palpable; Hudson can *feel* it.

Young Andy raises his glass to Bobby, noting it's his first drink all day. When Bobby asks where he's been all this time, young David explains that he couldn't come to the bar earlier, since their father, Hudson, had Andy's birthday money his mother had sent. Young Tom then delivers the coup de grâce: he starts to cry. And so it goes, with Hudson appearing to be a complete sot, not to mention a monster of a neglectful parent. When Hudson asks for rum, he gets a sneer, but when precious little Andy asks for gin, it's always, "Certainly, my little man. Do you know what they ought to do? They ought to put your healthy charming face on the label of those gin bottles instead of that idiotic collection of berries." And on it goes.

The nice people from the yacht buy it all, hook, line, and sinker. Finally one of the men catches on, guessing that it's a joke, but one girl isn't so sure, and she runs out, crying. At that point, the jig is up; they all feel bad and know it's time to end it. Apologies are issued, and there are no hard feelings; in fact, one of the girls in the group becomes friends with Davis and the boys.

The rummy scene in Mr. Bobby's bar is fairly hilarious, and I highly recommend you read it in its entirety. And I also urge you to find a true swizzle stick and have yourself a nice Rum Swizzle while doing so.

Sangria

1 liter of dry red wine

Juice of 2 lemons

Juice of 1½ oranges

¼-inch-thick slices of remaining half of orange

Combine all ingredients in a large pitcher, add several large ice cubes, stir, and serve. Serve on the rocks in wine or highball glasses. Garnish with additional fruit as desired.

SUGGESTED READING: *The Dangerous Summer* (Chapter 7), *A Moveable Feast* ("A False Spring")

n 1959, *Life* magazine asked Hemingway to cover Spain's summer bullfighting season, in particular, the much-hyped mano a mano matchup of Luis Miguel Dominguín and his brother-in-law Antonio Ordóñez, the two stars of the corrida.

For Hemingway, it would allow him the opportunity to not only return to "the country he loved more than any other except his own," but also reconfirm his stature as a great writer and an expert on bullfighting.[180] It would also be the last time his work would be published during his lifetime; *Life* magazine published it in September 1960, and it was posthumously published as *The Dangerous Summer*. As described by James Michener, "This is a book about death written by a lusty sixty-year-old man who had reason to fear

Luncheon at La Consula, Málaga, Spain, 1959. Bill Davis, Rupert Bellville, Ernest Hemingway, Mary Hemingway, and Juan Quintana. Ernest Hemingway Photograph Collection, John F. Kennedy Presidential Library and Museum, Boston.

that his own death was imminent."[181] In many respects, that summer was Hemingway's "last hurrah"; he died in July 1961.

Chapter 7 finds us in Alicante, near Valencia. The bullfighting that day was superb, and Hemingway and his entourage are ready for a lavish feast. They dine at Pepica's, having "sangria, red wine with fresh orange and lemon juice in it, served in big pitchers" as well as sausages, seafood, steaks, chicken, and more. Hemingway describes the meal as being "a very moderate meal by Valencian standards and the woman who owned the place was worried that we would go away hungry."[182]

Hemingway loved to drink wine with his meals, and from his years living in France he developed quite a palate. In his 1932 bullfighting treatise *Death in the Afternoon*, he describes wine as being "one of the most civilized things in the world and one of the most natural things of the world that has been brought to the greatest perfection," noting further that wine "offers a greater range for enjoyment and appreciation than possibly any other purely sensory thing which may be purchased." Sangria is a classic Spanish drink, basically a punch made of wine and fruit juice (usually citrus) at its simplest, or with the addition of other ingredients, such as Cognac, liqueurs, or the like. Like the paella it so deliciously accompanies, you needn't stick to a recipe; you use what you have on hand, a little of this, a little of that.

You might also try a fruit-and-wine drink Hemingway mentions in *A Moveable Feast*, when he and Hadley reminisce about "having fruit cup at Biffi's in the Galleria with Capri and fresh peaches and wild strawberries in a tall glass pitcher with ice." And don't feel compelled to use a vintage or expensive bottle; just a good, dry wine will do nicely. As Mary Hemingway once said, "We drink wine, not labels." By the way, if you're ever in Valencia, Pepica's is still there, located on the Paseo Neptuno, No. 6.

Scotch & Lime Juice

2–3 oz. Scotch
½ lime

Squeeze juice from a half lime into a rocks or Old Fashioned glass, drop in lime shell, add ice and Scotch, stir, and serve.

S un Valley, Idaho, is a resort community built by Averell Harriman and the Union Pacific Railroad as a way of introducing Americans to winter sports. Hemingway had been coming to Sun Valley since 1939. He loved it for its wild country, the hunting and fishing, and the people. In 1959 Ernest and Mary decided to drive out to nearby Ketchum to spend the fall months. Their friends Lloyd and Tillie Arnold found them a nice house to rent, and they made a road trip of it. They invited Key West friends Betty and Otto Bruce to join them on the long drive.

Ernest was enthralled by the appearance of the countryside. All across Iowa, Nebraska, and Wyoming, he counted and identified every bird he saw and kept a running record of the wild animals. He insisted on stopping at grocery stores in the smaller towns to buy apples, cheese, and pickles, which he washed down with Scotch and fresh lime juice.[183]

Shown above, Betty and Toby Bruce with Mary, during an epic 1958 cross-country road trip. Courtesy Bruce Family Archive.

As noted in the Physician, Heal Thyself chapter, by his late fifties, Hemingway was under doctor's orders to cut way back on his drinking. To paraphrase the beer jingle from the decade that followed, Scotch & Lime Juice became the one drink to have when having only one. Or perhaps two.

Pairing lime juice with an ounce or two of spirit, such as rum, is an age-old custom in the French Caribbean, although Papa might not approve of the added dash of simple syrup needed to make the classic Ti' Punch. It's a nice way of enjoying the flavors of a spirit, accentuated by the tartness of the lime and softened by the dilution of the ice.

Hemingway, circa 1947, at the bar of the Floridita. This is roughly where the statue of Hemingway now sits, on the left side of the bar. Ernest Hemingway Photograph Collection, John F. Kennedy Presidential Library and Museum, Boston.

Scotch with Lemon & Wild Strawberries

2 oz. blended Scotch

½ oz. fresh lemon juice

2 or 3 wild strawberries

Large chunk of ice

Squeeze a half lemon into a rocks glass, then drop in the lemon hull, too, and muddle it to extract essential oils. Also muddle several wild strawberries. Add a large chunk of ice, then the Scotch, and stir well.

SUGGESTED READING: "The Strange Country"

This is another Hemingway original. You'll find it in the posthumously published (and unfinished) short story "The Strange Country," which concerns two young lovers, Roger and Helen. It's actually a discarded fragment from an early draft of *Islands in the Stream*, but with Roger and Thomas Hudson swapping names. They're making their way from Miami to New Orleans by car. Along the way they stop over at diners, tourist cabins, and roadside motels, somewhat evocative of Nabokov's *Lolita*, but for the minor detail that Helen isn't Roger's preteen stepdaughter.

For Christmas and the New Year...

Time has branded

8 YEARS OLD

White Horse best

WHITE HORSE
CELLAR
De Luxe SCOTCH

PREMIUM QUALITY WITHOUT PREMIUM PRICE
BLENDED SCOTCH WHISKY • 86.8 PROOF • BROWNE VINTNERS CO., INC., NEW YORK

1941 White Horse Scotch ad. Courtesy Diageo.

It does have some degree of scandal to it, though: not only are they *not* married but Roger drinks while driving, for Pete's sake.

Along the way they drink Regal beer, another beer that reminds them of Regal (but the labels fell off, darn it), Greek retsina wine, and absinthe when they hit New Orleans. But their go-to road drink is a simple White Horse Scotch and soda, which they drink from enameled cups (Helena says they make the drinks taste "sort of slimy and slippery") while driving through the swamps and prairies of Florida and the Gulf Coast. Life was so much simpler then, eh? But while drinking one, Roger regales her with his recipe for Scotch with Lemon & Wild Strawberries, which he insists should be made using a tin cup: "But you ought to have ice cold spring water and the cup chilled in the spring. . . . If you have a lemon you cut half of it and squeeze it into the cup and leave the rind in the cup. Then you crush the wild strawberries into the cup and wash the sawdust off a piece of ice from the icehouse and put it in and then fill the cup with Scotch and then stir it till it's all mixed and cold."

Of course I can't condone Roger's behavior: he is very irresponsible to drink while driving. But he does recommend a nice drink here. The acidity and tartness of the lemon and the natural sweetness of the strawberry offer a nice complement to the smoky flavors of the Scotch. Whether or not it tastes better with ice from the icehouse, or in a tin or enameled cup, is likely a matter of personal taste, but I would recommend washing the sawdust off the ice first.

Tom Collins

TRADITIONAL
2 oz. London dry gin
¾ oz. fresh lemon juice
1 oz. simple syrup
2–4 oz. soda water

TOM COLLINS À LA HEMINGWAY
2 oz. London dry gin
¾ oz. fresh lime juice
2–4 oz. coconut water
2–3 dashes Angostura bitters

Vigorously shake all ingredients, then strain into an ice-filled collins glass. Garnish with a lime wedge or peel.

SUGGESTED READING: *The Garden of Eden* (Chapters 15 and 20), *Islands in the Stream* ("Bimini," Chapter 4, and "Cuba," Chapter 20)

The traditional Tom Collins is a classic drink. It's been around for well over one hundred years, though its origin is unclear. What is known for certain is that the "Great Tom Collins Hoax" swept the nation in 1874. It was essentially a practical joke, with one person telling someone else, "Have you seen Tom Collins? He's been saying nasty things about you, he's around the corner, go get him!" or the like. The unwitting victim would end up on a wild-

Photojournalist Robert Capa (right) and Hemingway at the bar at Trail Creek Cabin, Ketchum, Idaho, November 1940. Hemingway objected to Capa repeatedly photographing him while drinking during a *Life* magazine story assignment, as well as in other past instances. After this altercation, Capa relented and gave Hemingway the entire roll of film to be destroyed. Photo by Lloyd Arnold/Hulton Archive/Getty Images.

goose chase. It became a popular prank, with poor souls searching in vain for the elusive, nonexistent Tom Collins.

The drink itself first appeared in the 1876 edition of *The Bartender's Guide* by Jerry Thomas. Though the Tom Collins was originally made with Old Tom gin (a sweeter style), I suspect Hemingway would have made his with Gordon's gin, not to mention no sugar.

As two recipes are noted above, we'll begin with the traditional Tom Collins, which makes a couple of appearances in *The Garden of Eden*. The novel features David and Catherine Bourne. David is a writer, and he and his new bride are on an extended honeymoon on the Riviera. They come to meet and befriend a beautiful girl named Marita, who becomes a little bit more of a friend to them both, and a love triangle ensues. Complicating matters is the fact that Catherine is having a bit of a nervous breakdown. In Chapter 15, Catherine and Marita have gone out for the day while David works on his novel, and he ends his workday with a Tom Collins. He sits there at the bar, sipping his drink while looking into the bar mirror, questioning his behavior. He observes to his reflection, "I do not know if I'd have a drink with you or not if I'd met you four months ago."

In Chapter 20, David again spends the morning working, while Catherine and Marita go into Cannes for the day. David fixes himself a Scotch & Perrier, and has lunch while chatting with the hotel keeper. When the girls return, he fixes Catherine a Tom Collins while she's in the shower, offering it to her as she's toweling off, holding the cold glass "against the smooth dark skin of her belly."

The Tom Collins also makes an appearance in *Islands in the Stream*. The "Bimini" part concerns the artist Thomas Hudson, his friend Roger Davis, and Hudson's three sons. On the evening of the Queen's Birthday holiday (see the Gin & Tonic), they're hanging out on their friend Johnny Goodner's boat. Goodner enjoys a Tom Collins while eating stuffed Mexican peppers. With a drink in one hand and a chile pepper in the other, he says, "It's wonderful. . . . I bite just a little piece and it sets my mouth on fire and I cool it with this."

Apparently Goodner has these peppers specially made for him, stuffed with all kinds of things, from salmon to turtledove to bonito to bacalao. But his favorite of all is the one he holds in his hand, with the brown chupango sauce. "They give me a reason for drinking. . . . Have to cool my damned mouth."

The Tom Collins makes at least a nominal appearance later in *Islands*. In the "Cuba" part, Hudson is at home, and a gale is blowing outside. He's alone with his cats, in mourning, and drinking a

Scotch and soda. He decides to go into town, to the Floridita. But before he leaves, he asks his houseboy Mario to make him a modified Tom Collins. He savors the drink, noting that the coconut water is "still so much more full bodied than any charged water" could be, and how the Gordon's gin "[makes] it alive to his tongue and rewarding to swallow." Indeed, the drink "tastes as good as a drawing sail feels. . . . It is a hell of a good drink."

Note that this is not a traditional Tom Collins. Indeed, he's substituted lime for lemon, used coconut water for sparkling water, and added Angostura bitters. I'm guessing he left out the sugar, as well. In truth, this latter drink sounds more like the Green Isaac's Special, the drink Eddy makes in the "Bimini" part of the book (and later calls a Tomini). No matter, they're both delicious drinks, and I recommend them both highly.

Vermouth Panaché

2 oz. French (dry) vermouth

1 oz. Italian (sweet) vermouth

1 dash Angostura bitters

Lemon peel

Fill a collins glass with ice, add ingredients, stir, and serve.

SUGGESTED READING: *By-Line: Ernest Hemingway, To Have and Have Not* (Chapter 15), *A Farewell to Arms* (Chapter 8)

In April 1936, Hemingway wrote a feature article for *Esquire* titled "There She Breaches! or, Moby Dick Off the Morro."[184] The story centers around a 1934 fishing trip on board *Pilar* off the Havana coast. The sea was glass calm, and a spaghetti dinner was a half hour away from being served. It was time for a cocktail, so skipper Hemingway told his crew it was time for a drink. To a tall glass filled with ice, they added "French and Italian vermouth (two parts of French to one of Italian, with a dash of bitters and a lemon peel)." All of a sudden, this peaceful scene was broken by what one crew member thought was a cannonball hitting the water. "*Que canonazo!*" he shouted, saying it looked "like the spout from a twelve inch shell." In fact, it was a sperm whale that had just breached the surface. Instantly, chaos erupted as the crew scram-

Vintage Martini vermouth ad.
Courtesy Martini.

bled to react. Some wanted to chase it and shoot at it; Hemingway even entertained the idea of harpooning it. The whale eventually slipped away, leaving the crew to return to their no doubt diluted drinks.

We also find a simpler version of this drink being served to Helene Bradley in Chapter 15 of *To Have and Have Not* (though it's just the 2-to-1 French to Italian vermouth, with no mention of bitters or garnish).

After reading that *Esquire* piece, I wasn't sure what to call this drink. Initially I was set on calling it the Canonazo, but then I spent some time reviewing Hemingway's fishing logs from both the *Anita* (Joe Russell's boat) and the *Pilar*. The logs offer a wealth of information, not to mention just plain good reading. He'd write

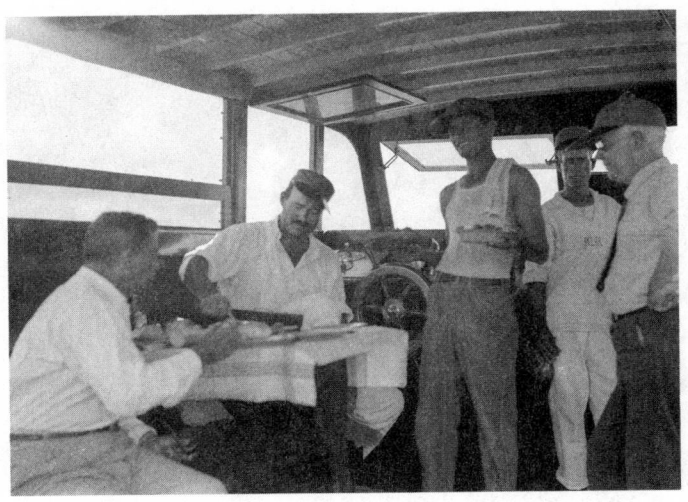

Chow time on *Pilar*, circa 1935. That's Carlos Gutierrez in the *Pilar* jersey, second from the right. Ernest Hemingway Photograph Collection, John F. Kennedy Presidential Library and Museum, Boston.

about not only epic battles with marlin, but also what they ate and drank on board.

I found an entry in the *Anita* log from 1933 where Hemingway refers to drinking something called a Vermouth Panaché. So I'm making an executive decision here and deeming it to be the same drink. Call it what you will.

Does the drink otherwise have a name? Well, sorta. It's very similar to a Prohibition-era cocktail called the Diplomate, which was published in the classic 1930 book *Cocktails*, written by someone known only as "'Jimmy' Late of Ciro's." The only difference is the substitution of Angostura bitters, in Hemingway's drink, for maraschino liqueur. Then there's a drink called the Duplex, if made without the inclusion of gin (as some recipes show it). And lastly, I'm reminded of the Old Hickory, said to have been enjoyed by Andrew Jackson during the Battle of New Orleans (1814–15). It's found in Stanley Clisby Arthur's 1937 classic, *Famous New Orleans Drinks & How to Mix 'Em*. The drink is an even blend of sweet and dry vermouth, with 1 dash orange bitters and 2 dashes Peychaud's bitters. While I doubt Jackson ever drank this (kinda early for vermouth to be available in New Orleans), it's delicious, nevertheless.

But who said it had to have a name? Hemingway often drank vermouth while at sea to deter seasickness (so he said). Having said that, he also called tequila his "steering liquor," hmmm. So, if you're going whale watching anytime soon, "bring out the bottles" and fix yourself . . . well, whatever it is you decide to call it.

Vermouth & Seltz

2 oz. vermouth (style depending on your taste)

3–4 oz. seltzer

Add ingredients to an ice-filled collins glass, stir, and garnish with orange wedge or peel.

SUGGESTED READING: "My Old Man," *The Garden of Eden* (Chapter 2)

This is a very simple, refreshing drink, and so easy to make. As I've noted, to think that Hemingway didn't care for vermouth, simply because he liked his Martini *very* dry, does an injustice to vermouth. He enjoyed it straight, in vermouth-only cocktails like the Vermouth Panache and in drinks like the Americano, Negroni, and Gambler's Delight. He even dreamed about vermouth while writing his play *The Fifth Column*, as he explains in a 1939 letter to his in-laws: "This morning I woke up dreaming that they had obtained new backing from a Vermouth Company and that the play was now to be called Cinzano Express. The first four scenes were to be the same but we should re-write the next to get the proper vermouth angle in."[185]

The Vermouth & Seltz makes an appearance in one of his earliest stories, "My Old Man" (1923). It's the tale of a father and son; the father is a jockey in Italy and later Paris, the son his naive sidekick. It is said to have been based on Tod Sloan, who may have been the world's first sports celebrity. In the late 1890s, Sloan revolutionized horse racing in England, winning a huge number of races.

As they say, familiarity breeds contempt, and the blue bloods that ran English horse racing became quite jealous of Sloan. They conspired to blackball him. He lost his license over a trumped-up charge of betting on himself, something other jockeys did, but on him it was the equivalent of a hanging offense.

Tod Sloan knocked around a bit, still retaining his international cachet. He tried his hand on Broadway, then in the movies, then he opened a bar in Paris (which became the legendary Harry's New York Bar, of all things). His celebrity fading, he ended up a ticket taker at the track in Tijuana and finally died of cirrhosis in 1933. We're ready for your close-up, Mr. Sloan, indeed.

In "My Old Man," Tod Sloan is reflected in both the father and the son—the father being the world-wise, possibly corrupt jockey, the son being the motherless lad that was Tod in his early years. We find the Vermouth & Seltz within the story, as the son tells of his father's habits and rituals as a jockey. Weight and con-

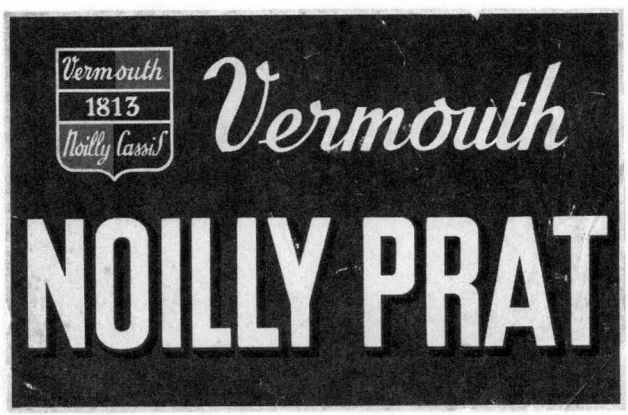

Vintage label. Courtesy Noilly Prat.

ditioning were always critical, so even when the jockeys went drinking, they had to keep it on the lighter side: "If a jock's riding for somebody too, he can't go boozing around because the trainer always has an eye on him if he's a kid and if he ain't a kid he's always got an eye on himself. So mostly if a jock ain't working he sits around the Café de Paris with the gang and they can all sit around about two or three hours in front of some drink like a vermouth and seltz and they talk and tell stories and shoot pool and it's sort of like a club or the Galleria in Milan."

In addition to being a light, lower-alcohol drink, the Vermouth & Seltz offers an excellent basis for discovering the many flavors of vermouth, from the drier French styles to the *bianco* to the sweeter Italians and to the more rosé-tinted offerings, such as Martini's spicy Rosato.

Villa America Special

1½ oz. Cognac or brandy
1 oz. Cointreau (or another liqueur of your choosing)
¾ oz. fresh lemon juice

Chill a cocktail glass. Rub rim of glass with lemon, then dip it in coarse sugar. Shake ingredients well with ice, then strain into chilled glass.

This is another of the cocktails of Hemingway's friend Gerald Murphy, one of the many American expatriates who came to France in the 1920s (see the Bailey). Gerald and his wife, Sara, befriended some of the greatest artists and writers of the Lost Generation. It's named for the Murphys' home on the French Riviera.

During a 1926 visit to Villa America, Hemingway's son Bumby had whooping cough and had to be quarantined. The Hemingways moved into a nearby villa rented by F. Scott Fitzgerald (he and Zelda had found a nicer one, it seems). Not letting quarantine stand in the way of a good time, the Hemingways and Murphys devised a way to have happy hour under otherwise unhappy conditions. As told by Hadley:

> And all of them would come over yardarm time and sit in their
> cars outside an iron grille fence and we would be up on this little,

tiny porch, and we'd all have drinks together, at a respectable distance, of course. And each empty bottle was put on a spike on the fence, and we really decorated the place in the course of a couple of weeks.[186]

The Murphys influenced Hemingway's life and his prose. While Fitzgerald admitted to Sara Murphy, "I used you again and again" in his novel *Tender Is the Night*, there are aspects of Sara and Gerald in "The Snows of Kilimanjaro" and *The Garden of Eden* as well.[187]

In the latter novel, the characters emulate Gerald's fondness for the classic blue-striped fisherman's shirt (which Hemingway also favored). Much of the novel takes place in and around Cannes, including one scene where the main characters are swimming near Eden Roc, a favorite spot of the Murphys. Hemingway also adopted, for better or worse, one of Gerald's mannerisms. It was during their 1926 trip to Pamplona that Hemingway picked up Gerald's habit of addressing young women by the term "daughter," and it

Vintage Cointreau ad, circa 1925. Courtesy Rémy Cointreau USA.

may have been Gerald who first called Hemingway "Papa" on that same trip.

The Murphys were quite fond of entertaining, be it a daytime gathering on the beach or an evening affair under the stars. As their daughter Honoria noted, "My father was, as in everything, very precise as he prepared his Villa America special, consisting of brandy, a liqueur, and lemon juice, which he poured from a silver shaker into long-stemmed glasses, the rims of which had been rubbed with lemon and dipped in coarse sugar."[188] Perhaps Gerald was serving this drink to the Hemingways and Fitzgeralds at "yardarm time."

Reading Honoria's description, I suspect that Gerald was mixing a recently invented drink, the immortal Sidecar, assuming the liqueur to be Cointreau. If not, however, then Gerald had apparently discovered that great bartending secret, that is, that the classic sour cocktail is a tremendous vehicle for swapping out components to create a nearly infinite range of drinks (see also the White Lady and Jack Rose).

The Sidecar debuted in 1922, in both Harry MacElhone's *Harry's ABC of Mixing Cocktails* and Robert Vermeire's *Cocktails: How to Mix Them*. Like many classic cocktails, its origins are unclear. The standard story concerns a bartender in Paris who made the drink by mistake, distracted by damage done to his motorcycle sidecar. MacElhone claimed he invented it at Harry's Bar in Paris, though some say Pat MacGarry created it at Buck's Club in London.

Many cocktail historians (Ted Haigh and Gary Regan among them) point to a drink from antebellum New Orleans as the Sidecar's likely progenitor. The Brandy Crusta, created by the celebrated New Orleans bartender Joseph Santini, also featured brandy, lemon, orange liqueur, and a sugared rim (yes, this practice goes back over 150 years). Santini was a bit of a bon vivant, so much so that upon his death, his coffin was too large for a hearse!

The Ritz Bar in Paris also claims to have been the home of the world's first Sidecar; it's certainly home to the world's *most expensive* one. The drink is served, of all places, at the Bar Hemingway, and it contains Cognac Ritz Paris 1865. It will set you back a mere $515. But you can make a perfectly good Sidecar, er, I mean Villa America Special, with any good VSOP Cognac.

Whiskey & Ginger Ale

2 oz. whiskey

4 oz. ginger ale

Fill a highball glass with ice, add ingredients, stir, and serve. Optionally garnish with a wedge (or peel) of lime.

SUGGESTED READING: *Islands in the Stream* ("Cuba"), "The Last Good Country"

This is one of the many Hemingway highballs. As is the case with the Whiskey & Soda, you're free to use whatever whiskey you prefer. The bite of the ginger is a nice complement to the spiciness of a good rye whiskey or the smokiness of Scotch. A lime wedge is especially good in this drink, as ginger and lime were made for each other.

The drink makes an appearance in the Nick Adams short story "The Last Good Country," a tale of a teenage boy who's being pursued by the law for deer hunting out of season. He and his kid sister, Littless, become fugitives and light out for the wilds of northern Michigan. Nick knows the woods like the back of his hand and is confident that he can elude the two pursuing game wardens. Before they leave, however, Nick and Littless come back

1937 Canada Dry ad. From the author's collection.

to their house, where the two wardens have set up a stakeout, waiting for Nick to return. Nick and Littless wait until dark; he wants to go and watch them drink in their house. The men are drinking Green River whiskey mixed with ginger ale, but soon run out of ginger ale and decide to turn in.

Before too long, of course, the local warden has fallen asleep at his post. Littless sneaks into the kitchen and steals everything they'll need for their getaway camping trip, leaving nothing for the men to eat in the morning. In addition to stealing flour, bread, bacon, butter, and other essentials, Littless steals some of the men's Green River whiskey, though she worries that the act renders her morally ruined. But she shrugs it off. As an aside, Hemingway's female characters are often maligned for lacking depth. Littless, I have to say, is one of my favorite Hemingway characters, male or female.

Nick catches three nice trout for dinner, and they fry them with bacon over the fire. After dinner, Littless falls asleep, and Nick reaches into the pack for the pint of whiskey, which he thinks smells good: "He dipped a half a cup of water out of the small pail he had brought from the spring and poured a little of the whiskey in it. Then he sat and sipped this very slowly, letting it stay under his tongue before he brought it slowly back over his tongue and swallowed it."

Nick is haunted by the idea that the game warden's son might know where they're hiding. A rivalry has existed between the two for some time, it seems. The story ends with Nick and Littless in

Vintage Green River playing card.
Courtesy John McCulloch Distillery.

camp, with Nick realizing that he'll "have to think about things now the rest of my life."

Green River whiskey, from Owensboro, Kentucky, was a popular brand before and after Prohibition. It started out in 1885 as a sour mash (like Jack Daniel's, similar to bourbon), then it became a blended whiskey. It was branded as "the whiskey without a headache" and "the whiskey without regrets," and it also went by "Mountain Dew." The brand was defunct for a time, but it's being made again now by John McCulloch Distillery, based in Martinsville, Ohio.

As for the recurring Hemingway character of Nick Adams, whiskey appears to be his favorite drink. I highly recommend to you the great coming-of-age short story "The Three-Day Blow," where Nick and his friend Bill put away a good bit of the stuff. But they're careful to drink only what's already open, since, after all, "opening bottles is what makes drunkards."

In *Islands in the Stream*, Whiskey & Ginger Ale makes an appearance in the "Cuba" part. Thomas Hudson is in Cojimar, the village near Havana where Hemingway kept *Pilar* and also the port where *The Old Man and the Sea* was based. It's just Hudson and his cat, Boise. Bad weather is blowing through. He's at home, preparing to leave for a day at the Floridita, but he's having a whiskey and mineral water, reminiscing about the day he first found Boise. He was at a local bar (perhaps La Terraza, Hemingway's favorite Cojimar haunt) with one of his sons. It was Christmas morning, the first Christmas of the war.

Hudson's son took a liking to a young cat that was hanging about the place and begged his father to adopt him. But Hudson was getting into a conversation with a local fisherman. As the two men began to talk, the son interjected, "Papa, before you and this gentleman start drinking, can we have this cat?" The answer of course was yes, after which the fisherman drank whiskey with ginger ale and Hudson drank whiskey with mineral water.

"Ginger ale makes me sick," Thomas Hudson said. "Let me have one with mineral water."

"It's very good for me," the fisherman said. "I like Canada Dry. Otherwise I don't like the taste of the whisky."

In real life, Hemingway had a cat named Boise, probably his favorite. But Hemingway had a *lot* of cats in Cuba, as many as fifty-seven at a time.[189] It should be noted that, in spite of what tour guides will tell you, he did *not* own any cats in Key West. All those adorable six-toed kitties swarming around the Hemingway house on Whitehead Street, allegedly descending from a "cat given to

Hemingway with sons Patrick and Gregory, and a few of the cats at the Finca Vigía, Cuba, circa 1946. Ernest Hemingway Photograph Collection, John F. Kennedy Presidential Library and Museum, Boston.

Hemingway by an old ship's captain"—it's all bunk. They are in fact cats, and they do have six toes. But they do not descend from Hemingway's cats because he did not own cats when he lived there (and cats don't swim). Both Patrick and Gregory Hemingway have gone on record as saying so.

Sorry, someone had to tell you. Go fix yourself a Whiskey & Ginger Ale, and don't forget to put out a bowl of milk for the kitties.

Floridita cocktail booklet, circa 1937. From the author's collection.

Whiskey & Soda

2 oz. whiskey or Scotch whisky

4 oz. seltzer or any sparkling water

Fill a highball glass with ice, add ingredients, stir, and serve. Optionally garnish with a wedge or peel of lemon or lime.

SUGGESTED READING: *Islands in the Stream* ("Bimini," Chapter 10; "Cuba"), *A Farewell to Arms* (Chapters 20 and 40), *The Sun Also Rises* (Chapters 2 and 19), *To Have and Have Not* (Chapter 24), *The Garden of Eden* (Chapters 9, 10, 11, 12, 17, 18, 20, 22, 23, 24, 26, 27, and 29), *A Moveable Feast* ("Evan Shipman at the Lilas," "Scott Fitzgerald"), *Green Hills of Africa* (Chapters 3, 6, 8, 10, and 13), *For Whom the Bell Tolls* (Chapter 32), *True at First Light* (Chapter 7), *Under Kilimanjaro* (Chapter 15), *The Fifth Column* (Act 3, scene 1), "The Snows of Kilimanjaro," "Night Before Battle"

This is another highball in the Hemingway oeuvre, and a classic at that. It's believed to be the original highball, invented by Patrick Gavin Duffy in the 1890s at the Ashland House in New York City. You might also know Mr. Duffy as the author of the *Official Mixer's Manual* (1934), one of the first post-Prohibition cocktail books and a staple behind any bar during the latter part of the twentieth century.

A simple enough recipe, right? Well, perhaps, but a little thought needs to go into deciding *which* whisk(e)y to use. Should it be Scotch (spelled "whisky") or one of the *other* whiskeys (spelled "whiskey"), namely bourbon, Tennessee sour mash (such as Jack Daniel's), rye, Canadian, Irish, or a blend? Of course, it depends on taste. Back in 1948, cocktail guru David Embury noted, "No one ever orders merely 'a Highball,' nor a 'whisky Highball,' nor even a 'Scotch Highball' or a 'Bourbon Highball.' The wise drinker does not even order 'a Scotch and soda' or 'a bourbon and ginger ale'; he names not only the type but also the *brand* of whisky along with the type and, perhaps, the brand of carbonated beverage."[190]

Hemingway often specified brands, such as Gordon's, Perrier, Schweppes, or Noilly Prat. But with his whiskey it's often just that—"whiskey"—leaving you to make the educated guess as to which kind. My sense is that it's typically Scotch, since the brands he *does* name, *when* he names them, are usually Scotches: White Horse, Haig & Haig Pinch, Old Parr, and Grand Macnish. As for Irish whiskey, there are only two mentions ("The Three-Day Blow" and *Islands in the Stream*). I'm only aware of one reference to rye (*Light of the World*) and no references to bourbon (though there's a bottle of Old Forester bourbon still waiting for him right where he left it back at the Finca Vigía in Cuba, along with a bottle of White Horse). Perhaps mindful of how other American authors (notably Faulkner) embraced bourbon, it may well be that it was a conscious decision on Hemingway's part to omit it from his prose.

So I submit to you, ladies and gentlemen of the jury, that Hemingway was a Scotch man. For what it's worth, according to *Pilar*'s bartender and cook, Gregorio Fuentes, Hemingway liked Dewar's White Label, Haig & Haig, or Johnny Walker in his Whiskey & Soda.[191] Having said all of this, you may use whatever whiskey you please in your Whiskey & Soda.

Although the Daiquiri, Martini, and Mojito get a lot more "publicity" as being Hemingway's favorite drinks, the Whiskey &

Soda certainly ranks up there. You'll certainly find many more references to it in his prose. The Daiquiri appears but once, in *Islands in the Stream*. The Martini is found six times (five novels, one short story). The Whiskey & Soda appears in no fewer than twelve of his works, not to mention numerous occasions in the *Anita* and *Pilar* logs. Yeah, he liked this one, I'd say.

In Chapter 40 of *A Farewell to Arms*, we find Frederic and Catherine in a hotel room in Lausanne, awaiting the birth of their baby. While Catherine unpacks, Frederic relaxes with the newspaper and a drink.

> I would have to tell them not to put ice in the whiskey. Let them bring the ice separately. That way you could tell how much whiskey there was and it would not suddenly be too thin from the soda. . . . Good whiskey was very pleasant. It was one of the pleasant parts of life.

In *A Moveable Feast* the whiskey is used as a symbol of protest, of all things. Hemingway and poet Evan Shipman are at Ernest's favorite café, the Closerie des Lilas, where Evan earlier discovered his new favorite waiter, Jean. Jean is upset that the café is calling for him to shave his beloved mustache. So, as a way of "sticking it to the man," Jean is serving Hemingway and Shipman extra portions of whiskey, on the house. At first they feel a bit guilty about accepting this windfall, not wanting to get Jean into trouble. They soon get over it, however, when they figure out that if they sip it carefully, the whiskey can last them a good long time.

When they eventually finish that round, they order another, and once again Jean tops off their glasses, to even more muted protestations from Shipman and Hemingway. "It's a good thing Dostoyevsky didn't know Jean," Evan said. "He might have died of drink." Hemingway halfheartedly objects, but Evan assures him that to drink the whiskey is simply their own way of supporting Jean's cause.

In *The Sun Also Rises*, Jake Barnes uses the Whiskey & Soda in a novel way. In Chapter 2, his friend Robert Cohn has dropped by uninvited, so Jake suggests they have a drink at the café downstairs. This is a trick Jake discovered for getting rid of unwanted drop-in guests. All you had to do was to go have a drink with them, then make up some story about how you had to get back to the office to send off some cables or the like. Jake reasoned that it was important for a person in the press to have methods such as this, albeit a shade dishonest.

As useful as it is for escaping social situations, Hemingway characters also use it as a way to escape from pain, as in "The Snows of Kilimanjaro." This is the story of a writer coming to terms with his impending death; a minor safari accident has caused terminal gangrene. Both the writer, Harry, and his wife, Helen, rely on Whiskey & Soda in dealing with their troubles. Harry rues his squandered talent, and all the things he'll never get to write. His wife has relied on it more in the past, as part of facing her day-to-day life: "She liked to read in the evening before dinner and she drank Scotch and soda while she read. By dinner she was fairly drunk and after a bottle of wine at dinner she was usually drunk enough to sleep."

In camp, Harry craves a drink, out of boredom or just to help with his pain. He asks for a drink, but his wife tells him he shouldn't, that it would be bad for his already-deteriorating health. They argue for a time, yet in the end he gets his drink. But he's disheartened: "So this was the way it ended in a bickering over a drink."

In an even more heart-wrenching scene, from Chapter 15 of *Islands in the Stream*, Thomas Hudson drowns his pain in Old Parr Scotch & Perrier. He's just learned of a tragic car accident in Biarritz, and he is returning to France for the funeral on an ocean liner. The long crossing gives him time to mourn and reflect on his loss, not to mention put away a lot of Scotch. Hudson learns the painful lesson that hell isn't necessarily as it has been described to us by Dante and other writers. Indeed, it could be a nice, comfortable stateroom on a favorite liner, taking you to a place you'd always loved, France.

Hudson understands he has to take it easy on the drinking, since it can "destroy the capacity for producing satisfying work." But since working is something he certainly cannot do now, he'll spend the next few days drinking, exercising, reading, and sleeping while making the crossing. So he calls for the steward and asks for a bottle of Perrier and some ice and cracks open a bottle of Old Parr Scotch. He then begins to read, or at least try to, a bundle of papers and magazines he picked up before departure from New York. He might make it, if he can just survive the next six days.

As so often was the case, this transatlantic crossing was mirrored in Hemingway's real life. It was January 1926, when Hemingway was grappling with the fact that he was married to Hadley, but in love with Pauline. He was tortured with guilt and self-loathing about one, while longing for the other. As it happened, he had to go to New York to work out the details of another divorce, with another "new girl" waiting in the wings. See, he was breaking up with Boni & Liveright, opting to go with Scribner, which would publish *The Torrents of Spring*, followed by *The Sun Also Rises*. Hemingway would use the long ocean passage on the *Mauretania* to sort things out. According to biographer Peter Griffin:

> He went aboard early, and this gave him the feeling of getting away. The days at sea could be a respite from the complications and the sorrow he had created in his life. Now all he needed were

his work and his whiskey. Of course, he could not write. So the drinks would have to do.[192]

There are far too many other references to Whiskey & Soda within the works of Hemingway, but I invite you to peruse the Suggested Reading list above to find other gems.

Selling It

Among whiskeys, Hemingway wrote about Old Parr, White Horse, Haig & Haig, and others. But it seems he didn't particularly care for Calvert; at least, he turned down the company's four-thousand-dollar offer to be in its popular "Man of Distinction" campaign. "I told them I wouldn't drink the stuff for four thousand dollars. I told them I was a champagne man. Am trying to be a good guy, but it's a difficult trade. What you win in Boston, you lose in Chicago."[193]

Note also that Hemingway offered a free "testimonial" for Gordon's gin, calling it "one of the sovereign antiseptics of our time" (see the Maestro Collins). Was Hemingway above being a corporate shill? Did he refuse commercial endorsement opportunities based on principle? Heck no. In 1948, he did an ad for a Parker ballpoint pen (though he usually did his writing with a No. 2 pencil), and in 1952, he did one for Ballantine Ale. Both ads used the same Hemingway photo—they just flipped the negative around (!). The ale ad's copy reads:

> *Bob Benchley first introduced me to Ballantine Ale. It has been a good companion to me ever since. You have to work hard to deserve to drink it. But I would rather have a bottle of Ballantine Ale than any other drink after fighting a really big fish. We keep it iced in the bait box with chunks of ice packed around it. And you ought to taste it on a hot day when you have worked a big marlin fast because there were sharks after him. You are tired all the way through. The fish is landed untouched by sharks and you have a bottle of Ballantine cold in your hand and drink it cool, light, and full-*

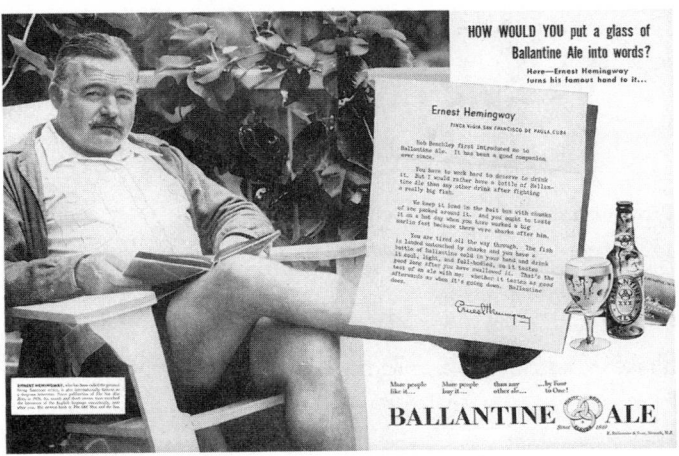

1952 Ballantine Ale ad. From the author's collection.

bodied, so it tastes good long after you have swallowed it. That's the test of an ale with me: whether it tastes as good afterwards as when it's going down. Ballantine does.

Come on, Hem, when you're out on the Gulf Stream, you're probably drinking Tropical, or more likely Hatuey beer from Havana (see *For Whom the Bell Tolls*, *To Have and Have Not*, and *The Old Man and the Sea*). Indeed, Hatuey (and Bacardi rum) held a ceremony for Hemingway in 1956 to thank him for the mentions and his patronage (not to mention to congratulate him on his Nobel Prize). Perhaps they didn't know about that Ballantine ad, or vice versa. As the man said, "What you win in Boston, you lose in Chicago."

Whiskey Sour

1½ oz. whiskey
Juice of ½ lemon
1 tsp. sugar or simple syrup

Shake well; strain into a chilled cocktail glass. Add a dash of seltzer if desired. Garnish with lemon peel.

SUGGESTED READING: *A Moveable Feast* ("Scott Fitzgerald")

The recipe shown above is the traditional Whiskey Sour, and you're free to use any whiskey you please. In *A Moveable Feast*, Hemingway refers to a drink as a "whisky sour," but it's more likely he was drinking a mixture of lemonade (in French, *citron pressé*), Scotch, and perhaps a little Perrier water. In other words, Hemingway likely didn't shake the drink as you would a true Whiskey Sour, just built it in the glass, but that's what he called it nevertheless.

In this book Hemingway writes at length about his relationship with F. Scott Fitzgerald. He tells of their first meeting, at the Dingo Bar, where Hemingway was sitting with some other people. One of them happened to be Duff Twysden, on whom Lady Brett Ashley in *The Sun Also Rises* was based (see the Jack Rose). In walked Scott. Hemingway knew of him; after all, he was already a successful writer. Scott drank Champagne, and then, before their eyes, Scott's appearance completely changed, as if he'd died right before them. He turned pale, his skin went taut, his eyes sank back into his head, and he passed out. Hemingway compared his appearance to that of a "death mask."

Hemingway wanted to get him to a hospital, but Scott's friend said it sometimes happened when he drank. So they put him in a taxi home. A few days later, Scott met Hemingway at the Closerie des Lilas, and they each had two Whiskey & Sodas. Nothing odd happened. It was during that encounter that Scott asked a favor of Hem. It seemed that his wife Zelda had been forced to leave their Renault automobile down in Lyon during some bad weather, and he wondered if Hem would be good enough to accompany Scott to Lyon to retrieve it. They could ride down together on the train, get the car, and then drive it back to Paris. Hemingway was enthusiastic about the trip, as it would give him a chance to spend time with a more accomplished writer. So he accepted.

The trip was nothing short of a disaster, something to laugh about years later, perhaps. Or write about. First off, Scott failed to meet Hemingway at the train station, so Hem had to foot the bill for his ticket. Once in Lyon, he couldn't find Scott, so he had to pay for that first night in the hotel. This was not what had been planned, and it was a little hard on the young, starving writer. But Hemingway made the most of it and ate a cheap dinner in an Algerian restaurant, engaging in conversation with a toothless fire-eater. He then returned to his hotel and read Turgenev. Good times. Scott finally showed up the next morning, but his words and manner made it appear that he felt it was Hemingway who'd stood up Scott. Hemingway was increasingly wondering why he'd said yes. But they had a nice big American breakfast, then a whiskey and Perrier, and felt much better. The plan was to hit the road after the hotel packed up a lunch for them to go.

When they got to the garage, Hemingway was shocked to discover that the car's top was missing. You see, the reason Zelda had ditched the car in Lyon was because she'd had the top cut off, because of some minor accident in Marseilles, and she refused to have it replaced. She liked convertibles, anyway, even if they had no top. So, off they started on their drive back to Paris in their topless French car. Then the rain came.

The rain caused them to stop just north of Lyon, and nearly a dozen times thereafter. Along the way, during breaks in the squalls or under the shelter of trees, they ate an excellent lunch of truffled roast chicken, washed down with white Mâcon wine. They had bought several bottles, which Hemingway would open as needed. Drinking wine straight from the bottle was particularly exciting for Scott, "as a girl might be excited by going swimming for the first time without a bathing suit."

And then the hypochondria set in. Scott became convinced that he'd contracted congestion of the lungs (he'd read about it somewhere), and he begged Hemingway to stop over at the next big town before he got a fever and became delirious. They stopped at a hotel, and Hemingway became doctor and nurse to Fitzgerald. Scott took to the bed, and while their rain-soaked clothing dried, Hemingway ordered lemonade and whiskey, which Scott dismissed as a folk remedy. It didn't stop him from drinking it, though. Scott continued to demand that he have his temperature taken, in spite of Hemingway's assurances that his forehead felt cool.

The waiter soon brought them two glasses of whiskey, fresh lemon juice, and ice, along with a bottle of Perrier. Although he also brought some aspirin, the waiter informed them that the pharmacy wasn't open, so no dice on getting a thermometer. Hemingway asked if there weren't some way he could borrow one, while Scott offered his best "baleful Irish look" to the waiter.

The waiter finally brought them a thermometer. Sort of. It was a huge affair with a wooden back, designed for bathtub water. Nevertheless, Hemingway shook it down as a doctor would, noting that luckily it wasn't a rectal thermometer. Scott wasn't amused. Hemingway placed it under Scott's arm, and whatever the temperature ended up being (it was centigrade, of course), Hemingway managed to convince Fitzgerald that it was normal. Scott remained convinced he was dying, and all the while the waiter kept bringing double Whiskey Sours.

Eventually the drinks worked their magic, and Scott felt good enough to go downstairs for dinner. There, they had a carafe of Fleurie with their snails, followed by a bottle of Montagny, "a light, pleasant white wine of the neighborhood" with their *poularde de Bresse*. Scott passed out at the table. After the waiter and he got Fitzgerald upstairs to bed, Hemingway went back down to the restaurant and finished the dinner, and of course the wine.

The next day they drove to Paris and the weather was beautiful. Hemingway said his good-byes to Scott and returned to his apartment. He was never so happy to be back home, and he and Hadley celebrated with a drink at the Closerie des Lilas. He told Hadley that he'd learned one thing: "Never to go on trips with anyone you do not love."

For the rest of their friendship, Hemingway worried not only about Fitzgerald's drinking, but also about Zelda's negative influence. He was convinced she was mentally ill (true enough), and further believed that she encouraged his drinking so as to diminish his abilities as a writer, so jealous was she of his success. Hemingway once said, "I told Scott that being a rummy made him very vulnerable—I mean, a rummy married to a crazy is not the kind of pari-mutuel that aids a writer."[94] Can't argue with that.

Harry's New York Bar, Paris

Apparently both Hemingway and Fitzgerald spent a bit of time at Harry's New York Bar, a Paris landmark located at 5 Rue Daunou, famously pronounced "Sank Roo Doe Noo." It was even part of the bar's advertising; visiting Americans were encouraged to "just tell the taxi driver *Sank Roo Doe Noo.*"

Speaking of the Whiskey Sour and Harry's, owner Harry MacElhone was quoted in 1951 as saying he missed the good old days when Hemingway and Fitzgerald were customers, and that "Hemingway could down 20 whiskey sours at one sitting and then go back to his hotel to work."[195] Hmmm . . .

The "Jumping" off place
"Harry's" New-York Bar
(CABARET)
5, Rue Daunou, 5
PARIS
Cable Address
" Cocktails "

I. B. F. HEADQUARTERS, TRAP. Nº 1

Vintage postcard, circa 1920. Harry's served as headquarters for the International Bar Flies, a whimsical institution headed by bartender Harry MacElhone. From the author's collection.

Back in the day, Hemingway was a regular customer; he considered Harry's to be "one of the few good, solid bars" in the world. According to Harry's lore, Hemingway once served as a most unusual bouncer, when an "ex-pug" (a former boxer, as in *pugilist*) visited the bar with an unwelcomed pet—a pet lion! Apparently the lion was a nice enough cat, "no growls or roars," but it had the annoying habit of . . . well, let's just say it wasn't housebroken. This was a bit off-putting for the clientele, so Harry had no choice but to ask the ex-pug to leave the lion at home next time. The next day, however, there he was, and there was his lion. And there again was the eventual mess on the floor. "This, of course, had a rather adverse effect on the trade," noted Hemingway. On the third day of this business, Hemingway intervened. "I went over, picked up the pug, who had been a welterweight, carried him outside, and threw him in the street. Then I came back and grabbed the lion's mane and hustled him out of there. Out on the sidewalk the lion gave me a look, but he went quietly."[196]

I'm not sure which tale is taller, the one about the twenty Whiskey Sours or the one about the lion. It's just my job to pass them along to you, dear reader.

Martha Gellhorn and Hemingway, 1941, in Hawaii, en route to China. Hemingway apparently had his fill of all of the hospitality they received in Hawaii, all the alohas and leis, and promised to "cool the next son of a bitch who touched him."[197] Courtesy Getty Images.

White Lady

1½ oz. London dry gin
1 oz. Cointreau
¾ oz. fresh lemon juice

Shake well with ice, strain into chilled cocktail glass. Optionally add an egg white for a frothier, creamier texture. Use pasteurized egg whites if concerned about raw eggs.

SUGGESTED READING: *Islands in the Stream* ("Bimini," Chapter 2)

The White Lady is a delightful cocktail that, I boldly predict, will soon enjoy a renaissance, as has occurred with the very similar Aviation and Bee's Knees. It is what's known as a *sour* cocktail, and once you've mastered the formula, you'll not only have a greater understanding of cocktails, but you'll be better prepared to create new ones of your own.

The basic sour is a three-part marriage of strong, sweet, and sour, shaken with ice and typically served "up" (strained, as opposed to on the rocks), in a chilled cocktail glass. In this case, it's gin (strong), Cointreau (sweet), and lemon juice (sour). Change the components and you have a Margarita (tequila, Cointreau, lime), Daiquiri (rum, simple syrup, lime), Whiskey Sour (whiskey, simple syrup, lemon), Sidecar (brandy, Cointreau, lemon), Jack Rose (applejack, grenadine, lime), and countless others. By plugging in different components, you can, as the great David Embury espoused, "roll your own."

Authorship of the White Lady is credited to either Harry Craddock, who ran the bar at the Savoy Hotel in London during the 1920s and '30s, or Harry MacElhone, a Scot who initially worked at Ciro's in London, then moved to Harry's New York Bar in Paris in 1923. We do know that MacElhone was the first to name a drink White Lady in 1911, but it was a different drink (crème de menthe in place of gin, and a lot more Cointreau). We also know that the current version of the drink first appeared in Craddock's epic 1930 bar guide, *The Savoy Cocktail Book*. Perhaps it's safe to say MacElhone invented it and Craddock *perfected* it.

Originally the bartender at New York's revered Hoffman House, Craddock went to London when Prohibition shuttered not only his bar but his profession. It's interesting to note that at the same time that many aspiring American writers, artists, and other creative ex-

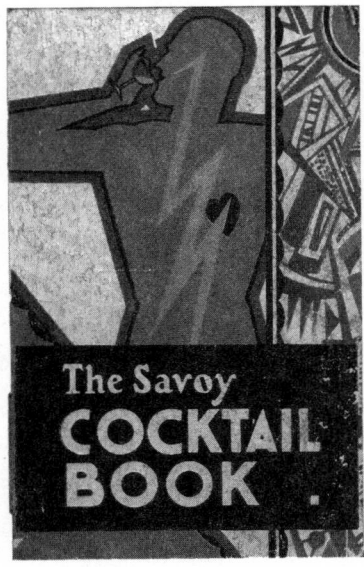

The Savoy Cocktail Book. From the collection of Nick Wineriter.

patriates were flocking to London, Paris, and elsewhere (Hemingway included), you had a similar exodus of another sort of artist, the craft bartender. Harry Craddock (London), Frank Meier (Paris), Eddie Woelke (Havana), and many others left the United States to ply their trade and give traveling Americans a taste of what they were missing back home. And, most important, to keep their skills sharp and carry the torch for the day that Prohibition ended.

The White Lady was named for the White Lady Banks Rose (*Rosa banksiae*), which was in turn named for the wife of famed English botanist Sir Joseph Banks. Banks was something of a bon vivant and was Captain James Cook's right-hand man during his epic circumnavigation aboard the HMS *Endeavour* (1768–71), during which Cook explored Brazil, Tahiti, New Zealand, Australia, and other exotic locales.

Speaking of islands, the White Lady cocktail is featured in *Islands in the Stream*. The opening chapters take place on Bimini, where Thomas Hudson lives and works as a painter. A Hemingway hero through and through, Hudson has three sons by two mothers. He typically works hard at his craft in the morning, then knocks off in the afternoon for some serious fishing and/or elbow bending. Hudson is eagerly anticipating the arrival of his sons for a summertime visit.

His houseboy, Joseph, offers to fix him a Gin & Tonic, but Hudson declines, saying he'll get a drink down at Mr. Bobby's, the local bar. Joseph suggests he have one at home first; not only will it be cheaper, but Bobby is in a foul mood from all the mixed drinks he's been forced to make for all these hoity-toitys who just arrived on a yacht. One of them even had the audacity to order "something called a White Lady." Instead of fixing her that White Lady, Bobby apparently "served her a bottle of that American mineral water with a lady in white kinda mosquito netting dress sitting by a spring."

Having heard this, Hudson is now determined to head for Mr.

Bobby's straightaway. But Joseph once again twists his arm into having a quick Gin & Tonic at home first. Hudson relents, and Joseph says, "Good thing. Because I already mixed it."

Ahhh, there's nothing so valuable as a bartender who anticipates his patrons' wants, eh? This isn't the only time when Joseph uses his keen powers of intuition, in spite of where the hands of the clock happen to be (as you can see in the Martini chapter in this book). Meanwhile, Mr. Bobby is strictly of the "shot-and-a-beer" bartending school, fed up with having to make fancy cocktails, especially if they're ordered by "that trash comes in on yachts." "Fix

Vintage White Rock ad. Note the "mosquito netting dress." From the author's collection.

your own damn drink. The hell with those fancy drinks," he later snorts at Hudson, who's had the audacity to order a Gin & Tonic with bitters (!). Of course, when the woman on the yacht wanted a White Lady, Mr. Bobby mistook her to mean White Rock, a popular soft drink brand of the day. One can just imagine her expression. And we're left to wonder if maybe he *knew* what a White Lady was, but was just too ornery or lazy to fix it.

This scene gives us one of many glimpses into Hemingway's work ethic: he typically worked hard in the mornings, and he never drank before noon, while he was writing, or late at night. You'll see this in *Islands in the Stream*, *The Garden of Eden*, *A Moveable Feast*, and elsewhere. According to his wartime friend Buck Lanham:

> Before he wrote a book he'd go into training. That is, he wouldn't take a drink until noon. . . . He'd swim forty laps in the morning and forty laps in the afternoon in a huge pool. And he'd look at his watch every two laps, waiting for that clock to move around. When it was eleven on the dot, you could see his major domo come out of the Finca up on the hill and start down with this big tray and a huge shaker of martinis, what he called "Montgomerys." And old Hemingstein would look at his watch and say, "Well, Buck, it's eleven o'clock. What the hell, it's twelve in Miami, let's have a drink." And he would. But it was real discipline for him to go that long in the morning without a drink. He was disciplined about his work.[198]

Of course, he sometimes cheated a bit. We see this several times in *Islands*; as I mentioned in the Martini chapter, Thomas Hudson and his friend Roger were backsliding into having a quick drink before noon. Of course, in this instance the drink is in celebration. Later in the novel, though (see the Whiskey & Soda), Hudson is in mourning and drinks to drown his sorrows, awakening in the

Hemingway, circa 1941, relaxing at the Finca Vigía. Ernest Hemingway Photograph Collection, John F. Kennedy Presidential Library and Museum, Boston.

middle of the night during a long transatlantic crossing. It seems that on this trip he breaks a couple of his rules, about drinking during the night and drinking before he's gotten any work done. But here he "felt the simple happiness of breaking training," the "first return of any purely animal happiness or capacity for happiness that he had experienced since the cable had come."

As a final note on the White Lady, it holds the honor of being the first cocktail served at the Savoy's American Bar when it reopened after a three-year, three-hundred-million-dollar renovation, on October 10, 2010 (that's 10/10/10, get it?). For the record, the Savoy uses a dash of egg white in its White Lady.

PAPA'S LEGACY

I've been blessed with many friendships among some of the world's greatest bartenders, writers, distillers, bar/restaurant owners, and other professionals from the world of drink. Hemingway had more than a few such friends of his own and is quoted as saying, "Don't bother with churches, government buildings or city squares, if you want to know about a culture, spend a night in its bars." Indeed, he advocated this noble profession to his friend Bill Smith in 1925: "Have you ever thought of tending bar? . . . Paris is louzy [sic] with American bars. Genial bartenders make a bar and command big wages, percentages and bonuses. Too many bars—not enough bar tenders with personality. You are the ideal bartender. There's nawthing [sic] I would rather do."[99] While I greatly enjoy my career as a member of the *legal* bar, I have to say I appreciate his sentiments.

I've also observed just how many of the world's cocktail luminaries have created either drinks inspired by Papa or their own "takes" on Hemingway classics. What follows is a compilation of some of the better ones I've encountered. To borrow that classic line from his short story "Hills Like White Elephants," "That's all we do, isn't it—look at things and try new drinks?" Submitted for your approval, here are a few.

Ernest's Advice

SONJA KASSEBAUM, cofounder/owner of North Shore Distillery, the first craft distillery in the Chicago area since Prohibition, and Sarah Macfarquhar, North Shore's ambassador

Inspiration: *"Hemingway's love of the beautiful pairing of absinthe and sparkling wine."*

1½ oz. Distiller's Gin No. 11
1 oz. fresh lemon juice
¾ oz. fennel simple syrup*
1–2 oz. sparkling wine
Spritzer of Sirène Absinthe Verte

Shake all ingredients (except for wine) with ice. Strain into a champagne flute and top with sparkling wine, then spritz one pump of absinthe over the top. Garnish with a lemon peel.

* To make the fennel simple syrup, simmer 1½ cups white sugar, 1 cup water, and 1 Tbsp. fennel seeds (or 1 tsp. ground fennel) for 5–7 minutes. Cool completely, then strain. Store in the refrigerator for up to 1 month.

Hemingway Daiquiri à la Voisey

CHARLOTTE VOISEY, portfolio ambassador at William Grant & Sons

Inspiration: *"Hemingway's classic Daiquiri recipe at the Floridita, Havana."*

4 Marasca cherries in syrup
2 oz. Flor de Caña Extra Dry Rum (4-year-old)
1 oz. fresh pink grapefruit juice
1 oz. fresh lime juice

Spoon cherries into a mixing glass, including the syrup they sit in. Muddle the cherries, then add the other ingredients, and shake this very well with ice. Strain twice, and serve up in a prechilled coupe. Garnish with a lime wheel speared by a fifth Marasca cherry on a pick.

Doctor's Orders 2.0

CHANTAL TSENG, bar manager at Mockingbird Hill, Washington, DC

Inspiration: *"This is my impression of the Physician, Heal Thyself, Hemingway's concoction of Sherry, Scotch, and Champagne."*

1½ oz. La Cigarrera Manzanilla
1 oz. Sherry-aged Scotch whisky (such as Glenfarclas 12-year-old)
1½ oz. Bohigas Gran Reserva Brut Cava sparkling wine

Build in a highball glass with ice. Garnish with lemon peel after expressing oils over the drink.

Blue-Green Isaac's Special

JEFF "BEACHBUM" BERRY, world-renowned Tiki expert; author of *Beachbum Berry's Grog Log, Potions of the Caribbean, Sippin' Safari*, et al.; and owner of Beachbum Berry's Latitude 29, New Orleans, Louisiana

Inspiration: *"A riff on the Green Isaac's Special, Hemingway's Bimini drink from* Islands in the Stream, *made with gin, lime, coconut water, and Angostura bitters."*

2 oz. Old Tom Gin (such as Hayman's)
½ oz. fresh lime juice
½ oz. orgeat syrup
¼ oz. blue curaçao
4 oz. coconut water

Shake well with ice, strain into a tall glass filled with fresh ice. Garnish with a spiral-cut lime peel.

The African Plateau (A Hemingway Daiquiri)

BRYAN DAYTON, owner/beverage director OAK at Fourteenth in Boulder, Colorado, and Acorn in Denver, Colorado; and *GQ* Magazine's Most Inspired Bartender, 2011

Inspiration: *"Hemingway's big-game hunting in Africa, merging his favorite Daiquiri with a celebration of the bounty and spices of the African plateau."*

1½ oz. Papa's Pilar Dark Rum
¾ oz. fresh lime juice
½ oz. falernum
¼ oz. spice allspice dram
¼ oz. simple syrup

Shake well with ice, strain into chilled cocktail glass.

Papa's New Negroni

BRYAN DAYTON

Inspiration: *"Hemingway's European adventures, a spicy twist on a classic, yet still retaining the bitters that he loved so much. I can see him waking early, pouring one of these before running with the bulls!"*

2 oz. rhum agricole (such as Rhum J.M)
1 oz. Domaine de Canton Ginger Liqueur
¾ oz. Campari
2 dashes grapefruit bitters

Stir all ingredients well with ice, then strain into a chilled cocktail glass. Garnish with grapefruit peel.

Fall of the Daiquiri

SIMON FORD, partner of the 86 Company; creator of Ford's Gin; and former brand ambassador for Plymouth Gin

Inspiration: *"A fable attached to Hemingway's statue at the Floridita in Havana. He's standing, not sitting. Why? Legend tells us that he once fell down drunk after too long a sitting, and since that fateful day he opted to stand, as a way of 'knowing when to say when,' so to speak. This commemorates that 'fall,' along with the inclusion of autumnal flavors."*

1½ oz. Caña Brava Rum
¾ oz. fresh lime juice
½ oz. Demerara syrup
¼ oz. St. Elizabeth's Allspice Dram
2–3 dashes fig bitters (or Angostura)

Shake well with ice, then strain into a rocks glass filled with fresh ice, or strain into a highball glass filled with crushed ice. Garnish with a lime wheel and a sprinkle of cinnamon.

Hemingway's Affairs

JULIO CABRERA, head bartender and managing partner at the Regent Cocktail Club Miami, and Bombay Sapphire's Most Imaginative Bartender, 2014

Inspiration: *"I wanted to create a take on the Hemingway Daiquiri especially enjoyable for women, so I added Moscato D'Asti, a sparkling sweet wine from Italy that matches perfectly with grapefruit, which made the drink less tart."*

1 oz. Bacardi Superior Rum
¼ oz. Luxardo maraschino liqueur
½ oz. fresh lime juice
¾ oz. fresh grapefruit juice
1½ oz. Moscato d'Asti
Basil leaf

Shake all the ingredients (except the Moscato and basil) well with ice, then strain into a chilled cocktail glass. Top with the Moscato d'Asti. Garnish with a small basil leaf, after smacking it to release aroma.

The Unrefined Pioneer

AARON JOSEPH, lead bartender at Wit & Wisdom, Four Seasons Hotel, Baltimore, Maryland; *Baltimore* magazine's Bartender of the Year, 2013, and People's Choice Award, 2014; and brand ambassador at Papa's Pilar Rum

Inspiration: *"The big, bold, passionate, and adventuresome life of Hemingway meets the Baltimore Southside Cocktail (rum, mint, lemon, simple syrup)."*

1 oz. Papa's Pilar Blonde Rum
½ oz. Papa's Pilar Dark Rum
½ oz. fresh lemon juice
¼ oz. fresh orange juice
½ oz. cane syrup
2 dashes chocolate bitters
8 mint leaves

Smack the mint leaves between your palms to release oils and aroma. Shake all ingredients well with ice, then double strain into a chilled champagne coupe. Garnish with a mint sprig.

Colada Cubana

JARED BROWN and **ANISTATIA MILLER**, drinks historians; publishers of Mixellany Ltd.; former directors of Exposition Universelle des Vins et Spiritueux; and cofounders of the Museum of the American Cocktail

Inspiration: *"Hemingway's love affair with Cuba, beginning in 1932 with his visits with 'Sloppy Joe' Russell. Like many Americans visiting during Prohibition, Hemingway undoubtedly became familiar with the original Piña Colada. This is our favorite version, based on a popular 1922 Cuban recipe. Piña colada translates to 'strained pineapple'; there was no coconut in the original."*

1⅔ oz. Havana Club Selección de Maestros (or another dry, dark aged
    rum, if you live in a deprived nation)
3⅜ oz. fresh pineapple juice
2 lime wedges
2 dashes Angostura bitters

Fill a rocks glass with ice. Stir. Strain out the melted water. Add the bitters, pineapple juice, and rum. Squeeze one of the lime wedges into the drink. Stir. Garnish with the other lime wedge, unsqueezed (which you may wish to squeeze after that first sip).

Solleone Cocktail

TODD APPEL, owner and bartender of Todd Appel Bar & Cocktail, Chicago, Illinois

Inspiration: *"Hemingway's love of Campari and gin, and grapefruit juice. Solleone means 'midday sun' or 'dog days of summer' in Italian. This cocktail is a perfect midsummer afternoon cooler, perhaps in Havana, on safari in Africa, or yachting on the Côte d'Azur."*

2 oz. London dry gin
½ oz. Campari
¾ oz. Appel's Grapefruit Cordial*
Grapefruit peel garnish

Shake well with ice. Serve up or on rocks. For a long drink, stir ingredients well with ice, then pour into a tall glass filled with ice and top with chilled soda.

* To make approximately 16 oz. of grapefruit cordial: Wash and zest 4 fresh grapefruits and set aside. Heat 8 oz. each of fresh strained grapefruit juice and lemon juice with 9 oz. of cane sugar. Heat the juice and sugar on low in a saucepan until it reaches 175 degrees. Stir often. Do not boil. Cool this to room temperature, then add grapefruit zest. Refrigerate for several hours, strain, and store in a glass bottle or jar in the refrigerator. Will keep for several months, if it lasts that long.

The Old Man and the Old Fashioned

DAVE RUSSELL, curator at RumGallery.com and cofounder of the International Rum Council

Inspiration: *"Like* The Old Man and the Sea, *this Rum Old Fashioned is simple when taken at face value, yet becomes more interesting as you look deeper into it—just like the allegorical struggles Hemingway presents in the story. In* The Old Man and the Sea, *Santiago personifies determination in the face of adversity, and the basic human need to rise up from indignity. At sea, one must endure the elements with only their wits and skill. We know Papa liked his whiskey, yet he wasn't afraid of inventing new drinks when necessary—such as when provisions run short while underway. Rum is plentiful in the tropics. No whiskey? No problem. I think this drink suits the story's character and the creator."*

2 oz. Papa's Pilar Dark Rum

½ tsp. Demerara or turbinado brown sugar

3 dashes Angostura bitters

Splash of soda water

Orange peel

Muddle sugar, bitters, and soda water in a rocks glass. Add a few large chunks of ice and the rum. Express oils from an orange peel over the drink, then wipe the outside of the orange peel around the rim of the glass to enhance aromas. Garnish with the orange peel.

The Dree

COLIN PETER FIELD, head bartender at the Hemingway Bar, Paris Ritz Hotel; ambassadeur for Air France; and author of *The Cocktails of the Ritz Paris*

Inspiration: *"Actually, this drink has never yet been made; I created it in my head. But it's a Hemingway drink, a new generation drink, to honor the new generation of Hemingways. Thus the name, Dree. Dree is very nice and always comes to the Hemingway Bar at the Ritz. We all like her."* Note: Dree Hemingway, fashion model and actress, is the daughter of Hemingway's granddaughter Mariel Hemingway (whose father was Jack, aka Bumby).

1¾ oz. lemon grass–infused white rum
⅓ oz. yuzu juice
½ oz. Limoncello di Sorrento

Shake well with ice, and strain into a chilled cocktail glass.

Muerte en la Mañana

JASON KOSMAS, cofounder of Employees Only; co-creator of the *Speakeasy* cocktail book; and co-owner of the 86 Company, makers of Ford's Gin, Caña Brava Rum, Tequila Cabeza, and Aylesbury Duck Vodka

Inspiration: *"Working on a tequila cocktail, I was inspired by Hemingway's love of grapefruit and anise/absinthe. I figured this might be the cocktail he would use to reset the clock in the morning."*

2 oz. Tequila Cabeza
¾ oz. honey syrup (1 part honey, 1 part water)
¼ oz. anise, absinthe, or pastis
3 dashes grapefruit bitters
1 grapefruit twist, for garnish
1 star anise pod, for garnish

Stir all ingredients well with ice in a mixing glass. Strain into a rocks glass with fresh ice. Garnish with grapefruit twist and star anise.

Cambodian Daiquiri

JASON KOSMAS

Inspiration: *"When asked to make a Southwest Asian cocktail, I took a Hemingway Daiquiri recipe and substituted pureed pineapple for the grapefruit, and added some Thai basil to give it a little zing. I've always liked the way pineapple and maraschino go together after tasting a Harlem cocktail."*

1½ oz. Caña Brava Rum (3-year-old)
½ oz. Luxardo maraschino liqueur
1 oz. pineapple puree
1 oz. lime juice
½ oz. simple syrup
5 Thai basil leaves, for shaking
1 Thai basil sprig, for garnish

Combine all ingredients including Thai basil in a cocktail shaker. Add ice and strain into a chilled cocktail glass. Garnish with Thai basil sprig.

Papa's Mimosa

CARLTON GROOMS, director of operations/rum maker for Hemingway Rum Company LLC, Papa's Pilar Rum, Key West, Florida

Inspiration: *"A great 'hair of the dog' drink and very popular in Key West today. Legend tells us it was created by bartender Frank Meier at the Hôtel Ritz, Paris. Some recipes allow for an additional touch of citrus via Cointreau or triple sec. I decided to add my own twist by coating the inside of a champagne flute with Papa's Pilar Blonde Rum. The rum has wonderful notes of grapefruit and citrus, a perfect complement to the cocktail."*

¼ oz. Papa's Pilar Blonde Rum

2 oz. Brut Champagne

2 oz. freshly squeezed orange juice

Coat the inside of a chilled champagne flute with rum. Add Champagne. Top with strained, freshly squeezed orange juice.

Death at Dusk

TED "DR. COCKTAIL" HAIGH, curator and cofounder of the Museum of the American Cocktail; graphic artist for *Boardwalk Empire, Ray,* and many other films and series; and author of *Vintage Spirits and Forgotten Cocktails*

Inspiration: *"Hemingway's most pungent drink, to match the force and brevity of his prose, is well-known as the Death in the Afternoon. I simply felt a little post-demise magic-hour chaser had long been wanting. I simply felt the need to grab that particular bull by the horns and supply it."*

2 oz. moonshine (Hudson New York Corn)
½ oz. freshly squeezed lime juice
½ oz. honey syrup (1 part honey, 1 part water)
1 dash Angostura aromatic bitters
Splash of Champagne (such as Veuve Clicquot)

Combine all ingredient except for the Champagne in a cocktail shaker with cracked ice. Shake, and strain into a small goblet. Douse with Champagne and gently stir.

Hemingway Daiquiri à la DeGroff

DALE "KING COCKTAIL" DEGROFF, James Beard Award-winning mixologist; author of *The Essential Cocktail* and *The Craft of the Cocktail*; founding president of the Museum of the American Cocktail; and creator of Dale DeGroff's Pimento Aromatic Bitters

Inspiration: *"The cocktail muse inspired the great Constantino Ribalaigua of the Floridita when he added fresh grapefruit juice and maraschino liqueur to the classic Daiquiri. The result is ambrosia. The drink was made as a frozen drink at the famous Floridita Bar in Havana and named Papa Doble (or Papa's Double) after Ernest Hemingway. The original recipe didn't call for any sugar, just a touch of maraschino, and it is always reprinted that way out of respect to Papa; Hemingway had an aversion to sugar. But you can be sure that for the average customer at the Floridita, the simple syrup was part of the recipe."*

1½ oz. white rum

¼ oz. Luxardo maraschino liqueur

½ oz. grapefruit juice

¾ oz. simple syrup

¾ oz. fresh lime juice

Shake ingredients and strain into chilled cocktail glass.

AUTHOR'S COMMENT: Bartenders have long complained that the Hemingway Daiquiri is too tart, since it's made without the usual sugar. Dale has fixed this little issue.

For the Love of Hemingway

TONY ABOU-GANIM, internationally recognized bartender and founder of the Modern Mixologist and author of *The Modern Mixologist: Contemporary Classic Cocktails* and *Vodka Distilled*

Inspiration: *"I too am a big fan of* Islands in the Stream *and used the Green Isaac's Special as inspiration for a drink I did on the television show* Iron Chef America: Battle Tropical, *with chef Shawn McClain. I was planning to serve a drink in a coconut, so I decided to use the fresh coconut water in this drink. It is basically a Green Isaac, but I cut back slightly on the lime juice, balanced that with a touch of simple syrup, substituted Peychaud's bitters for Angostura, and built it in the glass instead of shaking it, which I found made for a more balanced and complex version. I do hope you approve!"*

1½ oz. Bombay Sapphire gin

3–4 oz. fresh coconut water

¾ oz. fresh lime juice

½ oz. simple syrup

2 dashes Peychaud's bitters

Build in a tall highball glass. Stir to mix and garnish with lime slices and an edible tropical flower.

Pleasant Death in the Gulf Stream

PHILIP DUFF, owner of door 74 (Amsterdam), director of education for Tales of the Cocktail, and spirits educator

Inspiration: *"Hemingway's Death in the Gulf Stream."*

3 oz. genever (use one with the highest maltwine content you can find; an "oude" will do if there's no Corenwijn)

4 generous dashes Angostura aromatic bitters

1 oz. fresh lime juice

¼ oz. rich simple syrup (2 parts sugar, 1 part water)

Build in a tall glass full of finely cracked ice. Swizzle to mix.

The Sands Cocktail

MATTY GEE, owner of Juniper Tar, a new cocktail bar in San Antonio, Texas; formerly worked with Sasha Petraske at the legendary Milk & Honey for seven years, also the Gold Bar and the Top of the Standard, at the Standard Hotel in New York City

Inspiration: *"This is a Hemingway-themed variation on the classic Casino cocktail, and I was inspired to name it after the now-closed Sands Hotel and Casino, where the Rat Pack had their long entertaining residence."*

1½ oz. London dry gin

½ oz. Luxardo maraschino liqueur

½ oz. lemon juice

¾ oz. grapefruit juice

Shake well with ice, then strain into a chilled cocktail glass. Express oils from a lemon peel over the drink, then discard.

The Sun Also Rises

JIM MEEHAN, co-owner of the James Beard Award–winning bar PDT; creator of *The PDT Cocktail Book*; editor of numerous editions of *Food & Wine Magazine*'s annual cocktail book and *Mr. Boston's Bartender Guide*; and drinks editor for *Tasting Table*

Inspiration: *"Hemingway loved absinthe, which he mixed with Champagne in a cocktail he called the Death in the Afternoon. According to the 1935 cocktail book* So Red the Nose, or Breath in the Afternoon: *'After six of these cocktails the Sun Also Rises.' This inspired me to add absinthe to the classic Hemingway Daiquiri."*

2 oz. Banks 5-Island rum

¾ oz. fresh lime juice

½ oz. fresh grapefruit juice

½ oz. Luxardo maraschino liqueur

1 tsp. Vieux Pontarlier absinthe

Shake well with ice, then strain into a chilled coupe filled with crushed ice. No garnish.

The Never-Ending Story

LORENZO ANTINORI, bartender at Beaufort Bar in the Savoy Hotel, London

Inspiration: *"Created in 2013 as part of Beaufort Bar's signature cocktail menu, a tribute to famous guests of the Savoy. This drink celebrates Hemingway's love of rum and Cuba. It has the DNA of a Daiquiri, the chocolate suggests the Mulata, and the hint of absinthe recalls the Death in the Afternoon."*

1⅓ oz. Bacardi 1909
⅓ oz. dark cacao liqueur
⅔ oz. fresh lime juice
2 tsp. sugar
4 dashes absinthe

Shake all the ingredients and strain into a chilled coupette.

The Hemingwayesque Cocktail

ROCCO MILANO, beverage director, Barter Restaurant and Bar in Dallas, Texas

Inspiration: *"A combination of favorite Hemingway flavors. It's dry, very dry in fact. It will surprise you how subtly strong it is and how much flavor it has. The gin, acidity, and anise flavors all swirl upfront while the wine surprisingly hits with a delay showing mainly in the finish."*

4 oz. Tanqueray Rangpur gin

1 oz. sauvignon blanc

½ oz. fresh lime juice

1 tsp. Pernod

3 dashes Angostura aromatic bitters

Shake well with ice for 15 seconds. Strain into a chilled cocktail glass.

Faro Point

JILLIAN VOSE, bar manager at the award-winning Dead Rabbit Grocery & Grog, New York City; formerly bar manager at NYC's famous Death & Company

Inspiration: *"One of Hemingway's favorite bartenders was Constante Ribalaigua at the Floridita. Some of Constante's creations contained two different bases, so I created a drink in that same tradition. The Dead Rabbit specializes in Irish whiskey, but I wanted to get rum into the mix. I chose Teelings because this particular whiskey is aged in Flor de Caña rum barrels, so it seemed a no-brainer. The drink is a rum lover's introduction to Irish whiskey."*

1 oz. Teeling Small Batch Irish whiskey

1 oz. Plantation Barbados rum (5-year-old)

1 dash Dead Rabbit Orinoco bitters

1 dash Bittermens Xocolatl Molé bitters

¾ oz. fresh lemon juice

½ oz. banana simple syrup*

¼ oz. orgeat syrup

½ oz. Pineau des Charentes

Shake well with ice. Strain into a chilled cocktail glass. Garnish with grated nutmeg.

* To make the banana simple syrup:

2 cups white granulated sugar

2 cups water

1 ripe banana sliced into bite-size pieces

Add all ingredients to a pot and bring to a boil. Take off heat once syrup boils and let sit in refrigerator for 24 hours. Strain off banana and fortify with 1 oz. high-proof vodka or grain alcohol. Will last one week if refrigerated.

Hadley's Tears

JILLIAN VOSE, created while she was at Death & Company, New York City

Inspiration: *"Hemingway's first wife, Hadley, and her heartbreak in Paris."*

1 oz. Bols genever
1 oz. Appleton V/X Jamaican rum
¼ oz. sugar cane syrup
1 tsp. Galliano Ristretto
½ tsp. St. George absinthe
1 dash Bitter Truth aromatic bitters

Stir all ingredients with ice. Strain over fresh (and large) ice cubes in an Old Fashioned glass. Garnish with an orange twist.

Pauline Pfeiffer (Stockholm)

THOBIAS PETERSSON, beverage manager, and **PAOLO BAÑADOS**, bar manager, Bar Prinsen, Stockholm, Sweden

Inspiration: *"Pauline Pfeiffer was an American fashion journalist and the second wife of Hemingway. Pfeiffer's difficult labor with her son Patrick was the fictional basis for Catherine's death in the novel A Farewell to Arms. This apple libation is the perfect winter getaway cocktail with notes of apples, pears, and cardamom and a smooth apple finish."*

1⅔ oz. Busnel Calvados VSOP

7 green cardamom seeds

⅔ oz. fresh lime juice

⅔ oz. apple/pear syrup

⅙ oz. sugar

4 dashes Bob's cardamom bitters

⅔ oz. Loïc Raison la Cidraie (or any dry hard apple cider)

Build in a rocks glass with a large ice cube.

100 Days

DAVID ANDRLE, Hemingway Bar Prague, Prague, Czech Republic

Inspiration: *"Named after the hundred-day ultimatum that Hadley gave to Hemingway. If Hemingway could make it through one hundred days without seeing Pauline Pfeiffer, then she would grant him a divorce. Hadley thought that Hemingway was just crazy in love with Pfeiffer, but after the hundred days, he was still in love with her anyway, so she said yes and gave him freedom."*

1⅓ oz. Calvados VSOP

⅓ oz. bourbon infused with apple and cinnamon

⅔ oz. fresh lime juice

⅓ oz. Boudier Apple and Earl Grey Tea Liqueur

⅓ oz. simple syrup

1 dash Green Chartreuse

Shake well with ice, then strain into a chilled coupe. Garnish with a slice of dried apple caramelized with cinnamon and sugar.

Nick Adams's Medicine

ALEŠ PŮTA, Hemingway Bar Prague, Prague, Czech Republic

Inspiration: *"Nick Adams is a fictional (and somewhat autobiographical) character, the protagonist of many of Hemingway's short stories. This drink is inspired by Sam Ross's drink, Penicillin."*

1 slice fresh ginger
1⅔ oz. Chivas Regal Scotch (12-year-old)
⅓ oz. Galliano liqueur
⅔ oz. fresh lemon juice
1 oz. honey syrup (1 part honey, 1 part water)
⅓ oz. Ardbeg Scotch whisky

Shake all ingredients (except for the Ardbeg Scotch) well with ice, then strain into an Old Fashioned glass. Float the Ardbeg whisky on top. Serve with no garnish.

Pauline Pfeiffer (Prague)

DAVID ANDRLE, Hemingway Bar Prague, Prague, Czech Republic

Inspiration: *"This drink is as fashionable as its namesake. Pauline was an American journalist and Hemingway's second wife. She worked for Vogue magazine in Paris."*

3 fresh white grapes
1 teaspoon fresh lime juice
1 oz. Havana Club Añejo 3 Años rum (3-year-old)
⅓ oz. June liqueur
⅓ oz. Belvoir Elderflower Cordial
1 oz. cranberry juice

Muddle the grapes in a shaker. Add ice and other ingredients, then shake well. Double strain into a chilled goblet. Garnish with an orange peel.

And, last and likely least . . .

The Statin Islander

PHILIP GREENE

Inspiration: *"A grapefruit-free Hemingway Daiquiri. Some of us are on cholesterol meds, known as 'statin drugs,' and the label tells us to avoid grapefruit. Paul Harrington, who created the modern classic Jasmine cocktail, taught us how a little Campari and Cointreau magically create the flavor of grapefruit. So, as an homage to Paul and Papa, I give to you the grapefruit-free Hemingway Daiquiri. I also note, the touch of Cointreau or Ferrand Dry Curaçao addresses the 'too tart' complaint."*

1½ oz. Papa's Pilar Blonde Rum
½ oz. fresh lime juice
½ oz. Campari
¼ oz. Cointreau or Ferrand Dry Curaçao
1 tsp. Luxardo maraschino liqueur

Shake well with ice, then strain into a chilled cocktail glass.

GLOSSARY OF OTHER HEMINGWAY POTENT POTABLES

AMONTILLADO: A variety of Sherry, a fortified wine (wine with grape brandy added after fermentation) from Spain, approximately 18 percent alcohol. Found in *The Sun Also Rises*, Chapters 16, 19; *Death in the Afternoon*, Chapter 20.

EAU-DE-VIE: A brandy, that is, a distilled fruit juice. Literally, it means "water of life." Found in *A Moveable Feast* ("Miss Stein Instructs" and "A Strange Enough Ending").

FINE: Short for Fine Champagne Cognac, a blend of Grande and Petite Champagne Cognacs, with at least half coming from Grande Champagne. Found in *The Sun Also Rises*, Chapters 1, 8, 14; *The Garden of Eden*, Chapters 10, 14.

FRAMBOISE: A raspberry brandy, originally from France. Found in *A Moveable Feast* ("Miss Stein Instructs"). Gertrude Stein served framboise, mirabelle, and quetsch to guests in her salon. Hemingway noted that they "tasted like the fruits they came from, converted into a controlled fire on your tongue that warmed you and loosened it."

FUNDADOR: A style of brandy from Spain. The name comes from the Spanish word for "founder," since it was the first brandy to be marketed "Brandy de Jerez." Found in *The Sun Also Rises*, Chapter 17. Hemingway would often drink this on *Pilar*.

GRAPPA: A brandy from Italy distilled from pomace, the leftovers of the winemaking process, that is, the skins, pulp, seeds, and stems of the grape. Called marc in France. Often harsh in flavor. Found in *A Farewell to Arms*, Chapters 4, 12, 23, 33, 34; *Across the River and Into the Trees*, Chapters 12, 43; "Out of Season"; "A Way You'll Never Be."

IZARRA: A sweet herbal liqueur from the French Basque region around Bayonne. Found in *The Sun Also Rises*, Chapter 19. A waiter describes it to Jake Barnes as "made of the flowers of the Pyrenees. The veritable flowers of the Pyrenees. It looked like hair-oil and smelled like Italian *strega*."

KÜMMEL: A sweet liqueur flavored with caraway seeds, fennel, and cumin. It is popular in Germany and the Alps. Found in *A Farewell to Arms*, Chapter 22.

MARC/VIEUX MARC: Pronounced "marrh." Like Italian grappa, it is a brandy distilled from pomace, but made in France. Vieux marc is aged in oak barrels for at least five years. Found in *The Torrents of Spring*, Chapter 12; *A Farewell to Arms*, Chapter 41; *The Sun Also Rises*, Chapter 19; "The Strange Country."

MARSALA: A fortified wine (wine with grape brandy added after fermentation), originating in the town of Marsala, Sicily. Found in *A Moveable Feast* ("Miss Stein Instructs"); *A Farewell to Arms*, Chapters 19, 22; "Out of Season."

MIRABELLE: A liqueur made from yellow plums, originating in France. Found in *A Moveable Feast* ("Miss Stein Instructs"). See the note at "framboise," above.

PASTIS: A liqueur flavored with licorice and anise, originally made in France. Found in *The Garden of Eden*, Chapter 9.

QUETSCH: A liqueur made from purple plums, originating in Alsace. Found in *A Moveable Feast* ("Miss Stein Instructs"). See the note at "framboise," above.

SCHNAPPS: Depending on where it's from, it's either a spirit distilled from fruit (like an eau-de-vie), as in Germany and the Alps (spelled *Schnaps*), or a sweet, syrupy liqueur flavored with herbs or fruit (such as peppermint or peach). Found in *A Moveable Feast* ("There Is Never Any End to Paris"); "An Alpine Idyll."

STREGA: A yellowish herbal liqueur from the Campania region of Italy. Found in *A Farewell to Arms*, Chapter 3.

TIO PEPE: A proprietary brand of Sherry wine from Spain, dating back to 1844. Found in *The Garden of Eden*, Chapter 27.

ACKNOWLEDGMENTS

I'm profoundly grateful to Perigee, especially to my editor, Meg Leder, for all her patience, guidance, good humor, and support through this first-time author's travails. Also, a huge debt of gratitude is owed to my intrepid publishing agents, Jason Ashlock and Craig Kayser of Movable Type NYC. Thanks to you all for your hard work, for your brilliant direction and creativity, and for putting your faith in my project and in me.

I'd also like to thank the Hemingway Collection of the JFK Library, notably Susan Wrynn, Laurie Austin, Stephen Plotkin, Marti Verso, Mary Rose Grossman, Michael Desmond, Ed Le-Blanc, Nadia Dixson, and Lauren Pey. Thanks also to the Hemingway Foundation and Society, particularly Professor Kirk Curnutt. Profound thanks to my dear friends in the cocktail community, including Jill and Dale DeGroff, Ann Tuennerman, Ted Haigh, Robert Hess, Chris McMillian, Anistatia Miller, Jared Brown, Mardee Haidin Regan, Gary Regan, Dave Wondrich, Derek Brown, Angus Winchester, Charlotte Voisey, Jacob Briars, Leslie Pariseau, Karlyn Monroe, Lora Piazza, Joanne McKerchar, Sonya Perez, Sebastian Roncin, Manuela Savona, Dave Karraker, Tal Nadari, Lisa Laird Dunn, St. John Frizell, José Schiaffino, Jeff "Beachbum" Berry, Abby Vinyard, Maeve Hickey, Caitlin Davis, Paul Clarke, J. P. Caceres, and Joe Fee.

Thanks also to Arrigo Cipriani, Patricia Suau, Annie Sansone-Martinez, Shermane Billingsley, Marcie Rudell, Michael Shulman, Michelle Press, James DeMartini, Karin Peirce, Patricia Gurdick, Don Rebsch, Claudia and Craig Pennington, Benjamin "Dink" Bruce, Brewster Chamberlin, Donna Edwards, Wendy Tucker, Tom Hambright, Amanda Vaill, Laura Donnelly, Craig Boreth, Paul Hendrickson, Bob Panzer, Bill Smallwood, Sandra Hofferber, and Dr. Thomas Flynn.

NOTES

1. Barnaby Conrad III, *Absinthe: History in a Bottle* (San Francisco: Chronicle Books, 1988), 137.
2. Kirk Curnutt and Gail D. Sinclair, eds., *Key West Hemingway: A Reassessment* (Gainesville: University Press of Florida, 2009), 32.
3. Ernest Hemingway, *The Garden of Eden* (New York: Charles Scribner's Sons, 1986), 56.
4. David Embury, *The Fine Art of Mixing Drinks*, new rev. ed. (New York: Doubleday, 1958), 81.
5. Bernice Kert, *The Hemingway Women* (New York: Norton, 1983), 149.
6. Carlos Baker, *Ernest Hemingway: A Life Story* (New York: Charles Scribner's Sons, 1969), 130.
7. James R. Mellow offers more detail, notably that the old man was a Mr. Engelfield and that he wanted to be present when Hemingway's dressings were changed, as if taking some prurient pleasure from it. In *Hemingway: A Life Without Consequences* (Boston: Houghton Mifflin, 1992), 70.
8. Ernest Hemingway, *Dateline: Toronto—The Complete Toronto Star Dispatches, 1920–1924* (New York: Scribner, 1995), 182.
9. Ernest Hemingway, "The Great 'Apéritif' Scandal," in *Dateline: Toronto*, 182.
10. George Plimpton, "The Art of Fiction: Ernest Hemingway," *Paris Review* 5 (Spring 1958), reprinted in *Conversations with Ernest Hemingway*, edited by Matthew J. Bruccoli (Jackson: University Press of Mississippi, 1986), 120.
11. Letter from Cuba dated August 27, 1945, to Archibald MacLeish; found in the archives of the Hemingway Collection, JFK Library, Boston.

12. Carlos Baker, *Ernest Hemingway: A Life Story*, 171.

13. Gerald Murphy's recipe from Amanda Vaill, *Everybody Was So Young* (New York: Broadway Books, 1998), 162.

14. Calvin Tomkins in the introduction to *Making It New: The Art and Style of Sara and Gerald Murphy*, edited by Deborah Rothschild (Berkeley: University of California Press, 2007), 1.

15. Barbara Gamarekian, "In the Circle of a Charmed Life," *New York Times Book Review*, February 6, 1983, www.nytimes.com/books/98/05/24/specials/830206.html.

16. Ernest Hemingway, *A Moveable Feast*, restored ed. (New York: Scribner, 2009), 215.

17. Eric Felten, "He Was a Cocktail Artist," *Wall Street Journal*, March 14, 2009, http://online.wsj.com/article/SB123698213720424525.html.

18. Amanda Vaill, *Everybody Was So Young*, 5.

19. Arrigo Cipriani, *Harry's Bar: The Life and Times of the Legendary Venice Landmark* (New York: Arcade, 1996), 87.

20. Ibid., 64.

21. John DeMers, "Hemingway's Drink Charm Still Lingers," *Bend (OR) Bulletin*, October 15, 1986, http://news.google.com/newspapers?nid=1243&dat=19861015&id=94VTAAAAIBAJ&sjid=xIYDAAAAIBAJ&pg=5529,3112742.

22. Steven J. Austin, "Mariel Hemingway Applies a Fresh, Healthy Focus to Life," *Nevada Daily Mail*, March 21, 2007, http://news.google.com/newspapers?nid=1908&dat=20070321&id=sekfAAAAIBAJ&sjid=qtkEAAAAIBAJ&pg=1915,4589442.

23. Dale DeGroff, *The Essential Cocktail: The Art of Mixing Perfect Drinks* (New York: Clarkson Potter, 2008), 146.

24. George Jessel, *The World I Lived In* (Chicago: Regnery, 1975), 83–85.

25. Colin Peter Field, *The Cocktails of the Ritz Paris* (New York: Simon and Schuster, 2003), 6.

26. Letter to Bernard Peyton, April 5, 1947, in *Ernest Hemingway: Selected Letters, 1917–1961*, edited by Carlos Baker (New York: Scribner, 1981), 618–19.

27. Colin Peter Field, *The Cocktails of the Ritz Paris*, 18.

28. Ralph Ingersoll, "Story of Ernest Hemingway's Far East Trip," in *Conversations with Ernest Hemingway*, 34–35. Originally appears in *PM Magazine*, June 9, 1941.

29. Carlos Baker, *Ernest Hemingway: A Life Story*, 362.

30. A. E. Hotchner, ed., *The Good Life According to Hemingway* (New York: Ecco, 2008), 122.

31. Letter from Hemingway to Gingrich, July 24, 1933, archives, University of Delaware, www.lib.udel.edu/ud/spec/exhibits/hemngway/stories.htm.

32. John Drury, *Dining in Chicago: An Intimate Guide* (New York: John Day Co., 1931), 15.

33. David Embury, *The Fine Art of Mixing Drinks*, 3rd ed. (New York: Doubleday & Co., Inc., 1958), 25–26.

34. Eric Felten, "A Toast to April 15," *Wall Street Journal*, April 15, 2006, online at http://online.wsj.com/articles/SB114504694150826369.

35. Letter to William Smith, October 25, 1920, in *The Letters of Ernest Hemingway*, Vol. 1, 1907–1922 (Cambridge: Cambridge University Press, 2011), 248.

36. Ibid., 252.

37. Ernest Hemingway, *Dateline: Toronto—The Complete Toronto Star Dispatches, 1920–24* (New York: Charles Scribner's Sons, 1985), 58–59. A reprint of a news story appearing in the *Toronto Star Weekly*, November 6, 1920.

38. Letter to John Dos Passos, April 22, 1925, in *Ernest Hemingway: Selected Letters, 1917–1961*, edited by Carlos Baker (New York: Charles Scribner's Sons, 1981), 158.

39. Arrigo Cipriani, *Harry's Bar: The Life and Times of the Legendary Venice Landmark* (New York: Arcade, 1996), 25.

40. Ibid., 67.

41. Ernest Hemingway, *A Farewell to Arms* (New York, Charles Scribner's Sons, 1929), 37–38.

42. Ernest Hemingway, *Dateline: Toronto* (New York: Charles Scribner's Sons, 1985), reprint of a *Toronto Daily Star* story on May 2, 1922. At page 157.

43. Leicester Hemingway, *My Brother, Ernest Hemingway* (Cleveland: World, 1961), 120–21.

44. Ibid.

45. Ibid.

46. Denis Brian, *The True Gen: An Intimate Portrait of Hemingway by Those Who Knew Him* (New York: Dell, 1988), 84.

47. James R. Mellow, *Hemingway: A Life Without Consequences*, 425.

48. Stuart B. McIver, *Hemingway's Key West* (Sarasota, FL: Pineapple Press, 1993), 71.

49. Kirk Curnutt and Gail D. Sinclair, eds., *Key West Hemingway*, 26–27.

50. Ibid., 53.

51. Unpublished letter to Malcolm Cowley, April 9, 1948, Hemingway Collection, JFK Library, Boston.

52. Ernest Hemingway, *A Moveable Feast*, 184–85.

53. Peter Griffin, *Less Than a Treason: Hemingway in Paris* (New York: Oxford University Press, 1990), 152.

54. Anistatia Miller, Jared Brown, and Don Gatterdam, *Champagne Cocktails* (New York: Regan Books, 1999), 28.

55. Ibid.

56. Henry S. Villard and James Nagel, *Hemingway in Love and War: The Lost Diary of Agnes von Kurowsky* (Boston: Northeastern University Press, 1989), 185.

57. Peter Griffin, *Along with Youth* (New York: Oxford University Press, 1987), 104–12.

58. A. E. Hotchner, *Papa Hemingway* (New York: Random House, 1966), 33–34.

59. Wayne Curtis, *And a Bottle of Rum: A History of the New World in Ten Cocktails* (New York: Crown, 2006), 200.

60. Letter to John Dos Passos, April 12, 1936, *Selected Letters*, 447.

61. Wayne Curtis, *And a Bottle of Rum*, 203–7.

62. Jack Hemingway, *Misadventures of a Fly Fisherman: My Life With and Without Papa* (Dallas: Taylor, 1986), 248.

63. Wayne Curtis, *And a Bottle of Rum*, 170–71.

64. A. E. Hotchner, *Papa Hemingway*, 5.

65. Letter to Harvey Breit, February 24, 1952, *Selected Letters*, 754.

66. Unpublished letter to Mary Hemingway, September 29, 1945, Hemingway Collection, JFK Library, Boston.

67. Lillian Ross, *Portrait of Hemingway* (New York: Modern Library Paperback Edition, 1999), 56. Originally published in *The New Yorker*, May 13, 1950.

68. Sterling North and Carl Kroch, eds., *So Red the Nose, or, Breath in the Afternoon* (New York: Farrar & Rinehart, 1935), 1–2.

69. Carlos Baker, *Ernest Hemingway: A Life Story*, 208–9.

70. Sterling North and Carl Kroch, eds., *So Red the Nose*, 1–2.

71. Charles H. Baker Jr., *The Gentleman's Companion*, Vol. 2, *Being an Exotic Drinking Book*, 2nd ed. (New York: Derrydale Press, 1946), 31–32.

72. Ibid., 32.

73. Ibid.

74. René Villarreal and Raúl Villarreal, *Hemingway's Cuban Son: Reflections on the Writer by His Longtime Majordomo* (Kent, OH: Kent State University Press, 2009), 27.

75. Letter to Maxwell Perkins, August 2, 1943, *Selected Letters*, 547.

76. Carlos Baker, *Ernest Hemingway: A Life Story*, 372–73.

77. Spruille Braden quoted in Michael Reynolds, *Hemingway: The Final Years* (New York: Norton, 1999), 60.

78. Carlos Baker, *Ernest Hemingway: A Life Story*, 373.

79. Charles H. Baker Jr., *The Gentleman's Companion*, 34.

80. Letter to Howell Jenkins, February 2, 1925, *Selected Letters*, 149.

81. Letter to Jim Gamble, April 19, 1919. Letter courtesy Clarke Historical Library, Central Michigan University. Michael Federspiel, President, Michigan Hemingway Society, www.mynorth.com/My-North/August -2007/Hemingways-Young-Summers.

82. Carlos Baker, *Ernest Hemingway: A Life Story*, 210.

83. Mary Hemingway, *How It Was* (New York: Alfred A. Knopf, 1976), 429.

84. Ibid., 422.

85. Lee Alan Gutkind, *Hemingway's Wyoming*, Pittsburgh Press, February 21, 1971.

86. Letter to Henry "Mike" Strater, September 10, 1930, in *Ernest Hemingway: Selected Letters, 1917–1961*, edited by Carlos Baker (New York: Charles Scribner's Sons, 1981), 329.

87. Ed Spencer, *A History (More or Less) of the RDS, B-4, L-T and Hancock Ranches* (Cody, Wyoming: WordsWorth, 2006), 13.

88. Ernest Hemingway, *Green Hills of Africa* (New York: Charles Scribner's Sons, 1935), 22.

89. Mark Twain, *The Adventures of Huckleberry Finn* (New York: Penguin Classics, 2002).

90. Ernest Hemingway, *By-Line Ernest Hemingway* (New York: Charles Scribner's Sons, 1967), from a reproduction of an article titled "The Clark's Fork Valley, Wyoming," *Vogue*, February 1939.

91. Michael S. Reynolds, *Hemingway: The 1930s* (New York: Norton, 1997), 24.

92. Letter to Guy Hickok, July 27, 1928, in *Ernest Hemingway: Selected Letters, 1917–1961*, edited by Carlos Baker (New York: Charles Scribner's Sons, 1981), 281.

93. Letter to Waldo Peirce, August 9, 1928, in *Ernest Hemingway: Selected Letters, 1917–1961*, edited by Carlos Baker (New York: Charles Scribner's Sons, 1981), 282.

94. Ibid., 284.

95. Letter to John Dos Passos, April 12, 1932, in *Ernest Hemingway: Selected Letters, 1917–1961*, edited by Carlos Baker (New York: Charles Scribner's Sons, 1981), 356.

96. David Embury, *The Fine Art of Mixing Drinks*, 303.

97. Charles H. Baker Jr., *The Gentleman's Companion*, xvi.

98. Letter to Maxwell Perkins, December 26, 1931, *Selected Letters*, 346.

99. Norberto Fuentes, *Hemingway in Cuba* (Secaucus, NJ: Lyle Stuart, 1984), 101.

100. Ibid., 101–2.

101. From *St. Petersburg (FL) Independent*, August 6, 1940.

102. Joe Russell, quoted in the *St. Petersburg (FL) Independent*, August 6, 1940.

103. Letter to his cousin Bud White, January 29, 1931, from Hemingway Collection, JFK Library, Boston.

104. Toni D. Knott, *One Man Alone: Hemingway and "To Have and Have Not"* (Lanham, MD: University Press of America, 1999), 73–74.

105. Charles H. Baker Jr., *The Gentleman's Companion*, 59

106. Letter to Sherwood Anderson, December 23, 1921, *Selected Letters*, 59.

107. November 16, 1922, letter to Harriet Monroe, *Selected Letters*, 72.

108. December 26, 1921, letter to Howell Jenkins, *Selected Letters*, 60.

109. January 8, 1922, letter to Howell Jenkins, *Selected Letters*, 61.

110. Milt Machlin, "Hemingway Talking," in *Conversations with Ernest Hemingway*, 168. Originally appeared in *Argosy*, September 1958.

111. Letter to Janet Flanner, April 8, 1933, in *Ernest Hemingway: Selected Letters, 1917–1961*, edited by Carlos Baker (New York: Charles Scribner's Sons, 1981), 387.

112. Robert C. Ruark, "Once Wonderful Comic-Opera Paradise," *Spartanburg (NC) Herald*, May 1, 1963.

113. Robert C. Ruark, "Let's Spin a Yarn," *Reading (PA) Eagle*, May 1, 1963.

114. Mary Hemingway, *How It Was* (New York: Alfred A. Knopf, 1976), 330.

115. Interview with Hadley Mowrer in Denis Brian, *The True Gen*, 55–56.

116. Ernest Hemingway, *A Moveable Feast*, 24–25.

117. Ibid., 61.

118. Jack Hemingway, *Misadventures of a Fly Fisherman*, 248.

119. Jimmie Charters, *This Must Be the Place: Memoirs of Montparnasse* (New York: Collier Books, 1989), 1.

120. Ibid., 51.

121. Ernest Hemingway, "Marlin Off the Morro," *Esquire*, Autumn 1933.

122. Carlos Baker, *Ernest Hemingway: A Life Story*, 263.

123. A. E. Hotchner, *The Good Life According to Hemingway*, 101.

124. Stuart B. McIver, *Hemingway's Key West*, 53.

125. "Monologue to the Maestro: A High Seas Letter," *Esquire*, October, 1935, in *By-Line: Ernest Hemingway* (New York: Charles Scribner's Sons, 1967), 214.

126. Ibid.

127. Leicester Hemingway, *My Brother, Ernest Hemingway*, 114.

128. Arnold Samuelson, *With Hemingway: A Year in Key West and Cuba* (New York: Random House, 1984), 51–52.

129. Ibid., 101–3.

130. Ernest Hemingway, *By-Line: Ernest Hemingway*, 449, from a reproduction of a two-part *Look* magazine article, "The Christmas Gift," April 20 and May 4, 1954.

131. Ibid., 441.

132. Earl Wilson, "Writing Good: About to Bank Another Book," November 9, 1955, in *Conversations with Ernest Hemingway*, 103.

133. *Time*, December 13, 1954.

134. Letter to Charles Scribner, June 28, 1947, *Selected Letters*, 622–23.

135. A. E. Hotchner, *Papa Hemingway*, 107.

136. Ernest Hemingway, *By-Line: Ernest Hemingway*, 370–71, from a *Collier's* article, "Battle for Paris," September 30, 1944.

137. Carlos Baker, *Ernest Hemingway: A Life Story*, 417.

138. Alan Moorehead, *Eclipse* (London: H. Hamilton, 1945), 142.

139. Unpublished letter to Malcolm Cowley, April 9, 1948, from the Hemingway Collection, JFK Library, Boston.

140. Original manuscript, *Islands in the Stream*, Hemingway Collection, JFK Library, Boston.

141. René Villarreal and Raúl Villarreal, *Hemingway's Cuban Son*, 66–70.

142. Leonard Lyons, *Miami News*, April 21, 1948.

143. Letter to Charles Scribner, June 28, 1947, *Selected Letters*, 622–23.

144. Letter to Pauline Hemingway, June 28, 1947, from the Hemingway Collection, JFK Library, Boston.

145. Tillie Arnold, *The Idaho Hemingway* (Buhl, Idaho: Beacon Books, 1999), 86.

146. Ernest Hemingway, *By-Line Ernest Hemingway* (New York: Charles Scribner's Sons, 1967), from a reproduction of an article in *True* magazine, "The Shot," April 1951.

147. Letter to General E. E. Dorman-O'Gowan, June 13, 1951, in *Ernest Hemingway: Selected Letters, 1917–1961*, edited by Carlos Baker (New York: Charles Scribner's Sons, 1981), 729.

148. Dorice Taylor, *Ski Magazine*, October 1971.

149. Tillie Arnold, "Hemingway in Sun Valley," www.svguide.com/hemquotes.htm.

150. Lloyd Arnold, *High on the Wild with Hemingway* (Caldwell, Idaho: Caxton Printers Ltd., 1968), 54–55.

151. Lee Alan Gutkind, "Hemingway's Wyoming," *Pittsburgh Press*, February 21, 1971. Special thanks go to Chris Warren, owner of Hemingways Yellowstone.com, for tipping me off to this great story.

152. Carlos Baker, *Ernest Hemingway: A Life Story* (New York: Charles Scribner's Sons, 1969), 214–15.

153. David Nuffer, *The Best Friend I Ever Had* (self-published, 1988), 100.

154. A. E. Hotchner, *The Good Life According to Hemingway*, 101.

155. Quoted in Eric Felten, "A Cuban Summer Cooler," *Wall Street Journal*, August 4, 2007.

156. Brewster Chamberlin, August 6, 2011, email to the author.

157. Tom Miller, *Cuba: True Stories* (San Francisco: Travelers' Tales Inc., 2004), 146; Alfredo Jose Estrada, *Havana: Autobiography of a City* (New York: Palgrave Macmillan, 2008), 87; Tom Miller, *Trading with the Enemy: A Yankee Travels Through Castro's Cuba* (New York: Basic Books, 2008), 168.

158. A.E. Hotchner, *Papa Hemingway*, 158–160.

159. Interview with Juan Cobos, 1964, www.wellesnet.com/?p=183.

160. Arrigo Cipriani, *Harry's Bar*, 69–70.

161. Wikimedia Foundation, IBA Official Cocktails, Google eBook, http://books.google.com/books?id=lWuNTBCphpcC&printsec=frontcover&dq=iba+official+cocktails&hl=en&sa=X&ei=g4aUT_fwLYqZ6AH_mIWcBA&ved=0CDIQ6AEwAA#v=onepage&q=iba%20official%20cocktails&f=false, 89–90.

162. Gerald Clarke, *Capote: A Biography* (New York: Carroll and Graf, 1988), 175–76.

163. M. Thomas Inge, ed., *Truman Capote: Conversations* (Jackson: University Press of Mississippi, 1987), 228.

164. Carl Rollyson, *Nothing Ever Happens to the Brave: The Story of Martha Gellhorn* (New York: St. Martin's Press, 1990), 90.

165. Sharon Wells, *Sloppy Joe's: The First Fifty Years* (Key West: Key West Saloon, 1983), 19.

166. Stuart B. McIver, *Hemingway's Key West*, 52.

167. Based on Paula McLain's novel by that name.

168. A. E. Hotchner, *Papa Hemingway*, 154.

169. Earl Wilson, "Papa Hemingway Tells Why He Prefers Cuba," September 5, 1952, *Sarasota Herald-Tribune*, 11.

170. Ralph Blumenthal, *Stork Club: America's Most Famous Nightspot and the Lost World of Café Society* (Boston: Little, Brown, 2000); reprinted in *New York Times*, www.nytimes.com/books/first/b/blumenthal-stork.html.

171. Ibid.

172. Email exchange with Jeff "Beachbum" Berry, April 27, 2011.

173. José Antonio Schiaffino, *Cabo Blanco Fishing Club* (Lima: Empresa Tipsal S.A., 2011), interview with Alfred C. Glassell Jr., 90.

174. From the newspaper *Cronica*, June 18, 1956, and the magazine *Cultura Peruana*, date uncertain.

175. Carlos Baker, *Ernest Hemingway: A Life Story*, 533.

176. Annette Holzapfel and Stefan Ziemendor, "The Reincarnation of the Cabo Blanco," *Comercio*, June 25, 2001.

177. José A. Schiaffino, *El origen del Pisco Sour* (Lima: Heralmol S.R.L., 2006). José Antonio Schiaffino may be reached at museokontiki@hotmail.com.

178. John Dos Passos in Milt Machlin, *The Private Hell of Hemingway* (New York: Paperback Library, 1962), 116–17.

179. Letter to Patrick Hemingway, June 30, 1939, *Selected Letters*, 487.

180. Ernest Hemingway, *The Dangerous Summer* (New York: Scribner, 1985), dust jacket.

181. James A. Michener, foreword to Ernest Hemingway, *The Dangerous Summer*, 3.

182. Ernest Hemingway, *The Dangerous Summer*, 125.

183. Carlos Baker, *Ernest Hemingway: A Life Story*, 541.

184. Ernest Hemingway, "There She Breaches! or, Moby Dick Off the Morro," *Esquire*, April 1936. Reprinted in *By-Line: Ernest Hemingway*.

185. Letter to Mrs. Paul Pfeiffer, February 6, 1939, *Selected Letters*, 475.

186. Alfred G. Aronowitz and Peter Hamill, *Ernest Hemingway: The Life and Death of a Man* (New York: Lancer Books, 1961), 164.

187. Amanda Vaill, *Everybody Was So Young*, 264.

188. Ibid., 162.

189. Norberto Fuentes, *Hemingway in Cuba*, 26.

190. David Embury, *The Fine Art of Mixing Drinks*, 302–3.

191. Norberto Fuentes, *Hemingway in Cuba*, 101.

192. Peter Griffin, *Less Than a Treason*, 124.

193. Lillian Ross, *Portrait of Hemingway*, 56.

194. A. E. Hotchner, *The Good Life According to Hemingway*, 85.

195. "U.S. Tourists Lost Zip, Says Harry of Paris Bar," *Miami News*, June 29, 1951, http://news.google.com/newspapers?nid=2206&dat=19510629&id=Mp4yAAAAIBAJ&sjid=kukFAAAAIBAJ&pg=4503,7441885.

196. A. E. Hotchner, *The Good Life According to Hemingway*, 106.

197. Carl Rollyson, *Nothing Ever Happens to the Brave*, after page 206.

198. C. T. "Buck" Lanham, in Denis Brian, *The True Gen*, 187.

199. Letter to William B. Smith Jr., February 17, 1925, in *The Letters of Ernest Hemingway 1923–1925* (Cambridge: Cambridge University Press, 2013), 251.

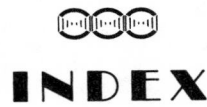

INDEX

Page numbers in *italics* indicate photos or illustrations

Daiquiri, Cuba, 76, 83–85
Daiquiris, 22, 58, 78, 82–90, *83*, *84*, *86*,
    87, *88*, *89*, *151*, 216, 293, 302, 305,
    307, 315, 318, 325, 332
The Dangerous Summer (Hemingway),
    xxi, 18, 247–48
Dark Laughter (Anderson), 146
Dateline: Toronto, xxi
Davis, Bill, 248, *248*
Dayton, Bryan, 305, 306
D-day, 92
Dead Rabbit Grocery & Grog, New York
    City, 325
Death, of Ernest, xvi
Death at Dusk, 317
Death & Company, New York City,
    325, 327
Death in the Afternoon, 4, 91–93
Death in the Afternoon (Hemingway), xv,
    96, 128, 248–49
Death in the Gulf Stream (Ernest
    Hemingway's Reviver), 94–98, *95*,
    96, 201. *See also* Pleasant Death in
    the Gulf Stream
Death in the Gulfstream (Peirce), 96
El Definitivo, 99–100
Degas, Edgar, 2, 224
DeGroff, Dale "King Cocktail," 27, 318
DeMers, John, 26
"The Denunciation" (Hemingway), 36,
    125, 128–31, 230, 232
DeVoto, Bernard, 181
Diamond, Legs, 73
The Dick Van Dyke Show (TV show), 80
Dingo American Bar, Paris, 165–67, 286
Dining in Chicago: An Intimate Guide
    (Drury), 38
"Dinner-Flowers-Gala," 21
Diplomate, 262
Divorces, xv, xvi
Doctor's Orders 2.0, 303
Domínguín, Luis Miguel, 247
Donayre, Jorge, 235, 236, *236*
Donn the Beachcomber, 224
door 74, Amsterdam, 320
Dos Passos, John, 7, 42, 77, 116, 123,
    139–40, 239–40
Dos Passos, Katy, 116
El Draque, 6, 86
The Dree, 313
Drinking, of Ernest, xii, xix, 145,
    226–27, *227*, 251, 257, 297–98
Drury, John, 38

Dry Martini, xi, 180–82, 206
Duff, Philip, 320
Duffy, Patrick Gavin, 151, 278
Duplex, 262

Eau-de-vie ("water of life"), 333
Eclipse (Moorehead), 183
Edgar, Carl "Odgar," 194, *194*
Education, xviii
Edward VIII (Duke of Windsor), 187–89
Egg whites, 233, 293
"E. Henmiway" Special, 82, *87*,
    87–88, 201
86 Company, 307, 314
Embury, David, 6–7, 38–39, 125, 132,
    181, 279, 293–94
Employees Only, 314
"The End of an Avocation" *A Moveable
    Feast* (Hemingway), 27
Ensslin, Hugo, 151
Ernest. *See* Hemingway, Ernest Miller
*Ernest Hemingway at Sloppy Joe's, Key
    West, Florida* (Peirce), 217
*Ernest Hemingway: Selected Letters,
    1917-1961*, xxi, 27, 179
Ernest Hemingway's Reviver (Death in
    the Gulf Stream), 94–98, *95*, *96*
Ernest's Advice, 301
The Essential Cocktail (DeGroff), 318
"Evan Shipman at the Lilas," *A Moveable
    Feast* (Hemingway), 278
Exposition Universelle des Vins et
    Spiritueux, 310

Fall of the Daiquiri, 307
"A False Spring," *A Moveable Feast*
    (Hemingway), 27, 49
*Famous New Orleans Drinks and How to
    Mix 'Em* (Arthur), 212, 263
A Farewell to Arms (Hemingway), xv,
    xvii, xviii, 49, 50–51, 61, 64, 66,
    67–69, 119, 123, 132–33, 179, 184,
    196, 278, 280, 328
A Farewell to Hemingway, 104–5
Faro Point, 325–26
Fascism, 128–30
Faulkner, William, 111, 145, 279
Favorite drink, of Ernest, 199–202,
    279–80
La Fée Verte (Green Fairy), 2, 3, 5
Felten, Eric, 22
Fennel simple syrup, 301
Fernandez, Manuel, 211

Ferrer, José, 178
Field, Colin Peter, 28–29, 313
The Fifth Column (Hemingway), xxi, 120, 229–30, 264, 278
Finca Vigía, Cuba, 11, *11*, 60, 102, *102*, 116, 188, *188*, 279
Fine, 333
Fine à l'eau (Brandy & Soda), 32–35, 62
The Fine Art of Mixing Drinks (Embury), 6–7
"Firewater" (Aguardiente), 6–7
Fishing, 53, *81*, 87, 92–93, 96, 97, *97*, 119–20, *120*, 122, 140, 170–71, *171*, 194, 215–16, 235, 239–41, 260–62, 284
Fitzgerald, F. Scott, 21, 22, 39, 40, 146, 165, 267, 268, 286–89, 290
Fitzgerald, Zelda, 21, 267, 287–88, 289
Flavor of the region (*terroir*), xviii, xx
Fleming, Ian, 10, 32
La Florida Bar "Floridita," Havana, 48, 83, *83*, *86*, 86–90, *87*, *89*, 148, *150*, 150–51, *151*, 199, 201, 212, 252, *252*, 277, *277*, 318, 325
Folly Ranch, 123
Ford, Ford Madox, 62–63
Ford, Simon, 307
"Ford Madox Ford and the Devil's Disciple," *A Moveable Feast* (Hemingway), 32, 61, 62
For the Love of Hemingway, 319
For Whom the Bell Tolls (Hemingway), xix, xxi, 1, 3–4, 60, 87, 115, 222, 229, 278, 285
For Your Eyes Only (Fleming), 32
Fox, Vollie, 194
Framboise, 333
France, xv, xvi, 1–2, 248, 267
Franco, Francisco, 128, 232
Franklin, Sidney, 104
French Revolution, 1
Fuentes, Gregorio, 137–39, 141, 279
Fundador, 333

Gable, Clark, 215
Gamble, Jim, 107, 108
Gambler's Delight, 107–9, *108*
Garate, José Andres, 200–201
The Garden of Eden (Hemingway), xix, xxi, 1, 2–3, 15, 16–17, 23, 32, 34–35, 49, 61, 63, 157–58, 179, 185–86, 223, 256, 257–58, 264, 268, 278, 297

Garden of Roses, Key West, 215
Gee, Matty, 321
Gellhorn, Martha (third wife), xvi, 31, 101, 103, 104, 128, 137, 190, *190*, 193, *193*, 203, 216, 292, *292*
Geneva Convention, 157
The Gentleman's Companion (Baker, Charles), 94–95, 104, 126, *126*
"Get a Seeing-Eyed Dog" (Hemingway), 43–45, 196
Gilbey's Gin, 174, *174*, 175, 243
Gilligan's Island, 116
Gimlet, 112–15
Gimlette, Thomas, 112
Gin, Lemon & Wild Strawberries, 119–21
"Gin and Cocoanut Water," 117–18
Gin & Angostura (Pink Gin, or Gin & Bitters), 229–31
Gin & Coconut Water, 116–18
Gingrich, Arnold, 37
Gin & Tonic, 125–31, *126*, *127*, *129*, *130*
Glassell, Alfred C., Jr., 235
Glühwein, 132–33
"A Good Café on the Place St.-Michel," *A Moveable Feast* (Hemingway), 142
"The Good Lion" (Hemingway), 8, 10, 205–6, 209
Goofy (horse), 196–98
Gordon's Gin, *45*, 59, *59*, *130*, 177, 179, 180, *180*, 188, *188*, 189, 206, 279, 284
Grant, Cary, 21
Grapefruit cordial, 311
Grapefruit-free daiquiri, 332
Grappa, 334
"The Great 'Apéritif ' Scandal" (Hemingway), 2
"Great Tom Collins Hoax," 256–57
Greene, Philip, 332
Green Fairy (*La Fée Verte*), 2, 3, 5
Green Hills of Africa (Hemingway), xv, xxi, 87, 112, 113, 119, 128, 278
Green Isaac's Special (The Tomini), 134–36
Green River whiskey, 272–74, *273*
Gregorio's Rx, 137–38
Greppi, Count, 67–69
Griffin, Peter, 282–83
Grog, 86
Grooms, Carlton, 316
Guest, Winston "Wolfie," 99–100, 101
Guillermo (friend), 90

Vodka Distilled (Abou-Ganim), 319
Voisey, Charlotte, 302
Vose, Jillian, 325–27

Wallace, Ivan, 196–97
Warburton, Mary, 28
War correspondent, xvi, xviii, *xxiii*, 128, 156, 182–83
War wounds, xv, 8, 51, 64, *64, 65,* 66, 69, 92, 107
"Water of life" (Eau-de-vie), 333
Wayne, John, 215
"A Way You'll Never Be" (Hemingway), 334
Welles, Orson, 208–9
Welsh, Mary (fourth wife), xvi, 29, 60, 89, *89,* 90, 111, 113, 116, 177, 237, 248, *248,* 249, 250, 251, *251*
Wheeler Shipyard, Brooklyn, 238
Whiskey & Ginger Ale, 271–76, *272, 273*
Whiskey & Soda, 278–83
Whiskey Sour, 286–89, 290, 291, 293
White, Bud, 140–41
White Christmas (film), 178
"White Christmas," 178
White Horse Scotch, 59, *59,* 254, *254*
White Lady, 293–98, 294, *296*
"The White Man's Burden" (Kipling), 85
White Rock, 295, 296, *296,* 297
The Wild Daiquiri (Papa Doble), 22, 82, 88–90, 318

William Grant & Sons, 302
Williams, Taylor "Bear Tracks," 191–92, 193, *193*
Williams, Tennessee, 111
Wilson, Bill, 39–40
Wilson, Earl, 220
Windham, Donald, 209
Wine, xix, 49–52, 132–33, 144, 226, 247–49, 288, 289, 334
"Wine of Wyoming" (Hemingway), 1
Wineskin (*bota*), 6, 7
With Hemingway (Samuelson), 173, 174
"With Pascin at the Dôme," *A Moveable Feast* (Hemingway), 32
Wit & Wisdom, Baltimore, 309
Woelke, Eddie, 295
Wondrich, David, 235
Woollcott, Alexander, 20
Work ethic, xix, 145, 297
Works, of Ernest, xxi. *See also specific works*
The World's Drinks and How to Mix Them (Boothby), 38
World War I, 92. *See also* Red Cross Ambulance Corps; war wounds
World War II, xviii, 15–16, 79–80, 101–3
Wormwood (*Artemisia absinthium*), 1, 2, 4, 5, 61, 211, 223
Wyoming, 119–24, *120,* 191, 196–98

Yellow journalism, 74